PHOENIX RESURRECTION

THE RETURN OF
JEAN GREY

MATTHEW ROSENBERG
WRITER

ISSUE #1

LEINIL FRANCIS YU
PENCILER

GERRY ALANGUILAN
INKER

ISSUE #2

CARLOS PACHECO
PENCILER

RAFAEL FONTERIZ
INKER

ISSUE #3

JOE BENNETT
PENCILER

LORENZO RUGGIERO
INKER

ISSUE #4

RAMON ROSANAS
ARTIST

ISSUE #5

LEINIL FRANCIS YU & JOE BENNETT
ARTISTS

GERRY ALANGUILAN & BELARDINO BRABO
INKERS

RACHELLE ROSENBERG
COLOR ARTIST

VC's TRAVIS LANHAM
LETTERER

LEINIL FRANCIS YU WITH **SUNNY GHO** (#1), **RACHELLE ROSENBERG** (#2),
ROMULO FAJARDO JR. (#3), **MARTE GRACIA** (#4) & **NOLAN WOODARD** (#5)
COVER ART

**CHRISTINA HARRINGTON
& CHRIS ROBINSON**
ASSISTANT EDITORS

DARREN SHAN
ASSOCIATE EDITOR

MARK PANICCIA
EDITOR

JEAN GREY CREATED BY STAN LEE & JACK KIRBY

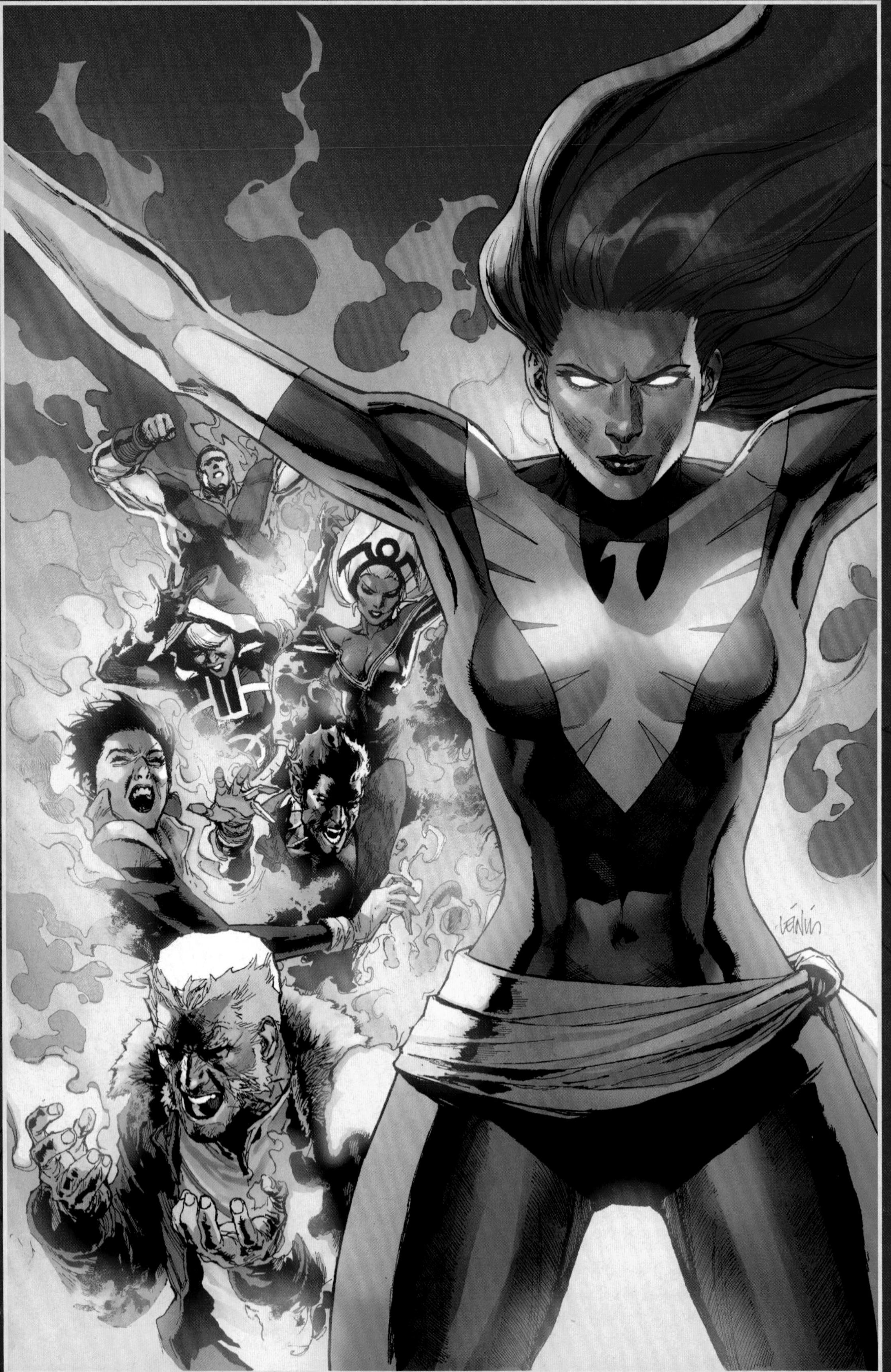

LEINIL

#1 VARIANT BY *LEINIL FRANCIS YU* & *SUNNY GHO*

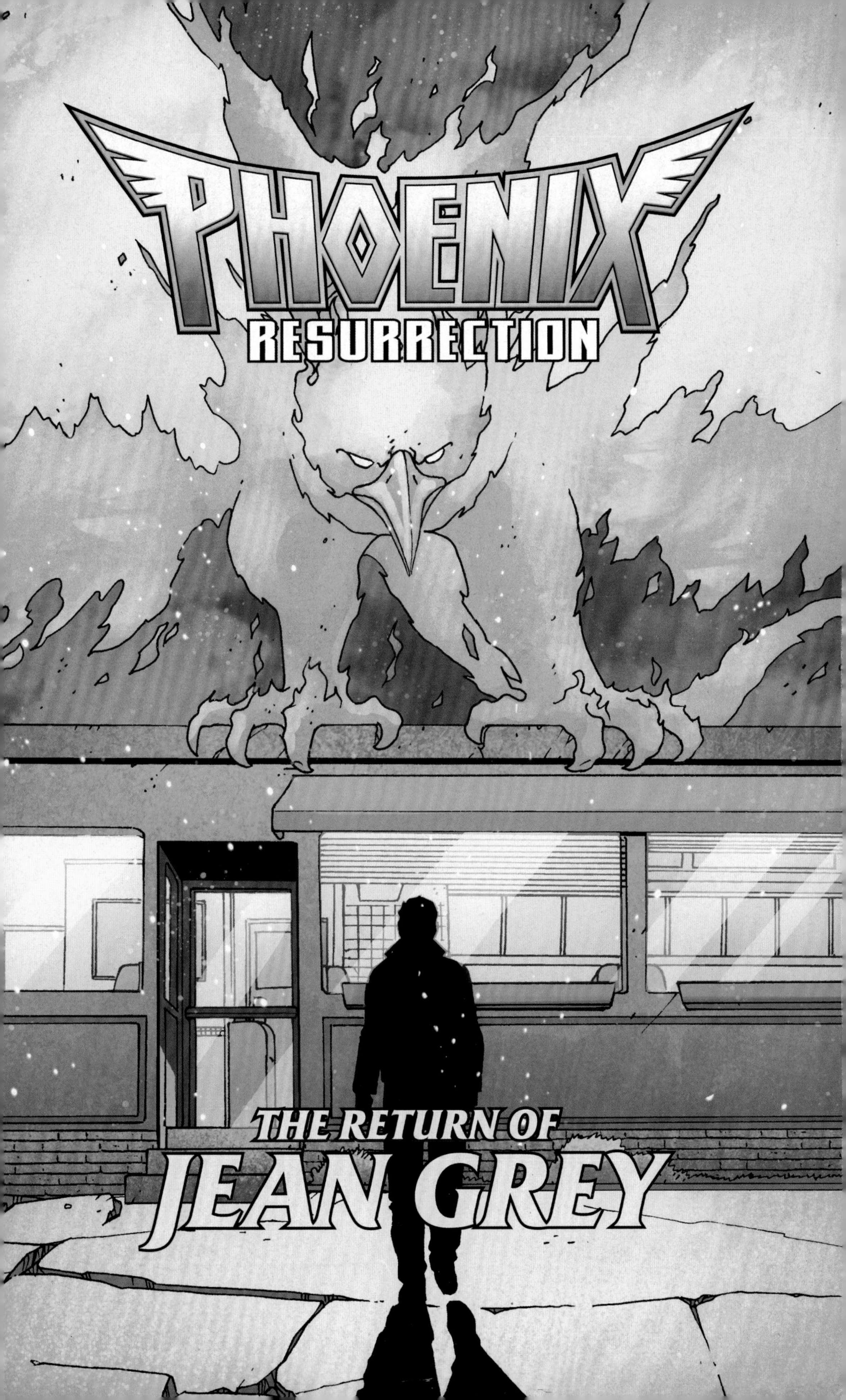
PHOENIX
RESURRECTION
THE RETURN OF
JEAN GREY

COLLECTION EDITOR **JENNIFER GRÜNWALD** ▪ ASSISTANT EDITOR **CAITLIN O'CONNELL**
ASSOCIATE MANAGING EDITOR **KATERI WOODY** ▪ EDITOR, SPECIAL PROJECTS **MARK D. BEAZLEY**
VP PRODUCTION & SPECIAL PROJECTS **JEFF YOUNGQUIST** ▪ SVP PRINT, SALES & MARKETING **DAVID GABRIEL**
BOOK DESIGNER **JAY BOWEN**

EDITOR IN CHIEF **C.B. CEBULSKI** ▪ CHIEF CREATIVE OFFICER **JOE QUESADA**
PRESIDENT **DAN BUCKLEY** ▪ EXECUTIVE PRODUCER **ALAN FINE**

PHOENIX RESURRECTION: THE RETURN OF JEAN GREY. Contains material originally published in magazine form as PHOENIX RESURRECTION: THE RETURN OF JEAN GREY #1-5. First printing 2018. ISBN 978-1-302-91163-8. Published by MARVEL WORLDWIDE, INC., a subsidiary of MARVEL ENTERTAINMENT, LLC. OFFICE OF PUBLICATION: 135 West 50th Street, New York, NY 10020. Copyright © 2018 MARVEL. No similarity between any of the names, characters, persons, and/or institutions in this magazine with those of any living or dead person or institution is intended, and any such similarity which may exist is purely coincidental. **Printed in Canada.** DAN BUCKLEY, President, Marvel Entertainment; JOHN NEE, Publisher; JOE QUESADA, Chief Creative Officer; TOM BREVOORT, SVP of Publishing; DAVID BOGART, SVP of Business Affairs & Operations, Publishing & Partnership; DAVID GABRIEL, SVP of Sales & Marketing, Publishing; JEFF YOUNGQUIST, VP of Production & Special Projects; DAN CARR, Executive Director of Publishing Technology; ALEX MORALES, Director of Publishing Operations; SUSAN CRESPI, Production Manager; STAN LEE, Chairman Emeritus. For information regarding advertising in Marvel Comics or on Marvel.com, please contact Vit DeBellis, Custom Solutions & Integrated Advertising Manager, at vdebellis@marvel.com. For Marvel subscription inquiries, please call 888-511-5480. **Manufactured between 2/23/2018 and 3/27/2018 by SOLISCO PRINTERS, SCOTT, QC, CANADA.**
10 9 8 7 6 5 4 3 2 1

1

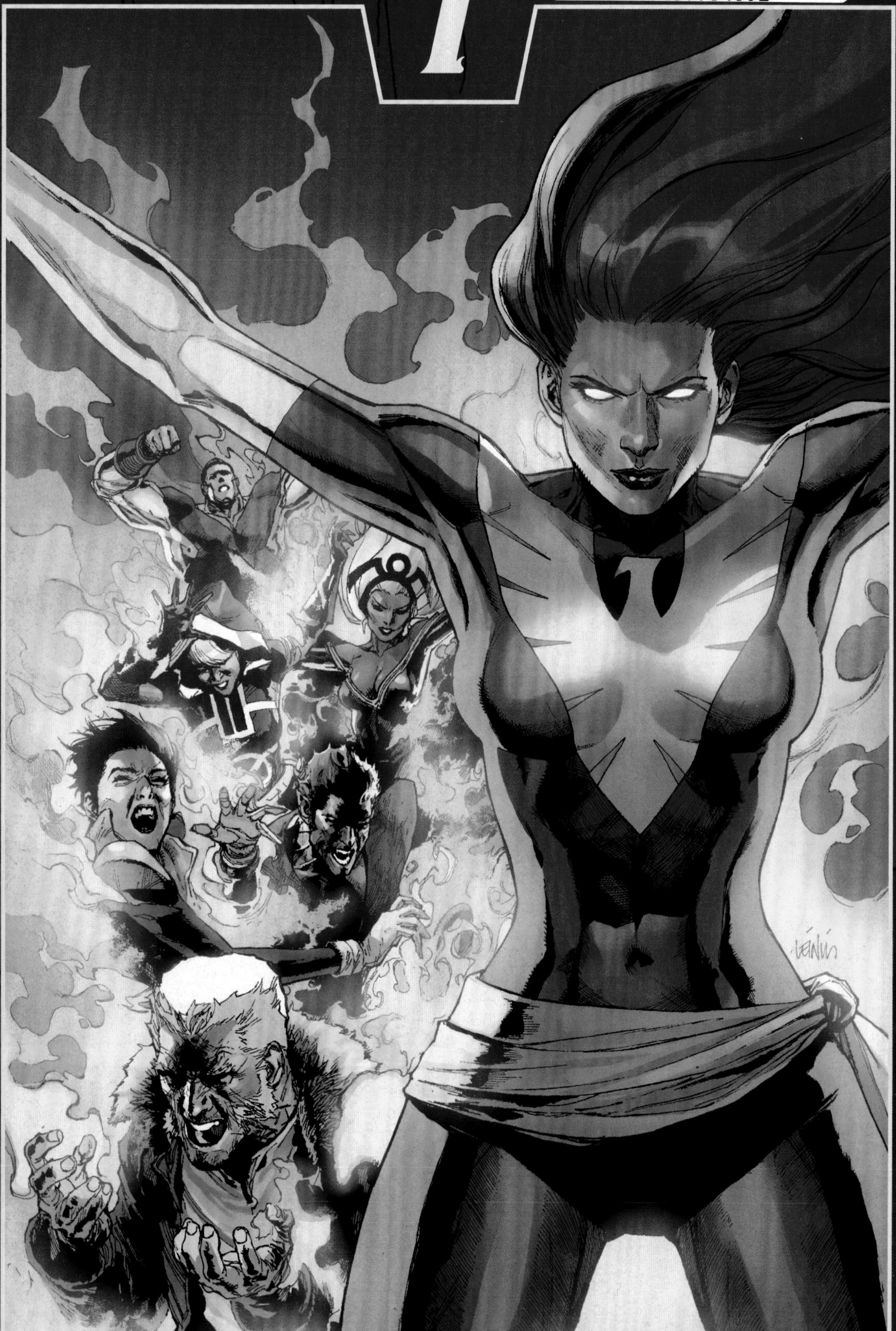

CHAPTER ONE: ***FRUSTRATE THE SUN***

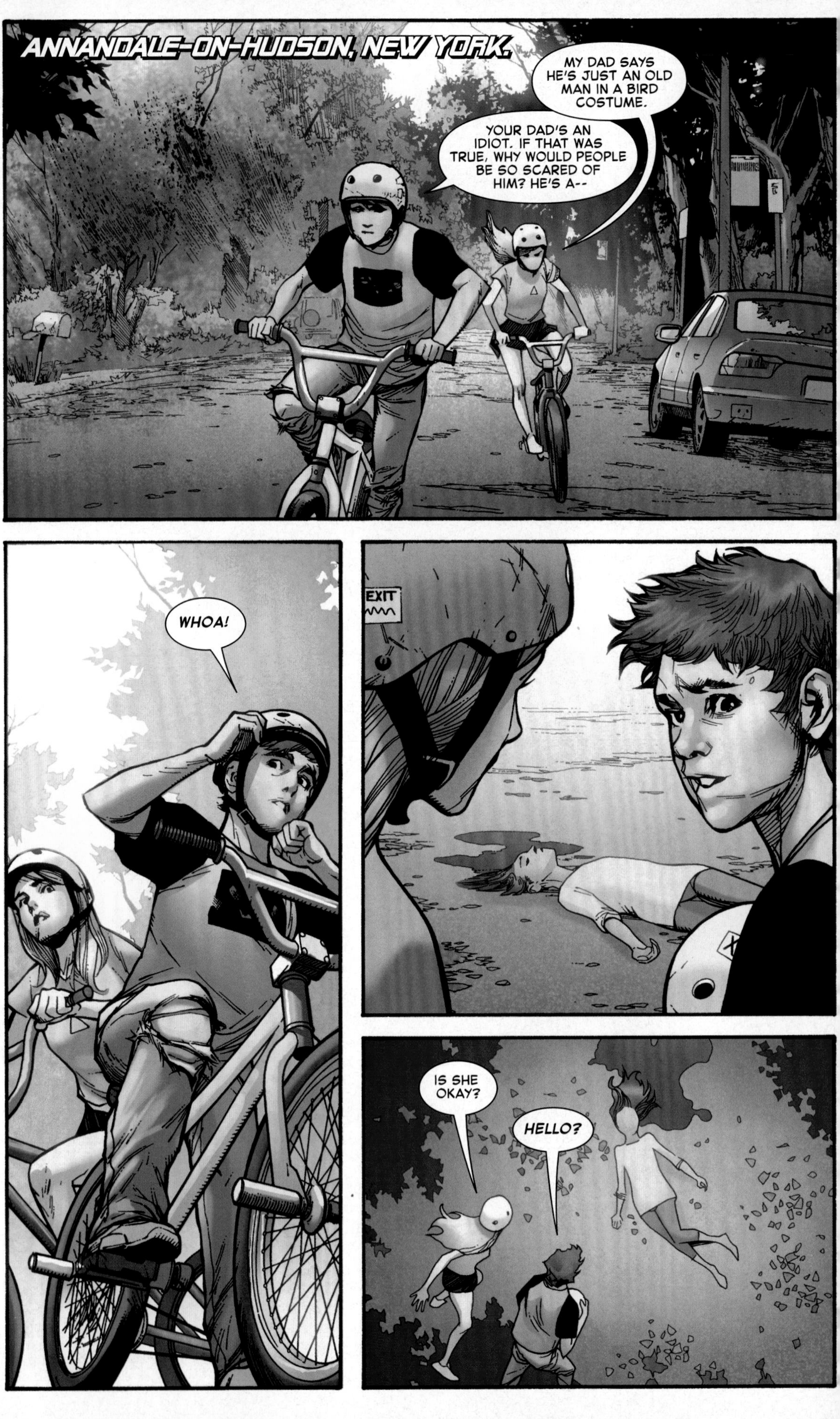

ANNANDALE-ON-HUDSON, NEW YORK.
MY DAD SAYS HE'S JUST AN OLD MAN IN A BIRD COSTUME.
YOUR DAD'S AN IDIOT. IF THAT WAS TRUE, WHY WOULD PEOPLE BE SO SCARED OF HIM? HE'S A--
WHOA!
EXIT
IS SHE OKAY?
HELLO?

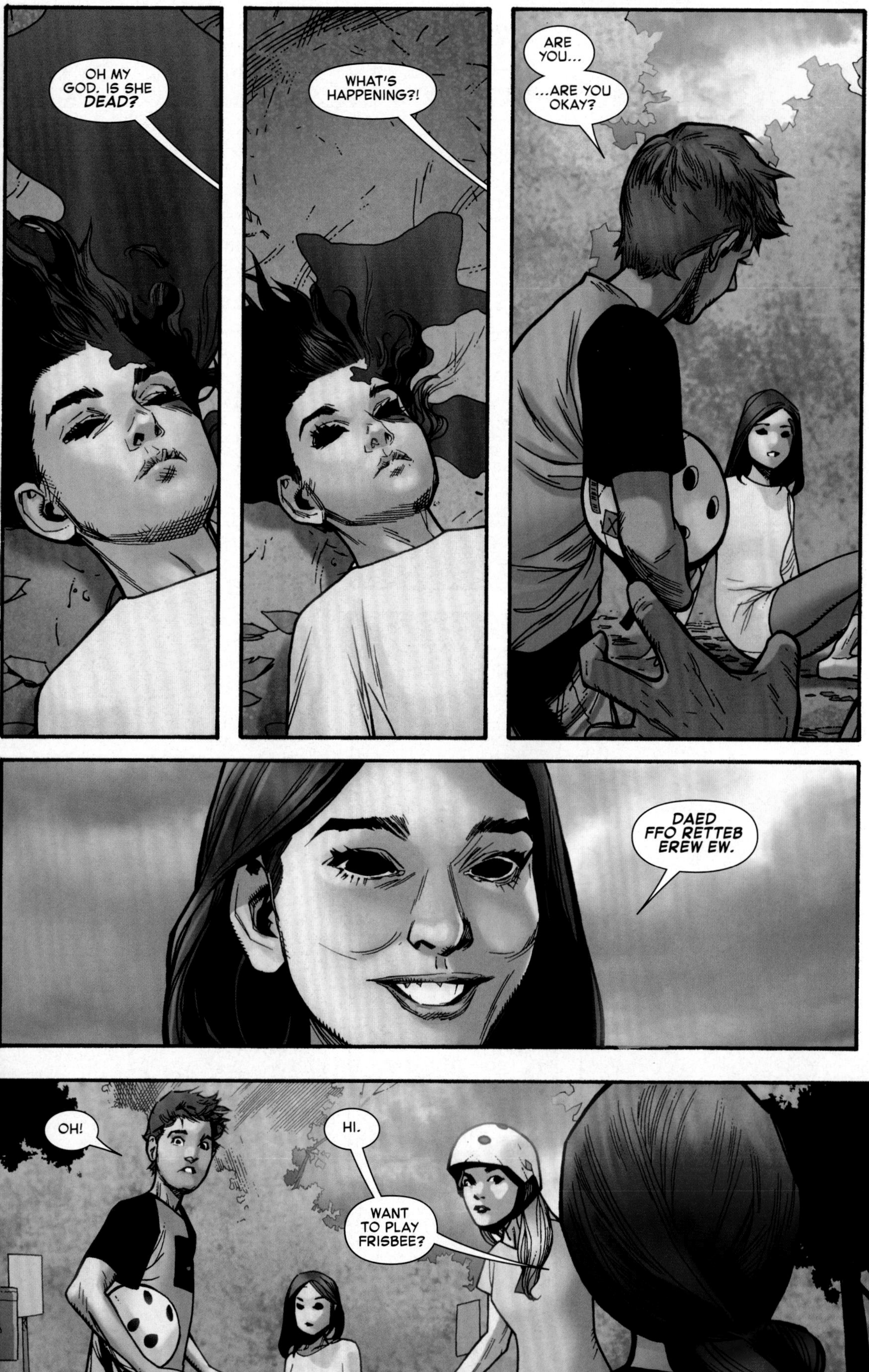
OH MY GOD. IS SHE DEAD?
WHAT'S HAPPENING?!
ARE YOU...
...ARE YOU OKAY?
DAED FFO RETTEB EREW EW.
OH!
HI.
WANT TO PLAY FRISBEE?

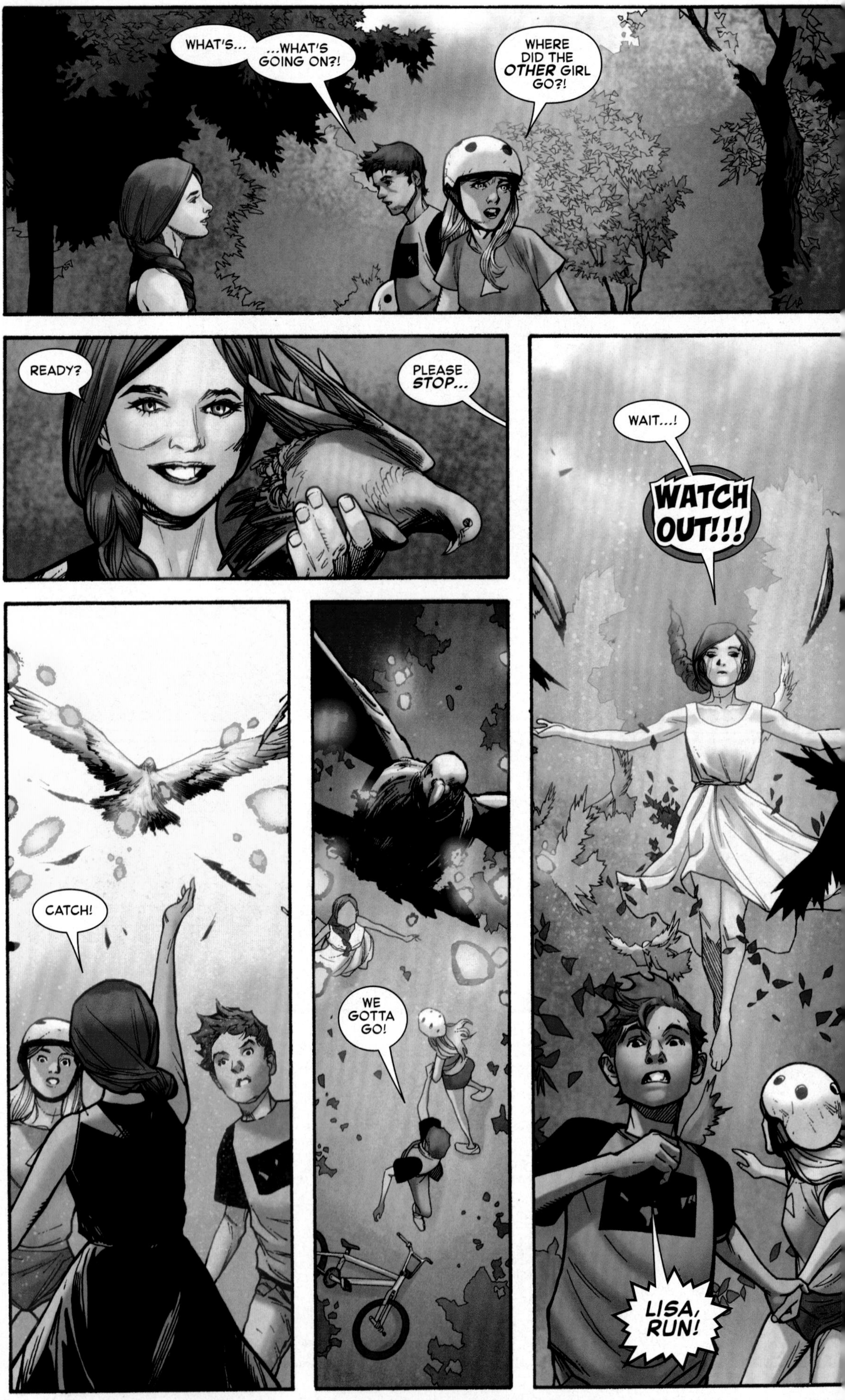
WHAT'S...
...WHAT'S GOING ON?!
WHERE DID THE OTHER GIRL GO?!
READY?
PLEASE STOP...
WAIT...!
WATCH OUT!!!
CATCH!
WE GOTTA GO!
LISA, RUN!

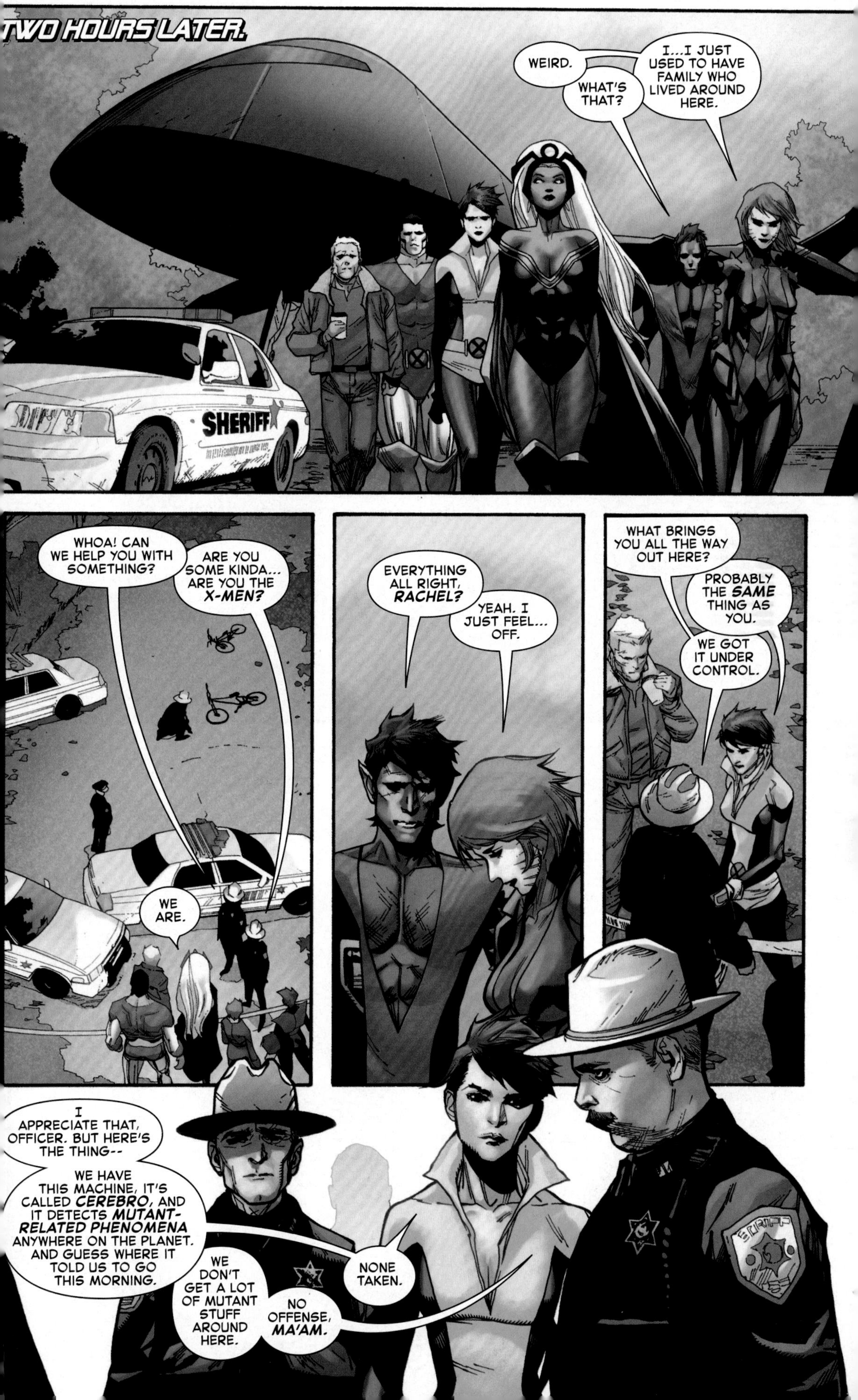
TWO HOURS LATER.
WEIRD.
WHAT'S THAT?
I...I JUST USED TO HAVE FAMILY WHO LIVED AROUND HERE.
SHERIFF
WHOA! CAN WE HELP YOU WITH SOMETHING?
ARE YOU SOME KINDA... ARE YOU THE X-MEN?
WE ARE.
EVERYTHING ALL RIGHT, RACHEL?
YEAH. I JUST FEEL... OFF.
WHAT BRINGS YOU ALL THE WAY OUT HERE?
PROBABLY THE SAME THING AS YOU.
WE GOT IT UNDER CONTROL.
I APPRECIATE THAT, OFFICER. BUT HERE'S THE THING--
WE HAVE THIS MACHINE, IT'S CALLED CEREBRO, AND IT DETECTS MUTANT-RELATED PHENOMENA ANYWHERE ON THE PLANET. AND GUESS WHERE IT TOLD US TO GO THIS MORNING.
WE DON'T GET A LOT OF MUTANT STUFF AROUND HERE.
NO OFFENSE, MA'AM.
NONE TAKEN.

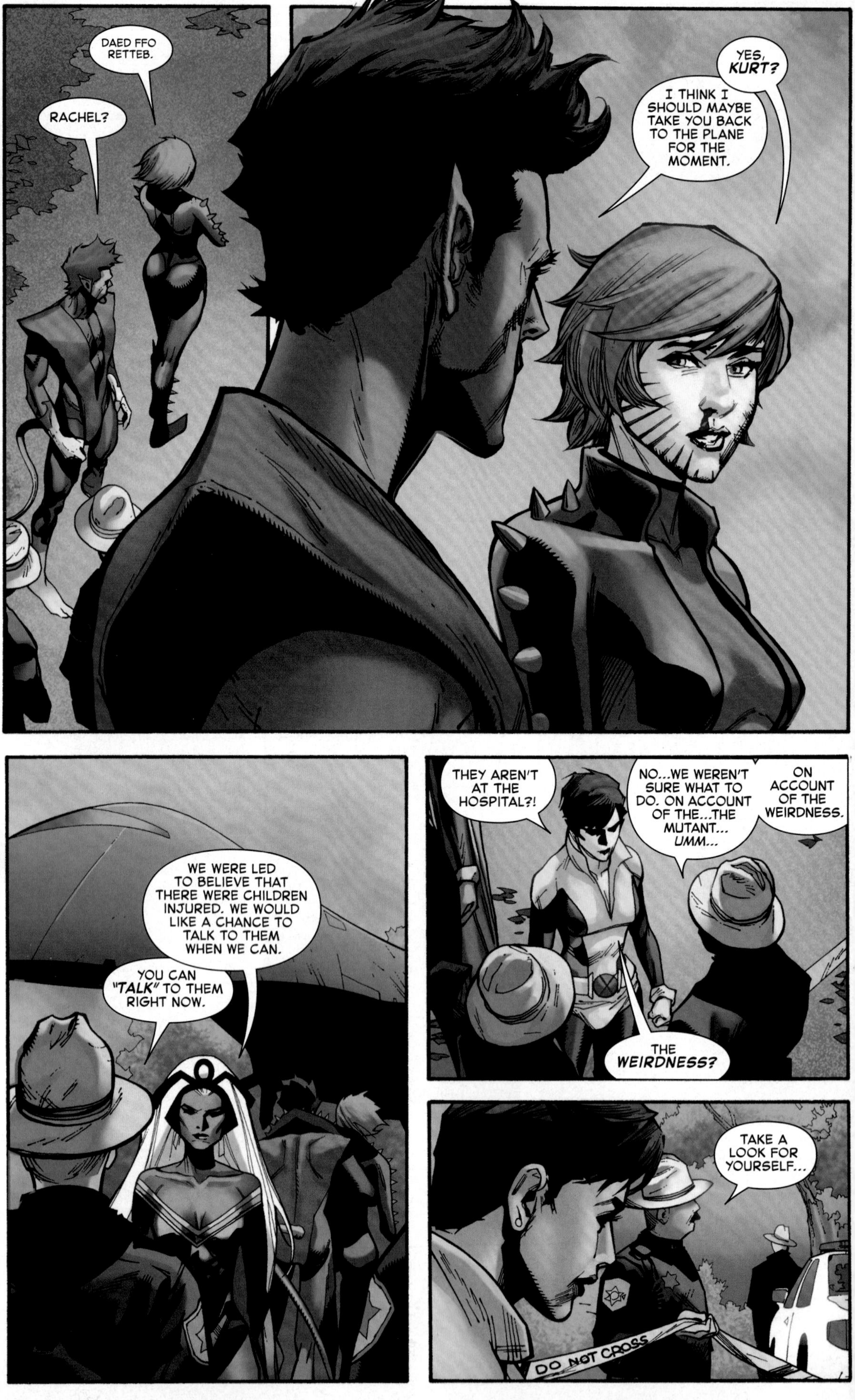

DAED FFO RETTEB.
RACHEL?
YES, *KURT?*
I THINK I SHOULD MAYBE TAKE YOU BACK TO THE PLANE FOR THE MOMENT.
WE WERE LED TO BELIEVE THAT THERE WERE CHILDREN INJURED. WE WOULD LIKE A CHANCE TO TALK TO THEM WHEN WE CAN.
YOU CAN "*TALK*" TO THEM RIGHT NOW.
THEY AREN'T AT THE HOSPITAL?!
NO...WE WEREN'T SURE WHAT TO DO. ON ACCOUNT OF THE...THE MUTANT... *UMM...*
ON ACCOUNT OF THE WEIRDNESS.
THE *WEIRDNESS?*
TAKE A LOOK FOR YOURSELF...
DO NOT CROSS

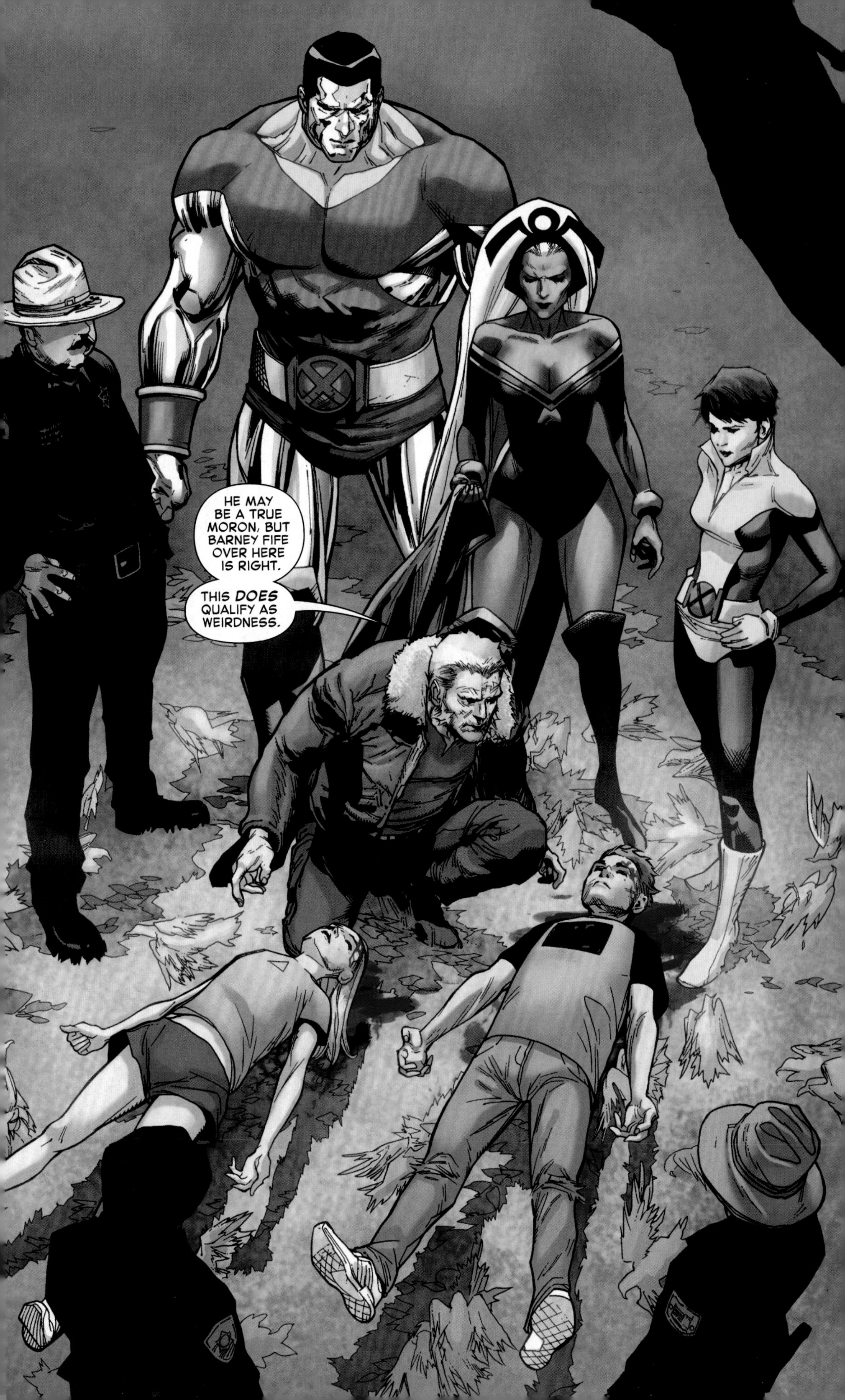
HE MAY BE A TRUE MORON, BUT BARNEY FIFE OVER HERE IS RIGHT.
THIS DOES QUALIFY AS WEIRDNESS.

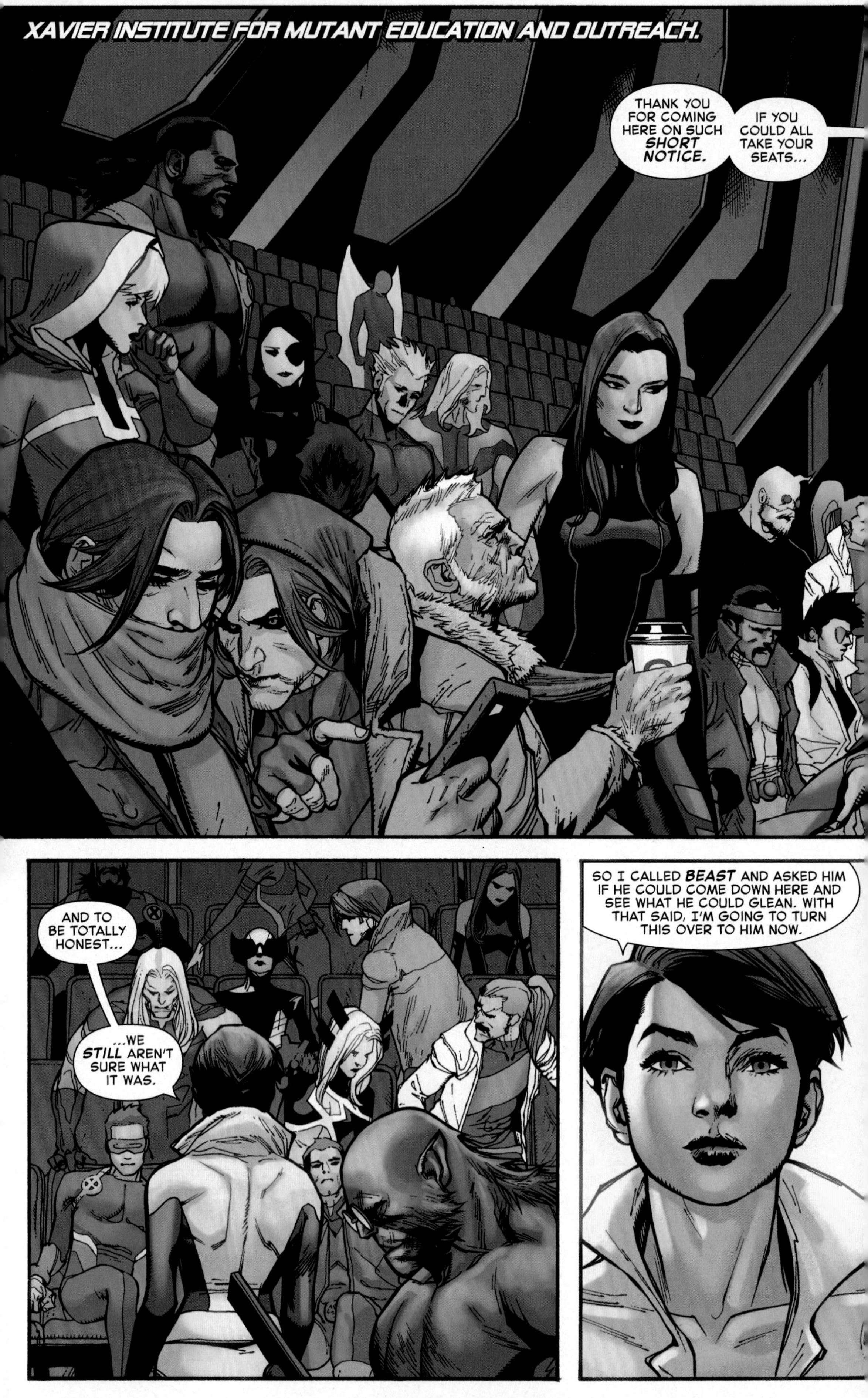
XAVIER INSTITUTE FOR MUTANT EDUCATION AND OUTREACH.
THANK YOU FOR COMING HERE ON SUCH SHORT NOTICE.
IF YOU COULD ALL TAKE YOUR SEATS...
AND TO BE TOTALLY HONEST...
...WE STILL AREN'T SURE WHAT IT WAS.
SO I CALLED BEAST AND ASKED HIM IF HE COULD COME DOWN HERE AND SEE WHAT HE COULD GLEAN. WITH THAT SAID, I'M GOING TO TURN THIS OVER TO HIM NOW.

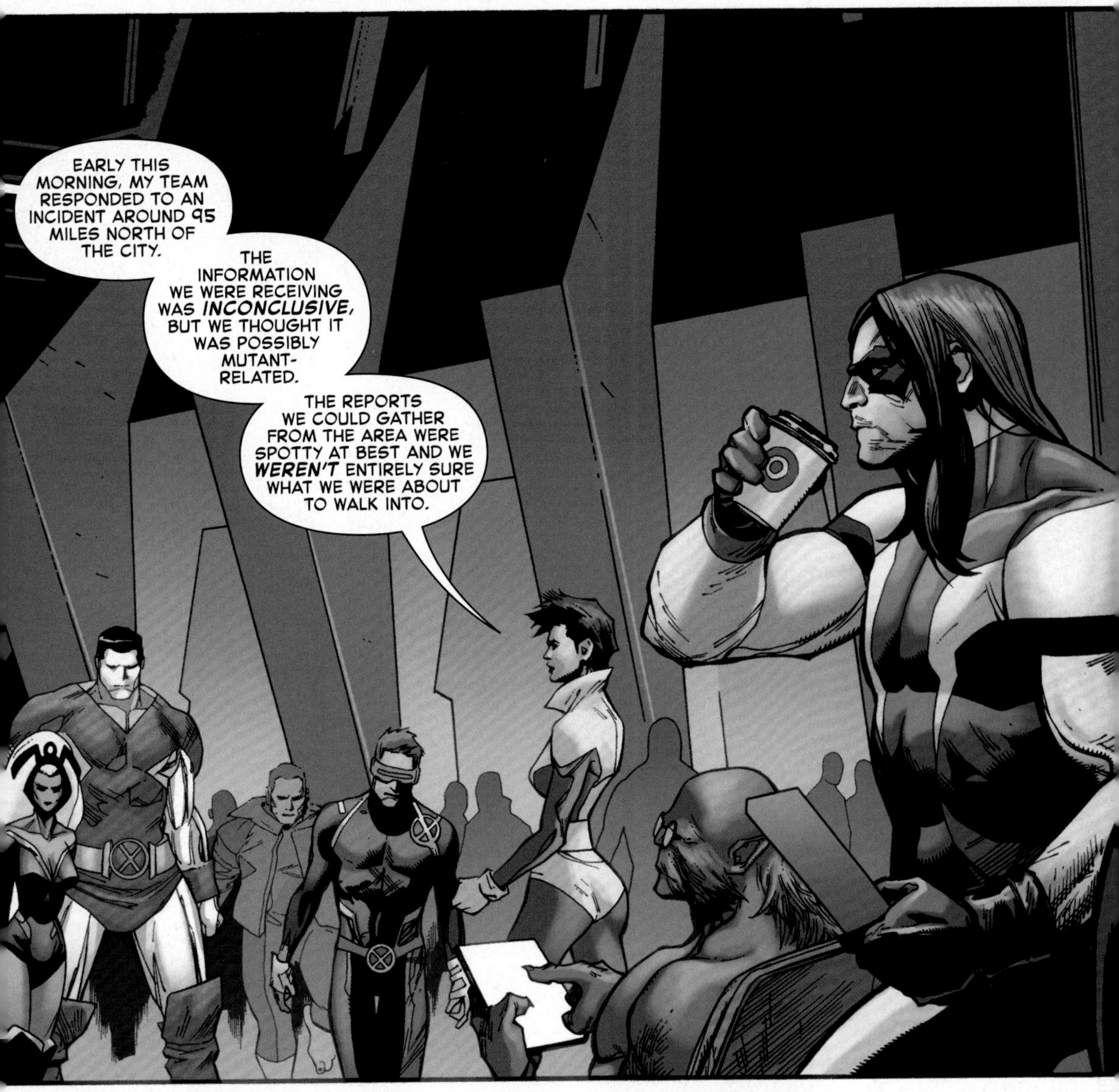
EARLY THIS MORNING, MY TEAM RESPONDED TO AN INCIDENT AROUND 95 MILES NORTH OF THE CITY.
THE INFORMATION WE WERE RECEIVING WAS *INCONCLUSIVE*, BUT WE THOUGHT IT WAS POSSIBLY MUTANT-RELATED.
THE REPORTS WE COULD GATHER FROM THE AREA WERE SPOTTY AT BEST AND WE *WEREN'T* ENTIRELY SURE WHAT WE WERE ABOUT TO WALK INTO.

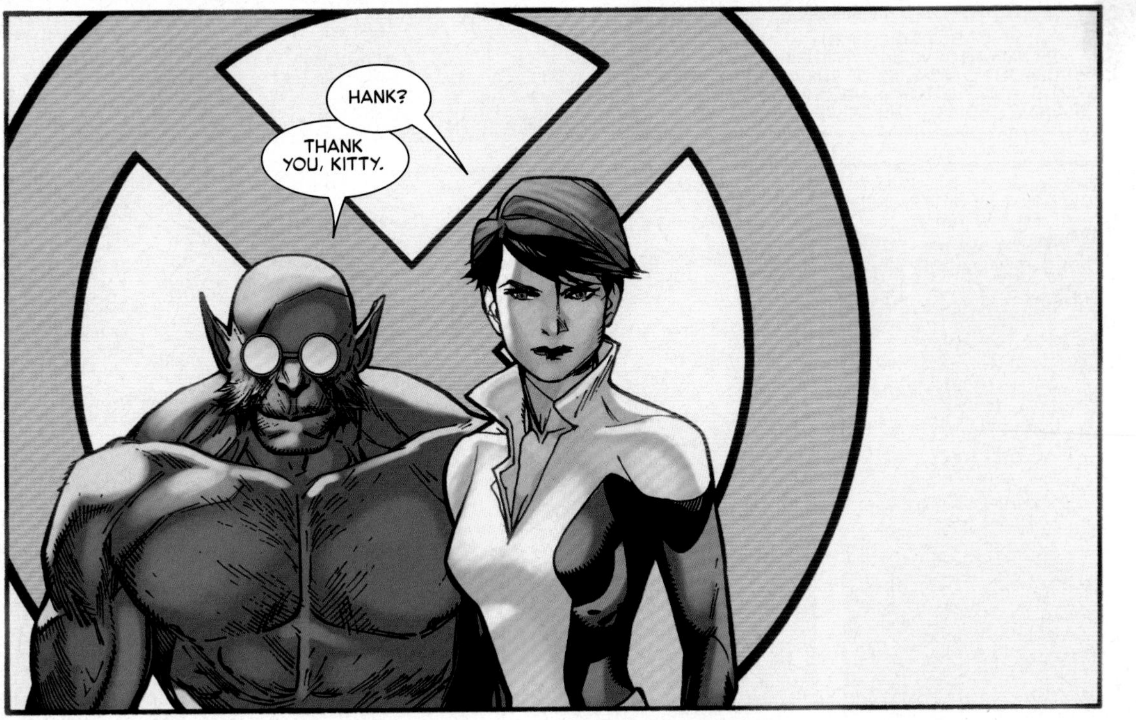
HANK?
THANK YOU, KITTY.

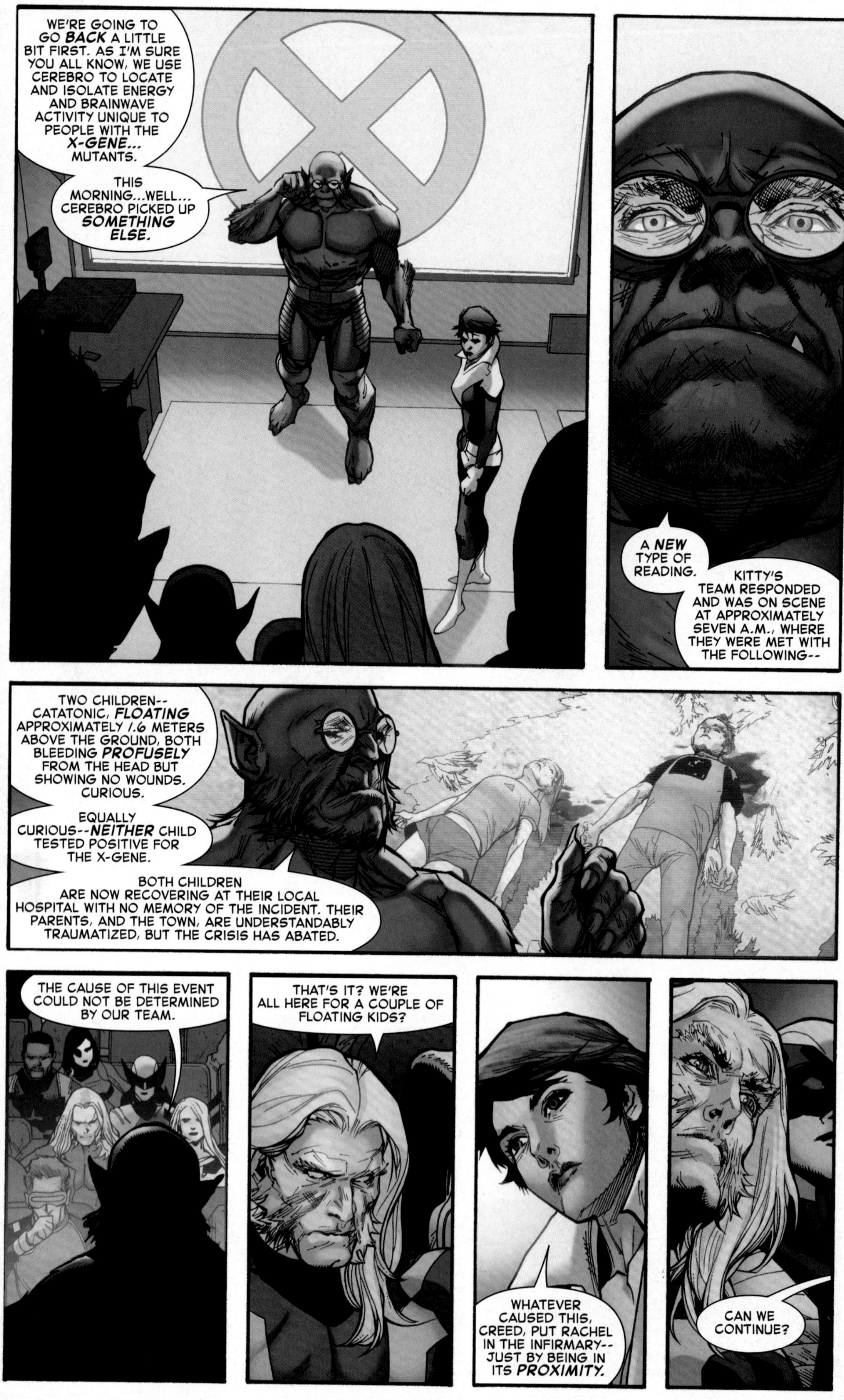
WE'RE GOING TO GO BACK A LITTLE BIT FIRST. AS I'M SURE YOU ALL KNOW, WE USE CEREBRO TO LOCATE AND ISOLATE ENERGY AND BRAINWAVE ACTIVITY UNIQUE TO PEOPLE WITH THE X-GENE... MUTANTS.
THIS MORNING...WELL... CEREBRO PICKED UP SOMETHING ELSE.
A NEW TYPE OF READING.
KITTY'S TEAM RESPONDED AND WAS ON SCENE AT APPROXIMATELY SEVEN A.M., WHERE THEY WERE MET WITH THE FOLLOWING--
TWO CHILDREN-- CATATONIC, FLOATING APPROXIMATELY 1.6 METERS ABOVE THE GROUND, BOTH BLEEDING PROFUSELY FROM THE HEAD BUT SHOWING NO WOUNDS. CURIOUS.
EQUALLY CURIOUS--NEITHER CHILD TESTED POSITIVE FOR THE X-GENE.
BOTH CHILDREN ARE NOW RECOVERING AT THEIR LOCAL HOSPITAL WITH NO MEMORY OF THE INCIDENT. THEIR PARENTS, AND THE TOWN, ARE UNDERSTANDABLY TRAUMATIZED, BUT THE CRISIS HAS ABATED.
THE CAUSE OF THIS EVENT COULD NOT BE DETERMINED BY OUR TEAM.
THAT'S IT? WE'RE ALL HERE FOR A COUPLE OF FLOATING KIDS?
WHATEVER CAUSED THIS, CREED, PUT RACHEL IN THE INFIRMARY-- JUST BY BEING IN ITS PROXIMITY.
CAN WE CONTINUE?

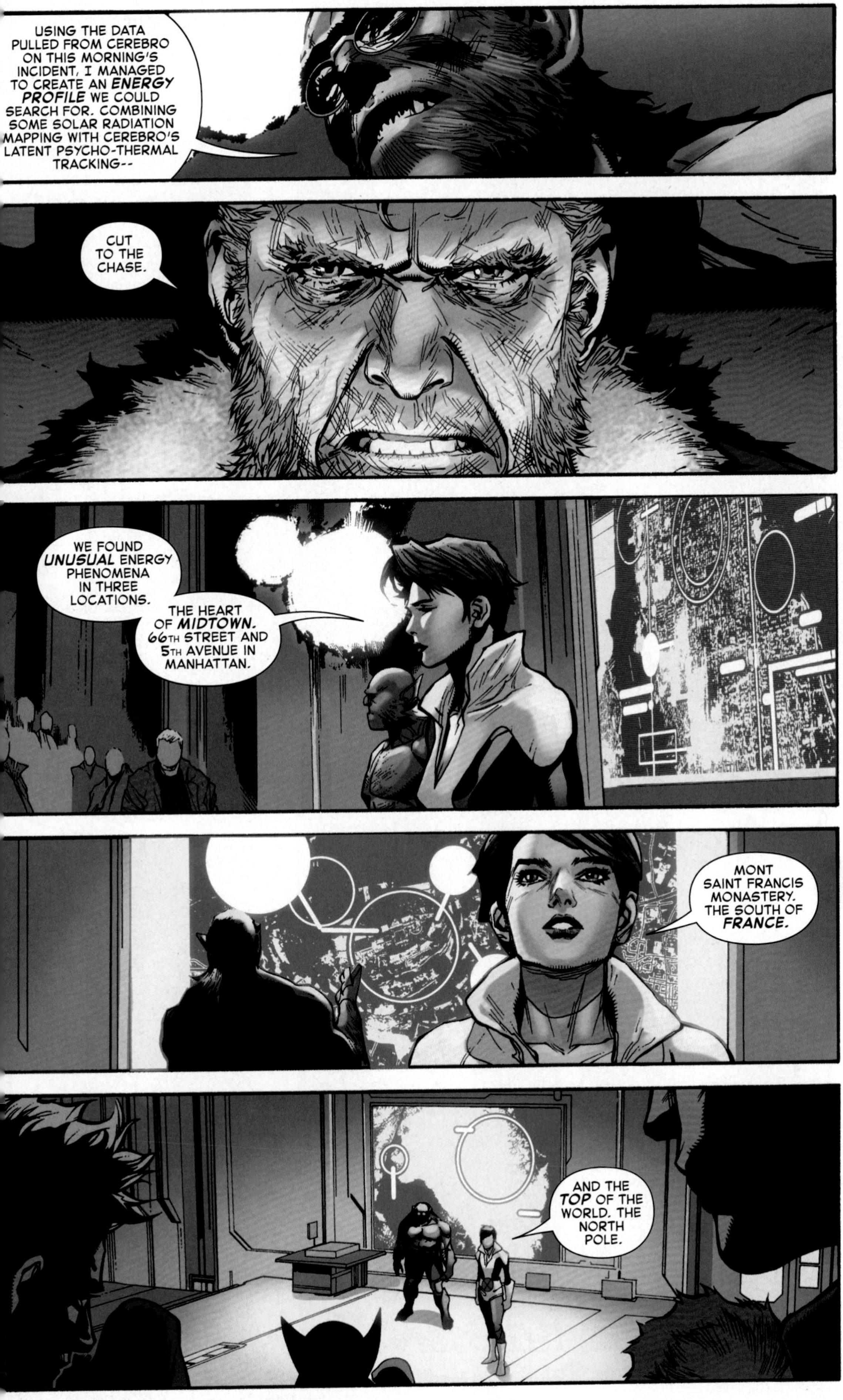
USING THE DATA PULLED FROM CEREBRO ON THIS MORNING'S INCIDENT, I MANAGED TO CREATE AN ENERGY PROFILE WE COULD SEARCH FOR. COMBINING SOME SOLAR RADIATION MAPPING WITH CEREBRO'S LATENT PSYCHO-THERMAL TRACKING--
CUT TO THE CHASE.
WE FOUND UNUSUAL ENERGY PHENOMENA IN THREE LOCATIONS.
THE HEART OF MIDTOWN. 66TH STREET AND 5TH AVENUE IN MANHATTAN.
MONT SAINT FRANCIS MONASTERY. THE SOUTH OF FRANCE.
AND THE TOP OF THE WORLD. THE NORTH POLE.

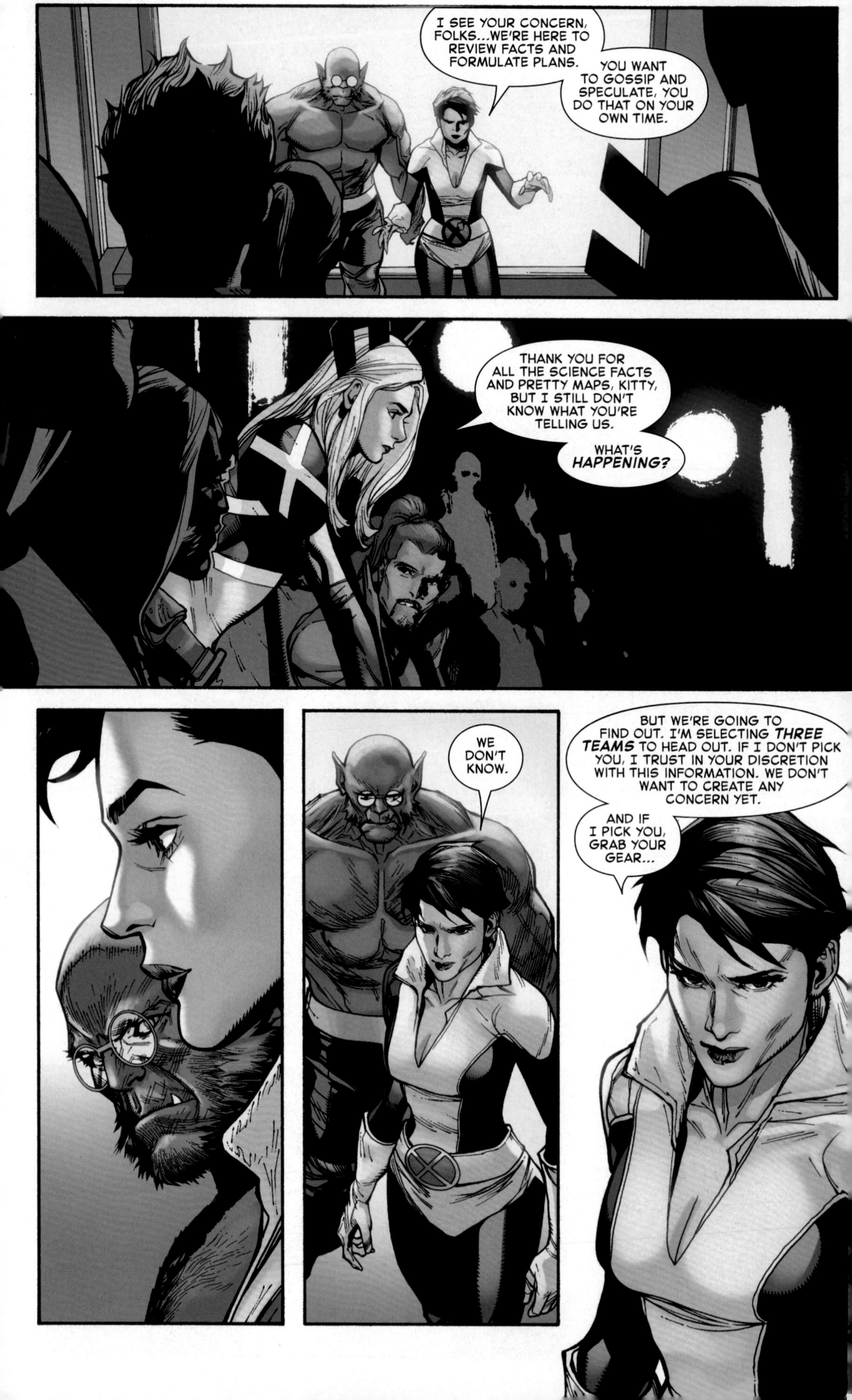
I SEE YOUR CONCERN, FOLKS...WE'RE HERE TO REVIEW FACTS AND FORMULATE PLANS.
YOU WANT TO GOSSIP AND SPECULATE, YOU DO THAT ON YOUR OWN TIME.
THANK YOU FOR ALL THE SCIENCE FACTS AND PRETTY MAPS, KITTY, BUT I STILL DON'T KNOW WHAT YOU'RE TELLING US.
WHAT'S *HAPPENING?*
WE DON'T KNOW.
BUT WE'RE GOING TO FIND OUT. I'M SELECTING *THREE TEAMS* TO HEAD OUT. IF I DON'T PICK YOU, I TRUST IN YOUR DISCRETION WITH THIS INFORMATION. WE DON'T WANT TO CREATE ANY CONCERN YET.
AND IF I PICK YOU, GRAB YOUR GEAR...

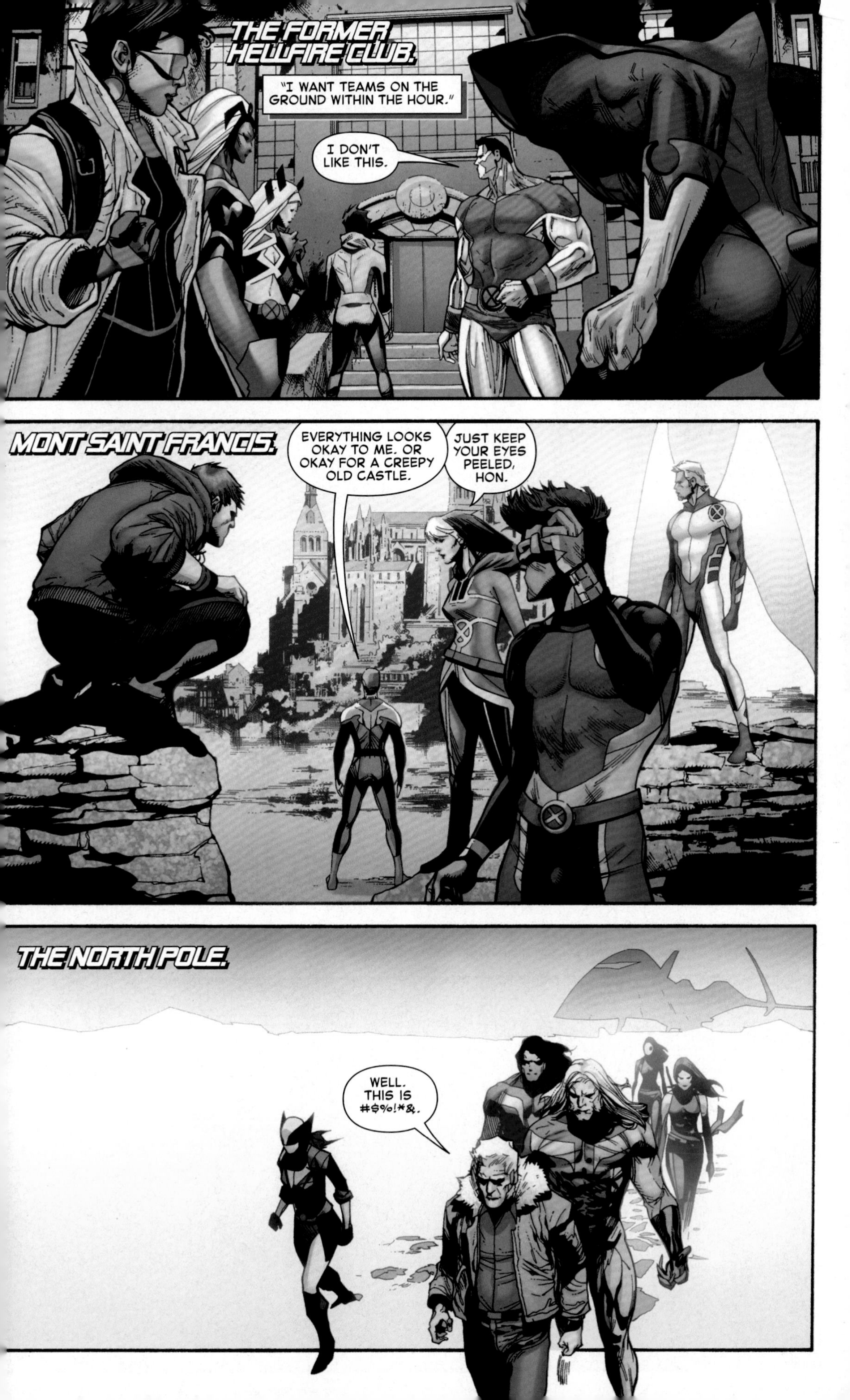
THE FORMER HELLFIRE CLUB.
"I WANT TEAMS ON THE GROUND WITHIN THE HOUR."
I DON'T LIKE THIS.
MONT SAINT FRANCIS.
EVERYTHING LOOKS OKAY TO ME. OR OKAY FOR A CREEPY OLD CASTLE.
JUST KEEP YOUR EYES PEELED, HON.
THE NORTH POLE.
WELL. THIS IS #$%!*&.

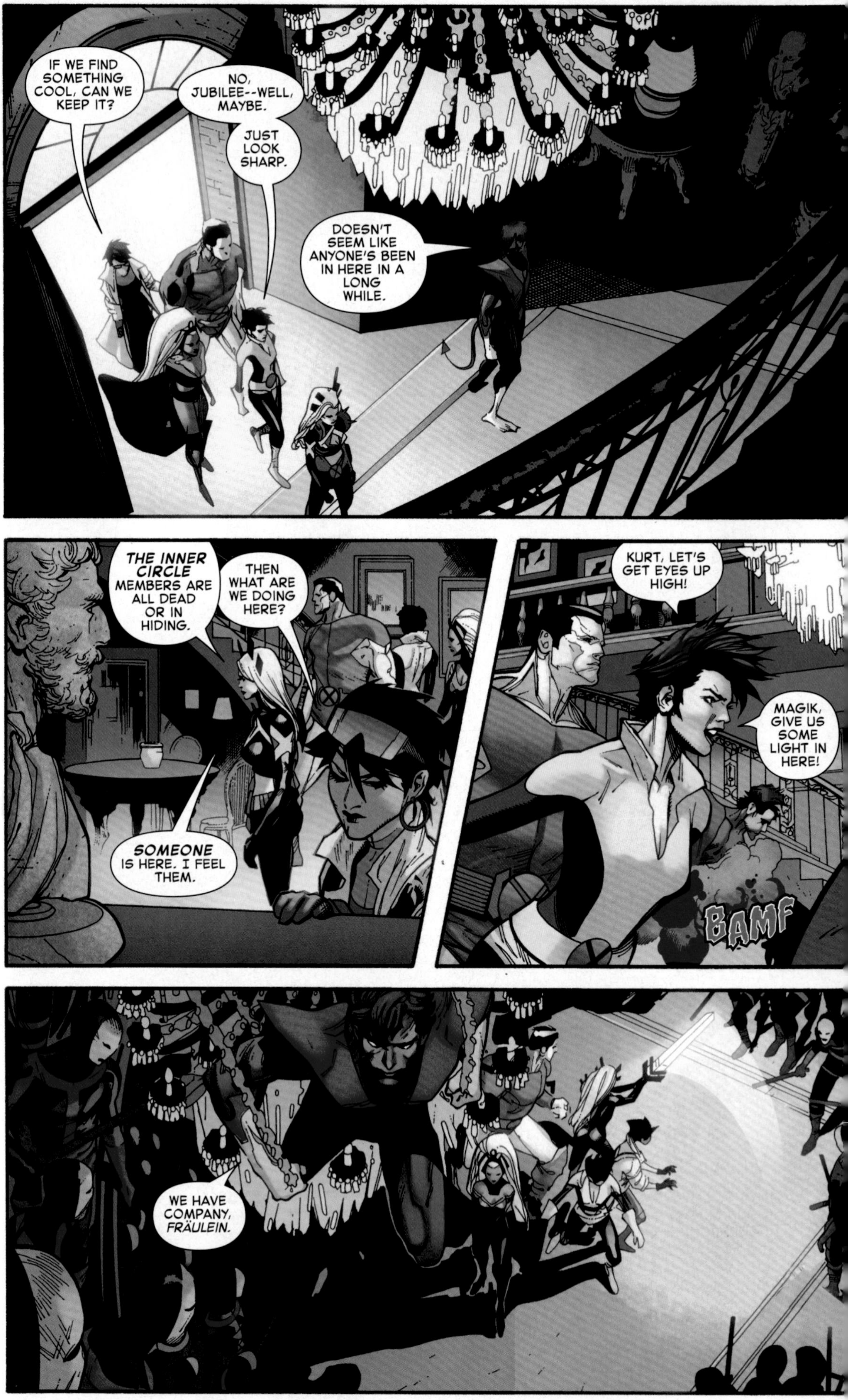
IF WE FIND SOMETHING COOL, CAN WE KEEP IT?
NO, JUBILEE--WELL, MAYBE.
JUST LOOK SHARP.
DOESN'T SEEM LIKE ANYONE'S BEEN IN HERE IN A LONG WHILE.
THE INNER CIRCLE MEMBERS ARE ALL DEAD OR IN HIDING.
THEN WHAT ARE WE DOING HERE?
SOMEONE IS HERE. I FEEL THEM.
KURT, LET'S GET EYES UP HIGH!
MAGIK, GIVE US SOME LIGHT IN HERE!
BAMF
WE HAVE COMPANY, FRÄULEIN.

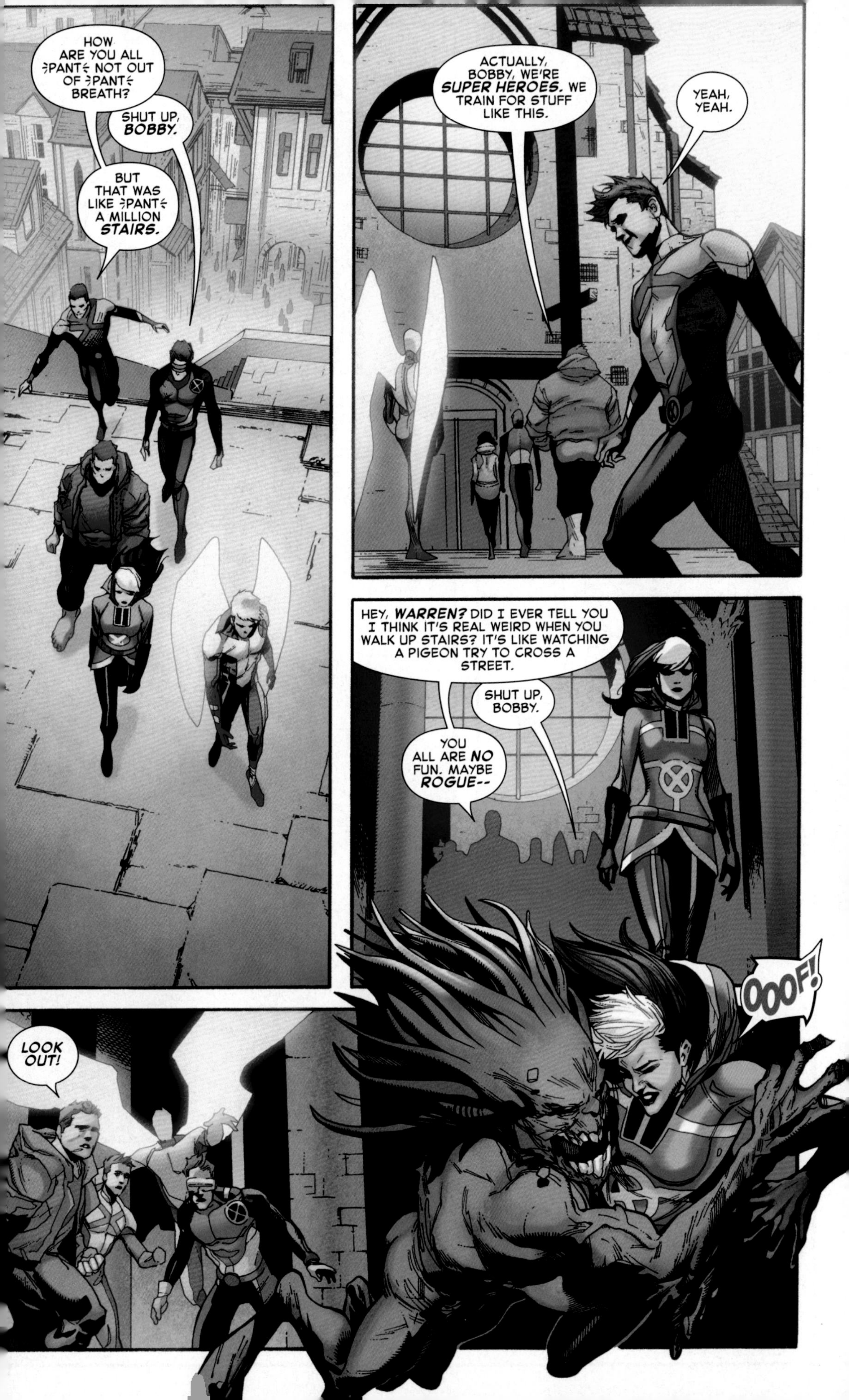

HOW ARE YOU ALL ⁼PANT⁼ NOT OUT OF ⁼PANT⁼ BREATH?
SHUT UP, BOBBY.
BUT THAT WAS LIKE ⁼PANT⁼ A MILLION STAIRS.
ACTUALLY, BOBBY, WE'RE SUPER HEROES. WE TRAIN FOR STUFF LIKE THIS.
YEAH, YEAH.
HEY, WARREN? DID I EVER TELL YOU I THINK IT'S REAL WEIRD WHEN YOU WALK UP STAIRS? IT'S LIKE WATCHING A PIGEON TRY TO CROSS A STREET.
SHUT UP, BOBBY.
YOU ALL ARE NO FUN. MAYBE ROGUE--
LOOK OUT!
OOOF!

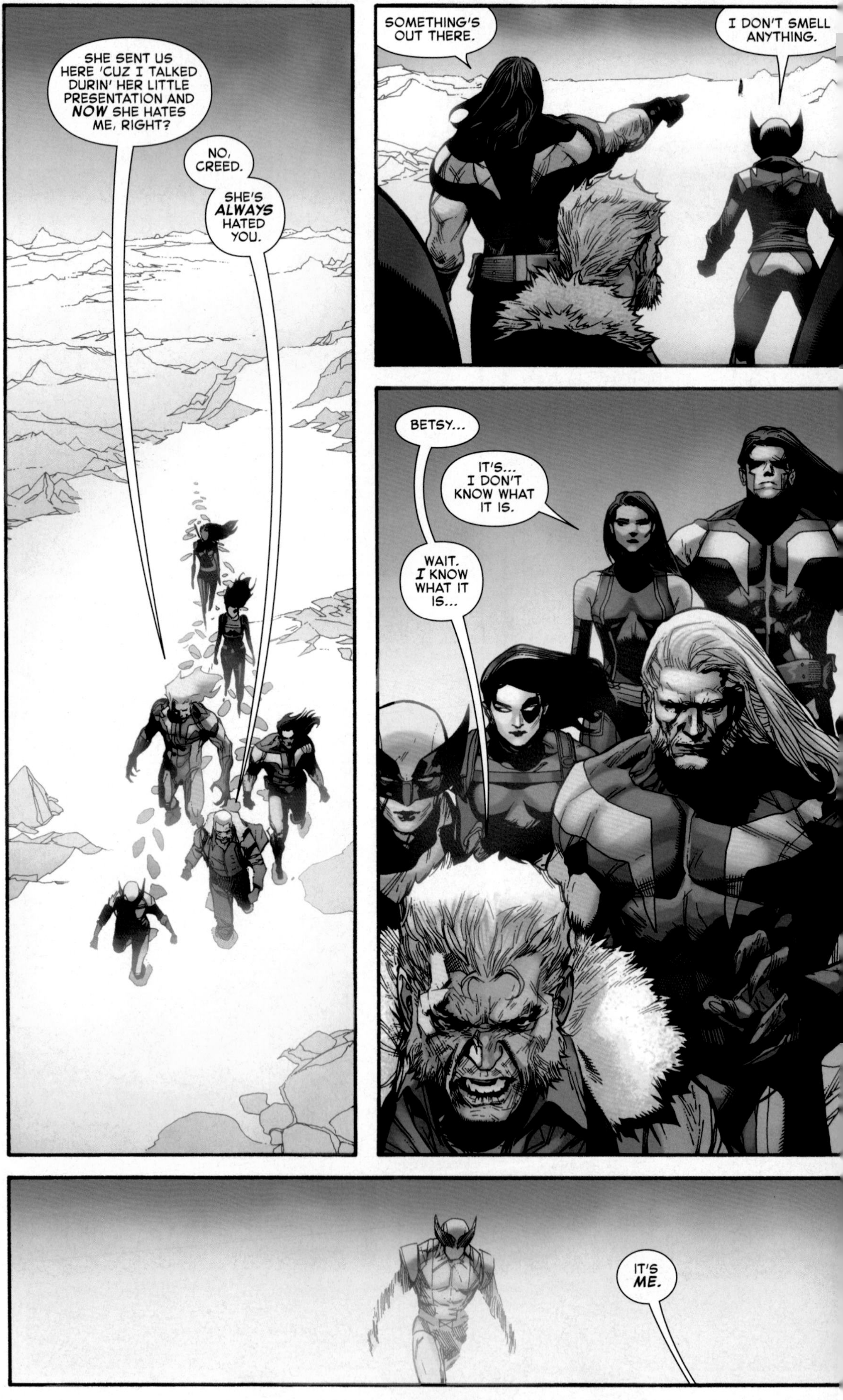
SHE SENT US HERE 'CUZ I TALKED DURIN' HER LITTLE PRESENTATION AND NOW SHE HATES ME, RIGHT?
NO, CREED.
SHE'S ALWAYS HATED YOU.
SOMETHING'S OUT THERE.
I DON'T SMELL ANYTHING.
BETSY...
IT'S... I DON'T KNOW WHAT IT IS.
WAIT. I KNOW WHAT IT IS...
IT'S ME.

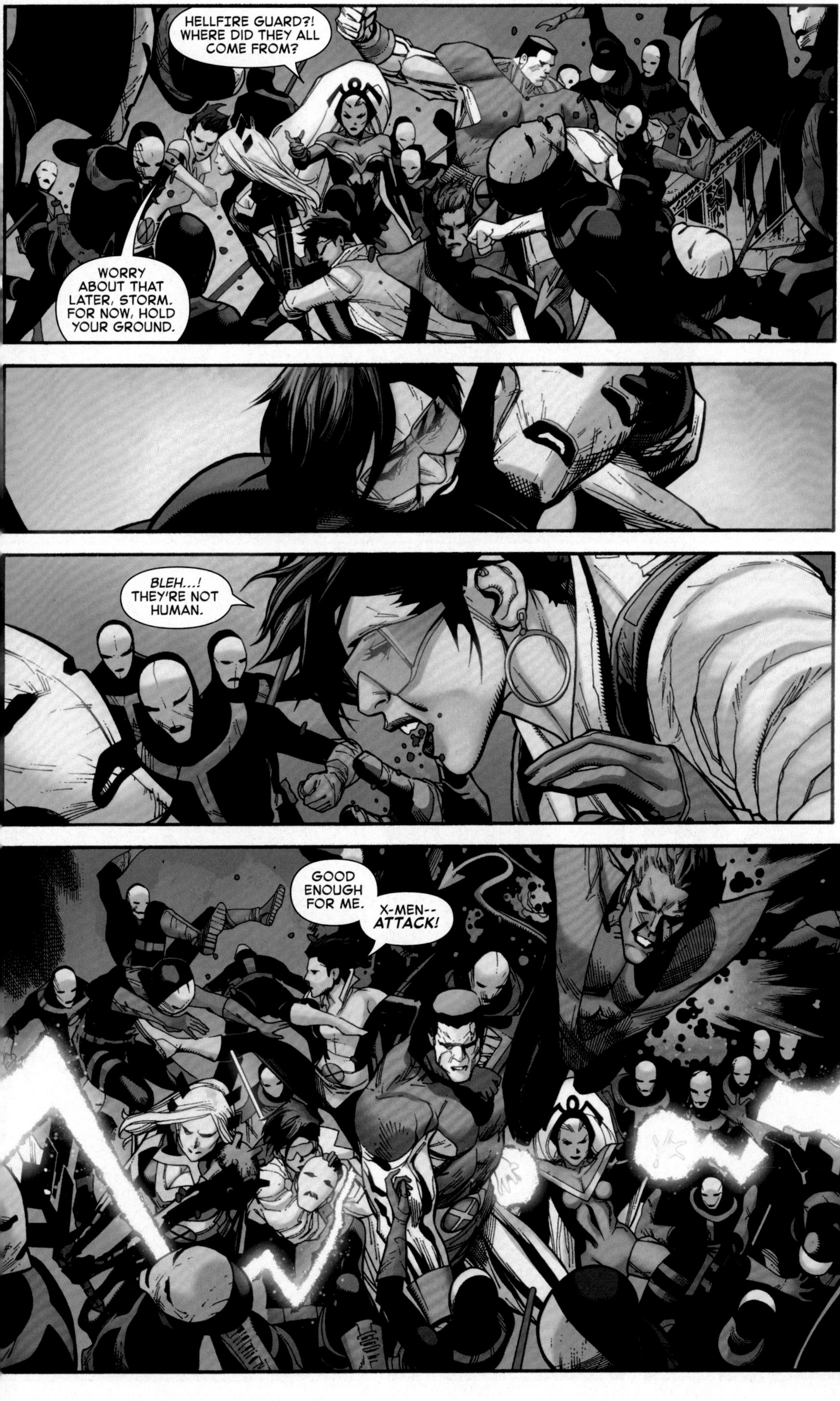
HELLFIRE GUARD?! WHERE DID THEY ALL COME FROM?
WORRY ABOUT THAT LATER, STORM. FOR NOW, HOLD YOUR GROUND.
BLEH...! THEY'RE NOT HUMAN.
GOOD ENOUGH FOR ME.
X-MEN-- ATTACK!

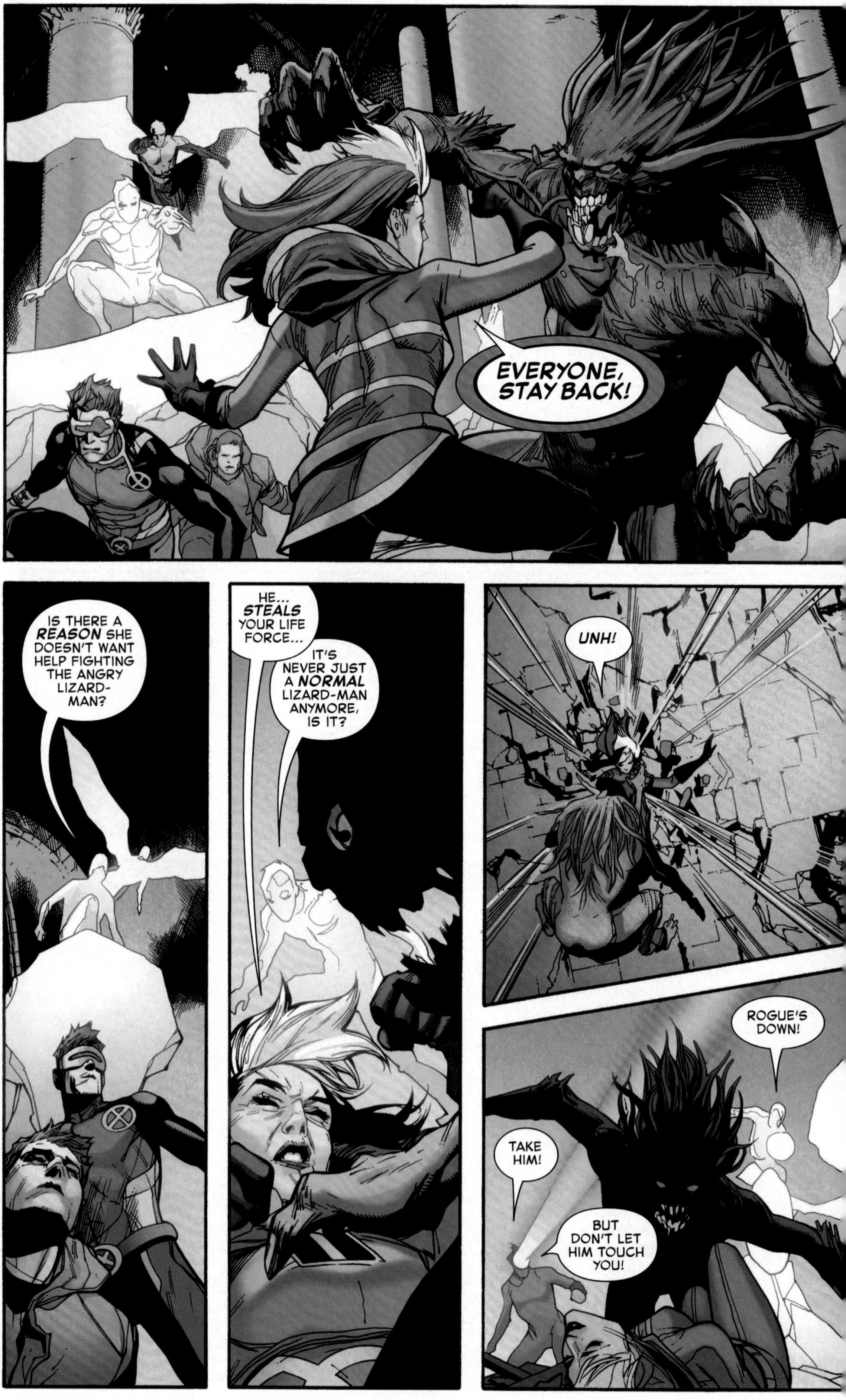
EVERYONE, STAY BACK!
IS THERE A REASON SHE DOESN'T WANT HELP FIGHTING THE ANGRY LIZARD-MAN?
HE... STEALS YOUR LIFE FORCE...
IT'S NEVER JUST A NORMAL LIZARD-MAN ANYMORE, IS IT?
UNH!
ROGUE'S DOWN!
TAKE HIM!
BUT DON'T LET HIM TOUCH YOU!

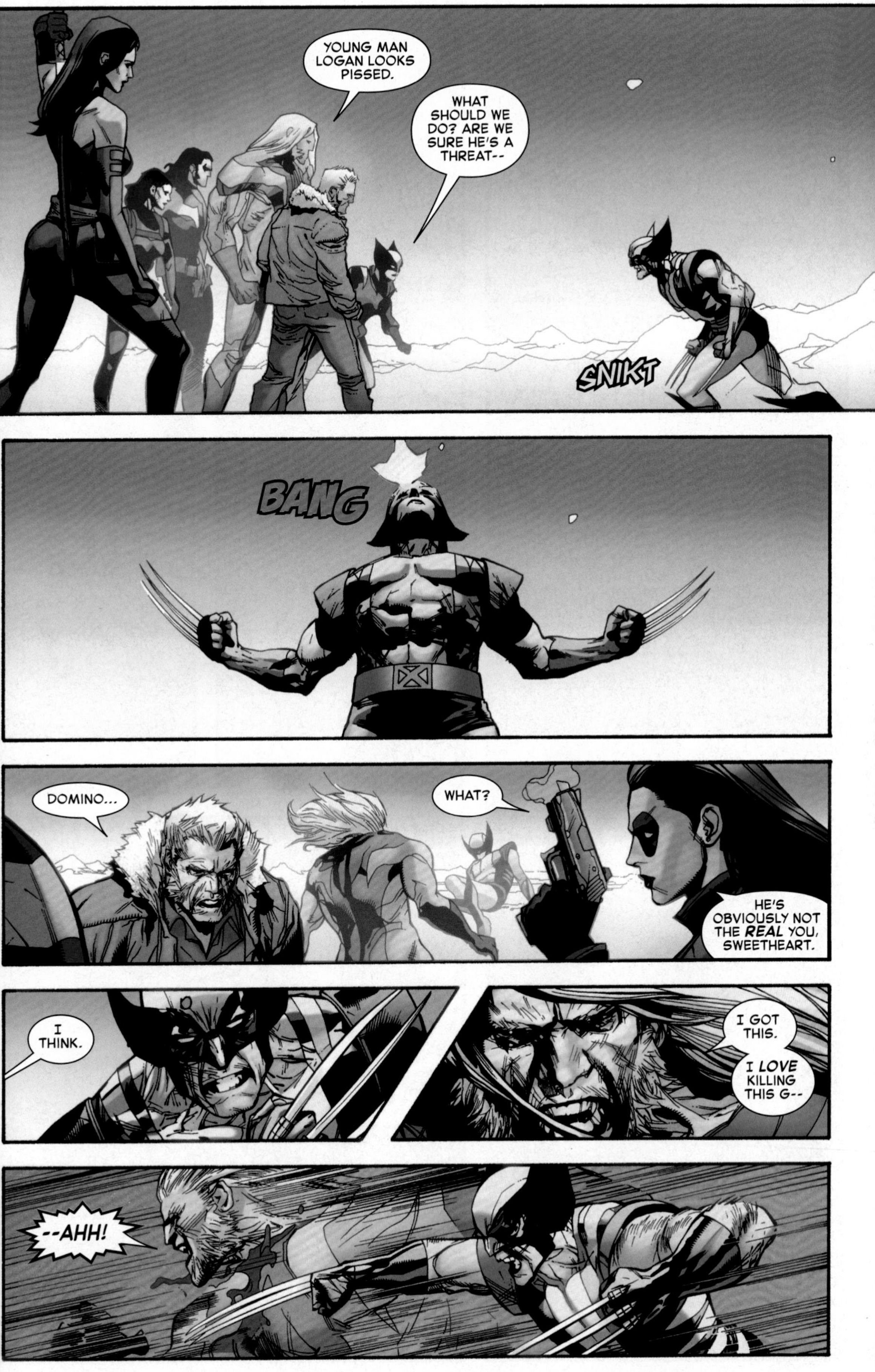

YOUNG MAN LOGAN LOOKS PISSED.
WHAT SHOULD WE DO? ARE WE SURE HE'S A THREAT--
SNIKT
BANG
DOMINO...
WHAT?
HE'S OBVIOUSLY NOT THE REAL YOU, SWEETHEART.
I THINK.
I GOT THIS.
I LOVE KILLING THIS G--
--AHH!

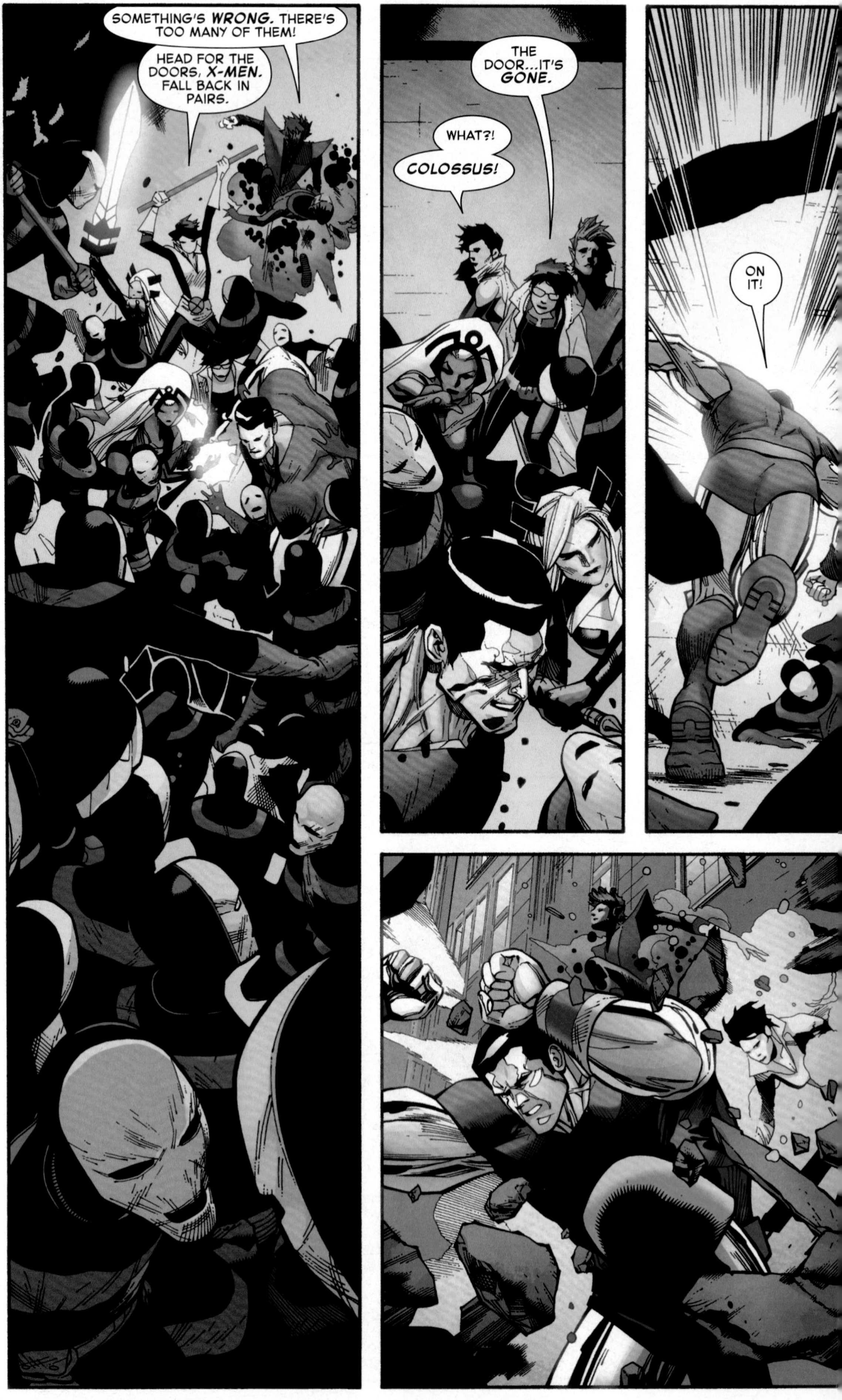
SOMETHING'S WRONG. THERE'S TOO MANY OF THEM!
HEAD FOR THE DOORS, X-MEN. FALL BACK IN PAIRS.
THE DOOR...IT'S GONE.
WHAT?!
COLOSSUS!
ON IT!

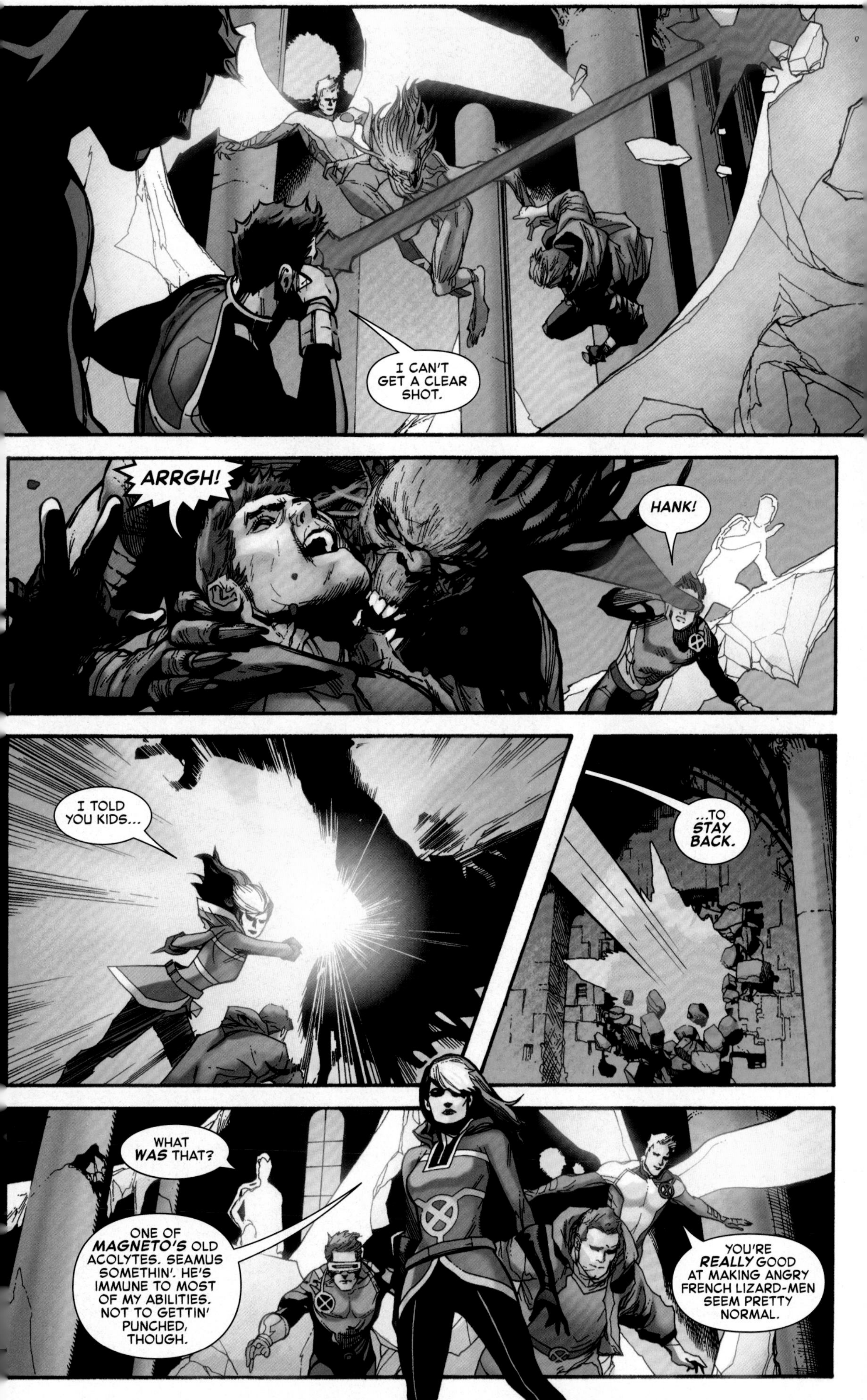
I CAN'T GET A CLEAR SHOT.
ARRGH!
HANK!
I TOLD YOU KIDS...
...TO STAY BACK.
WHAT WAS THAT?
ONE OF MAGNETO'S OLD ACOLYTES. SEAMUS SOMETHIN'. HE'S IMMUNE TO MOST OF MY ABILITIES. NOT TO GETTIN' PUNCHED, THOUGH.
YOU'RE REALLY GOOD AT MAKING ANGRY FRENCH LIZARD-MEN SEEM PRETTY NORMAL.

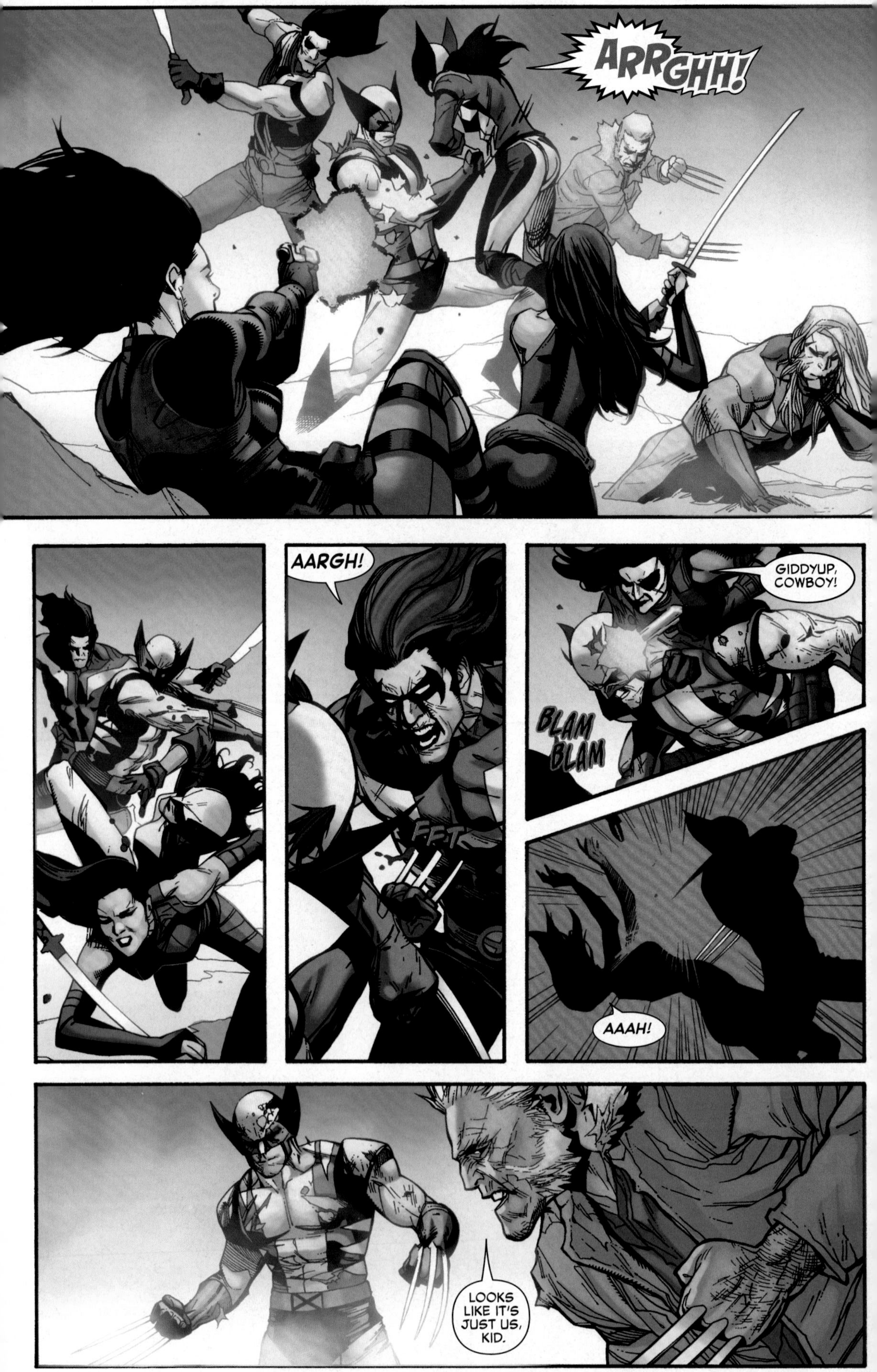
ARRGHH!
AARGH!
FFT
GIDDYUP, COWBOY!
BLAM BLAM
AAAH!
LOOKS LIKE IT'S JUST US, KID.

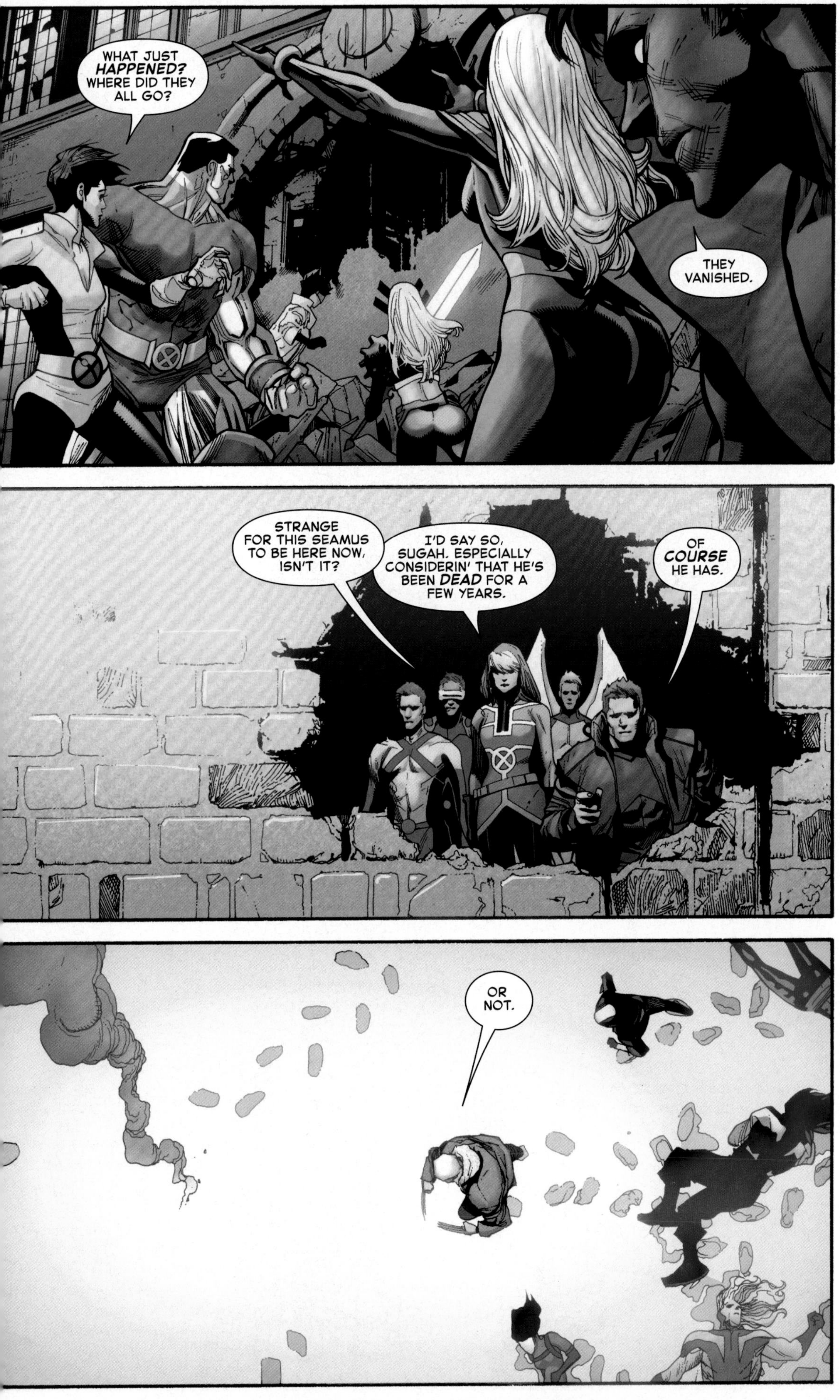
WHAT JUST HAPPENED? WHERE DID THEY ALL GO?
THEY VANISHED.
STRANGE FOR THIS SEAMUS TO BE HERE NOW, ISN'T IT?
I'D SAY SO, SUGAH. ESPECIALLY CONSIDERIN' THAT HE'S BEEN DEAD FOR A FEW YEARS.
OF COURSE HE HAS.
OR NOT.

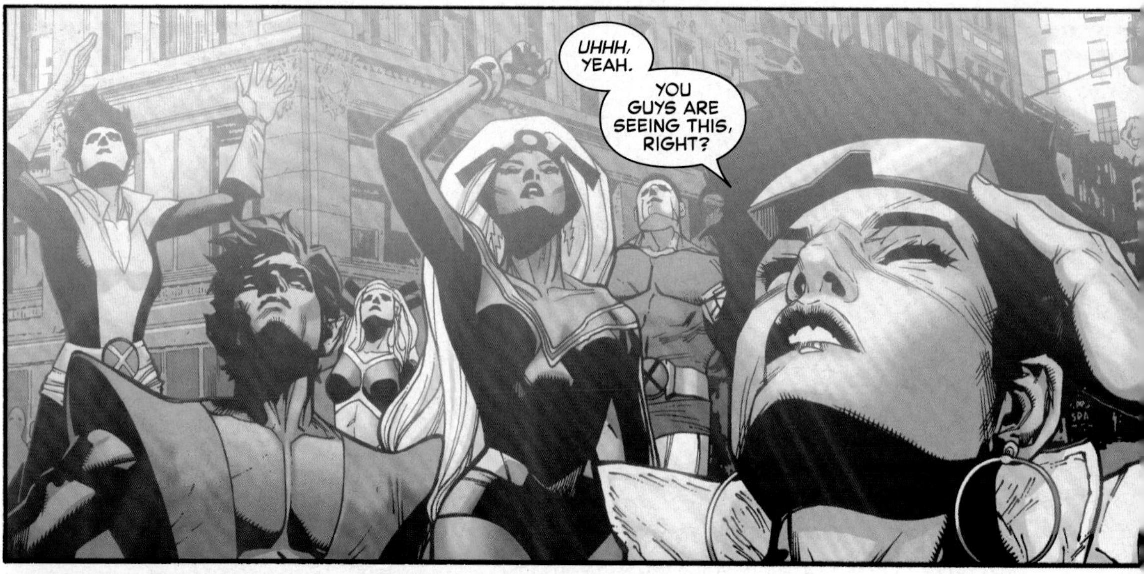
UHHH, YEAH.
YOU GUYS ARE SEEING THIS, RIGHT?
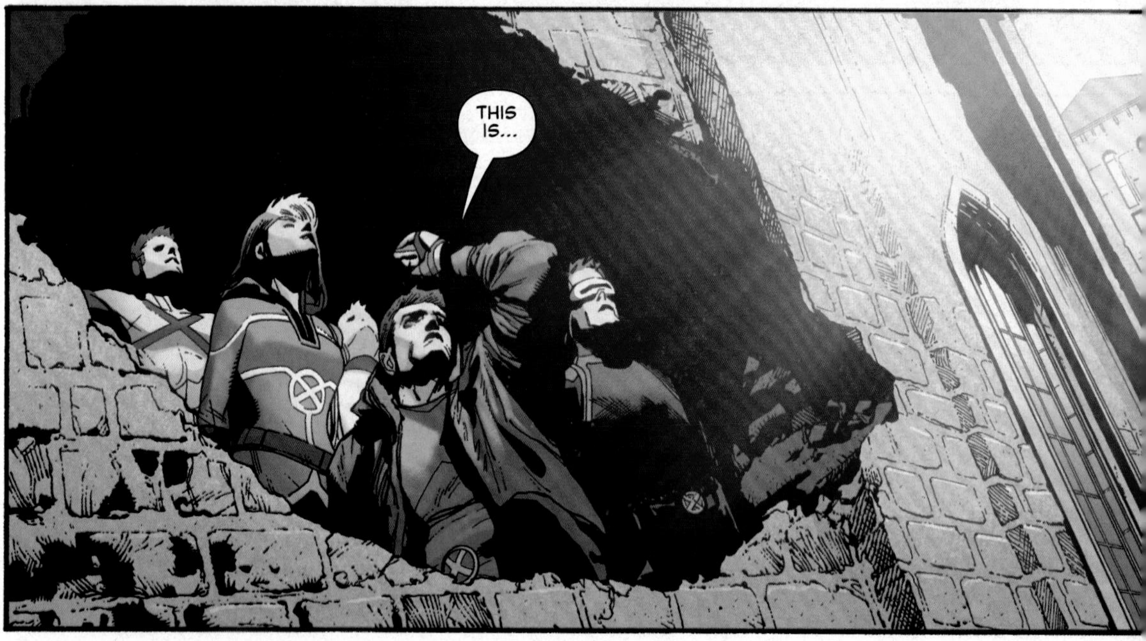
THIS IS...
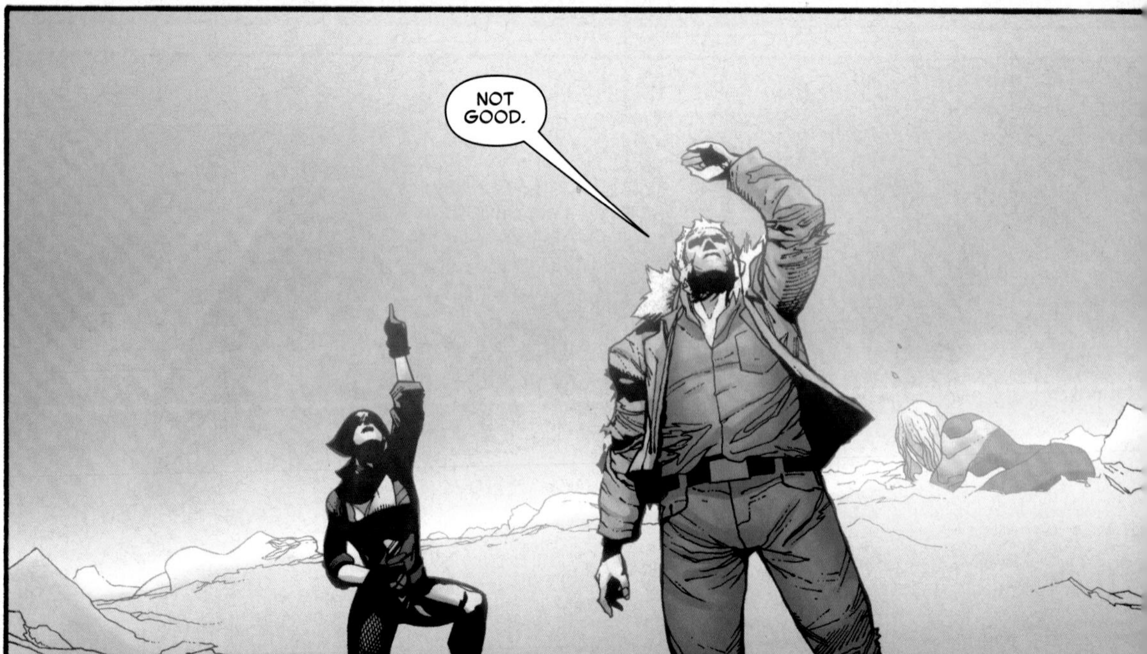
NOT GOOD.

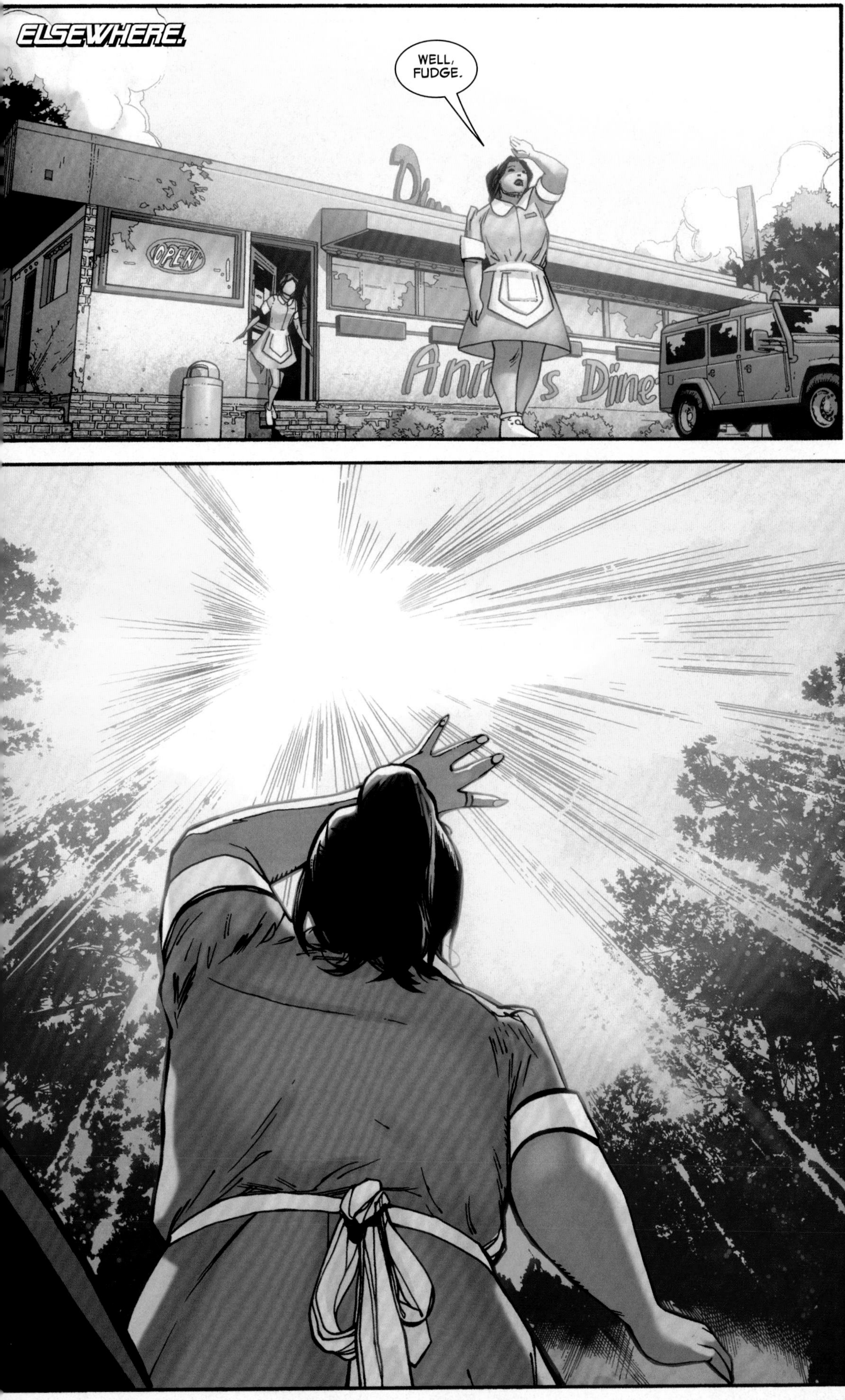
ELSEWHERE.
WELL, FUDGE.
OPEN
Ann s Dine

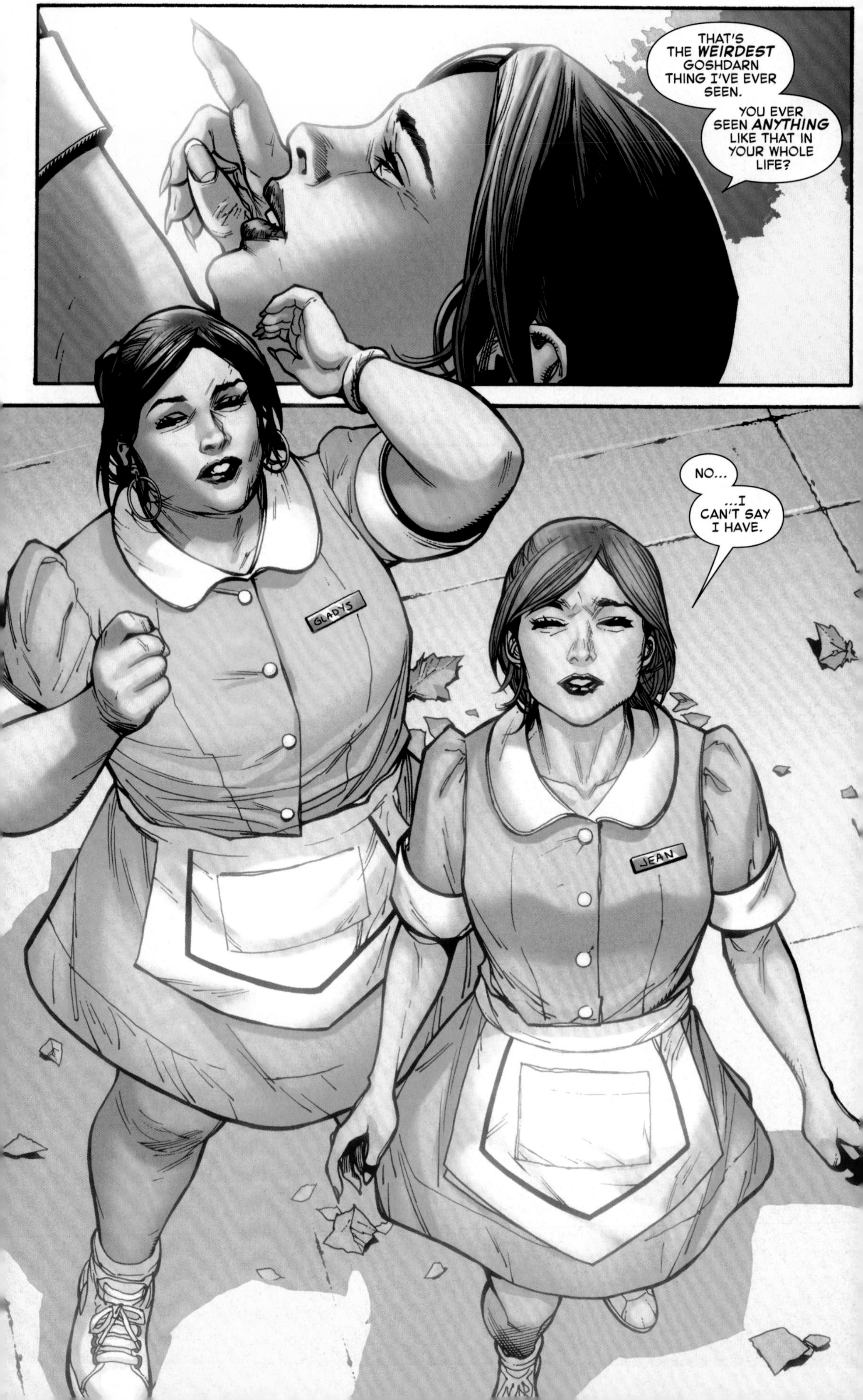

THAT'S THE WEIRDEST GOSHDARN THING I'VE EVER SEEN.
YOU EVER SEEN ANYTHING LIKE THAT IN YOUR WHOLE LIFE?
NO...
...I CAN'T SAY I HAVE.
GLADYS
JEAN

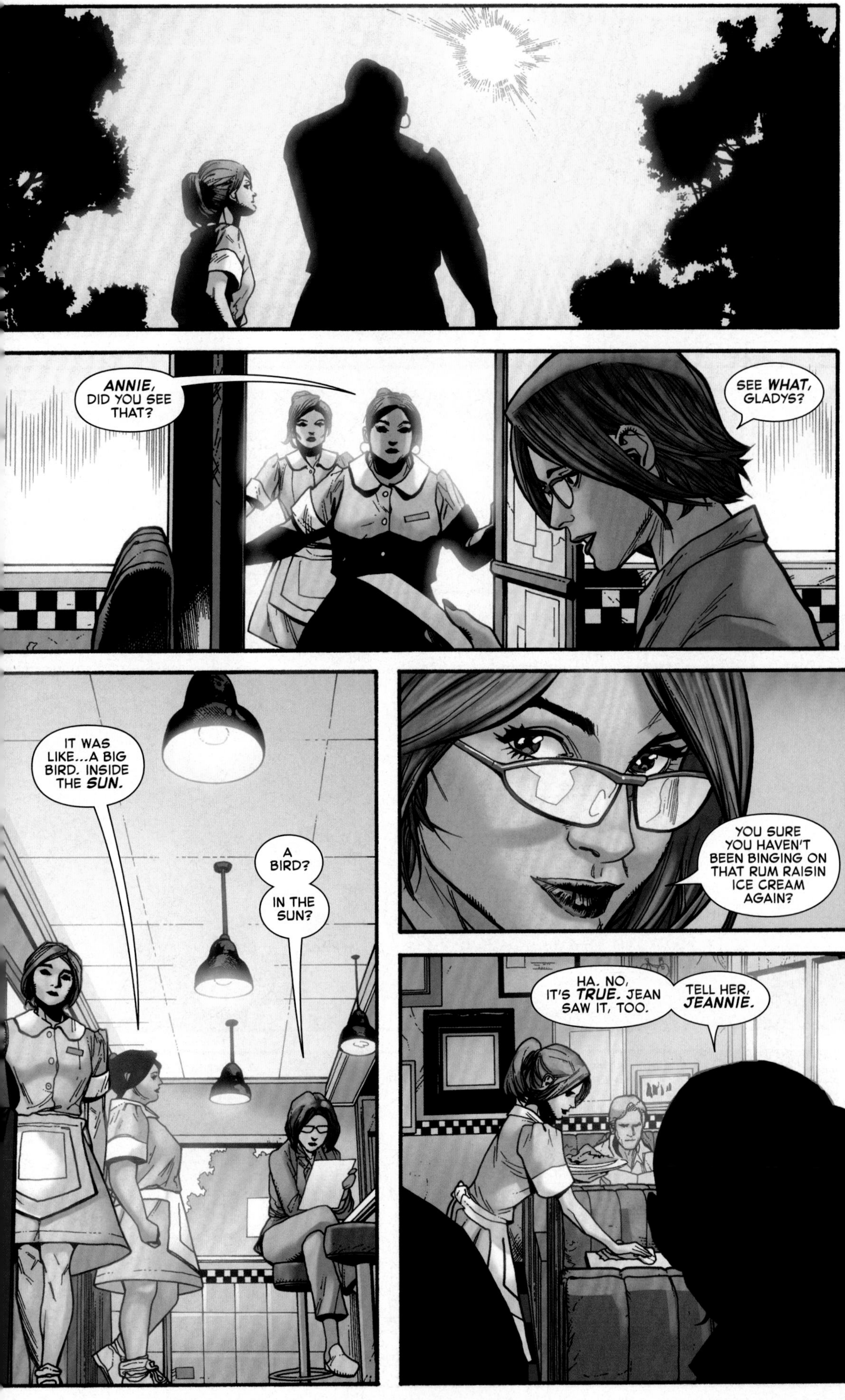
ANNIE, DID YOU SEE THAT?
SEE WHAT, GLADYS?
IT WAS LIKE...A BIG BIRD. INSIDE THE SUN.
A BIRD?
IN THE SUN?
YOU SURE YOU HAVEN'T BEEN BINGING ON THAT RUM RAISIN ICE CREAM AGAIN?
HA. NO, IT'S TRUE. JEAN SAW IT, TOO.
TELL HER, JEANNIE.

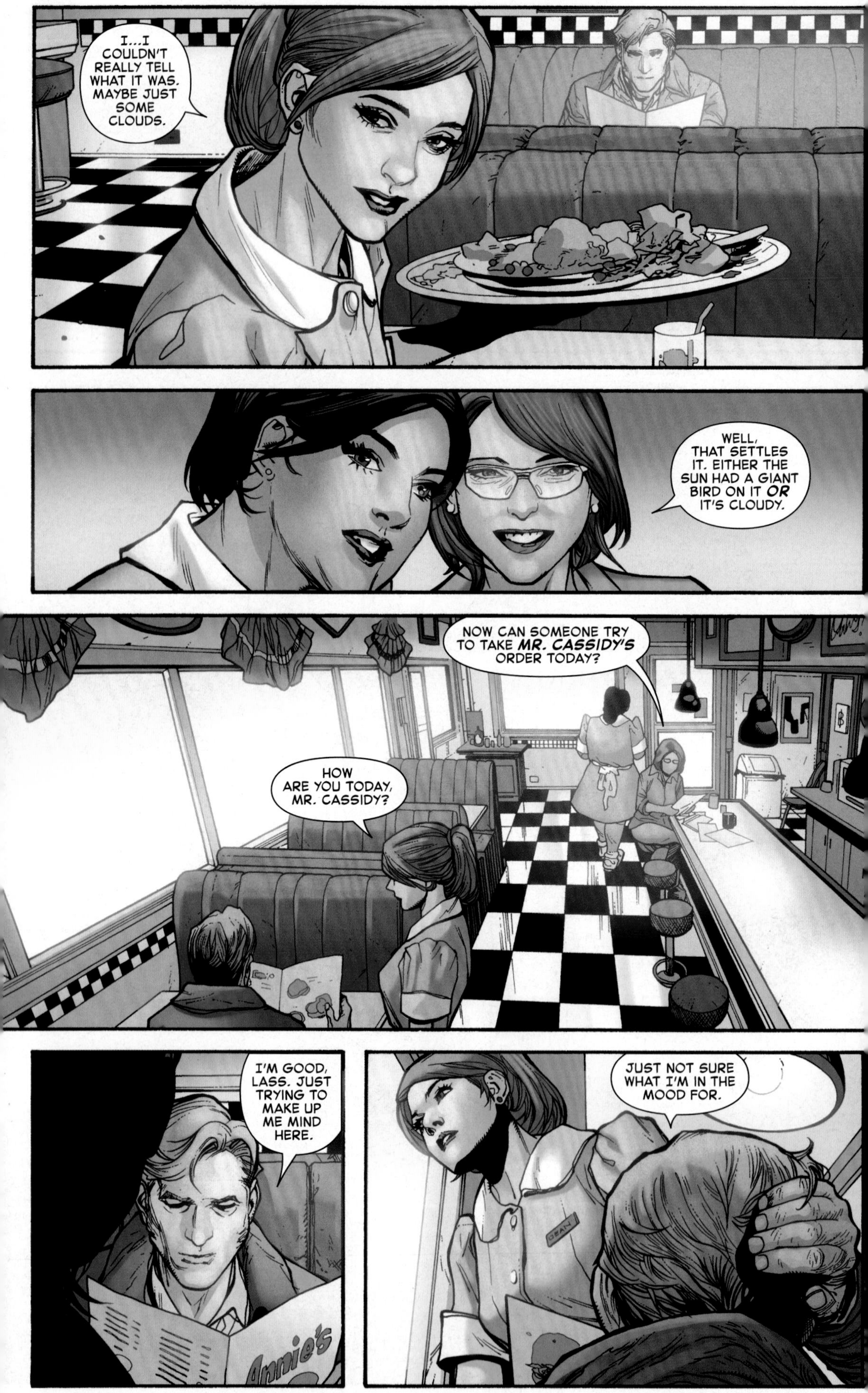

I...I COULDN'T REALLY TELL WHAT IT WAS. MAYBE JUST SOME CLOUDS.
WELL, THAT SETTLES IT. EITHER THE SUN HAD A GIANT BIRD ON IT OR IT'S CLOUDY.
NOW CAN SOMEONE TRY TO TAKE MR. CASSIDY'S ORDER TODAY?
HOW ARE YOU TODAY, MR. CASSIDY?
I'M GOOD, LASS. JUST TRYING TO MAKE UP ME MIND HERE.
JUST NOT SURE WHAT I'M IN THE MOOD FOR.
Annie's

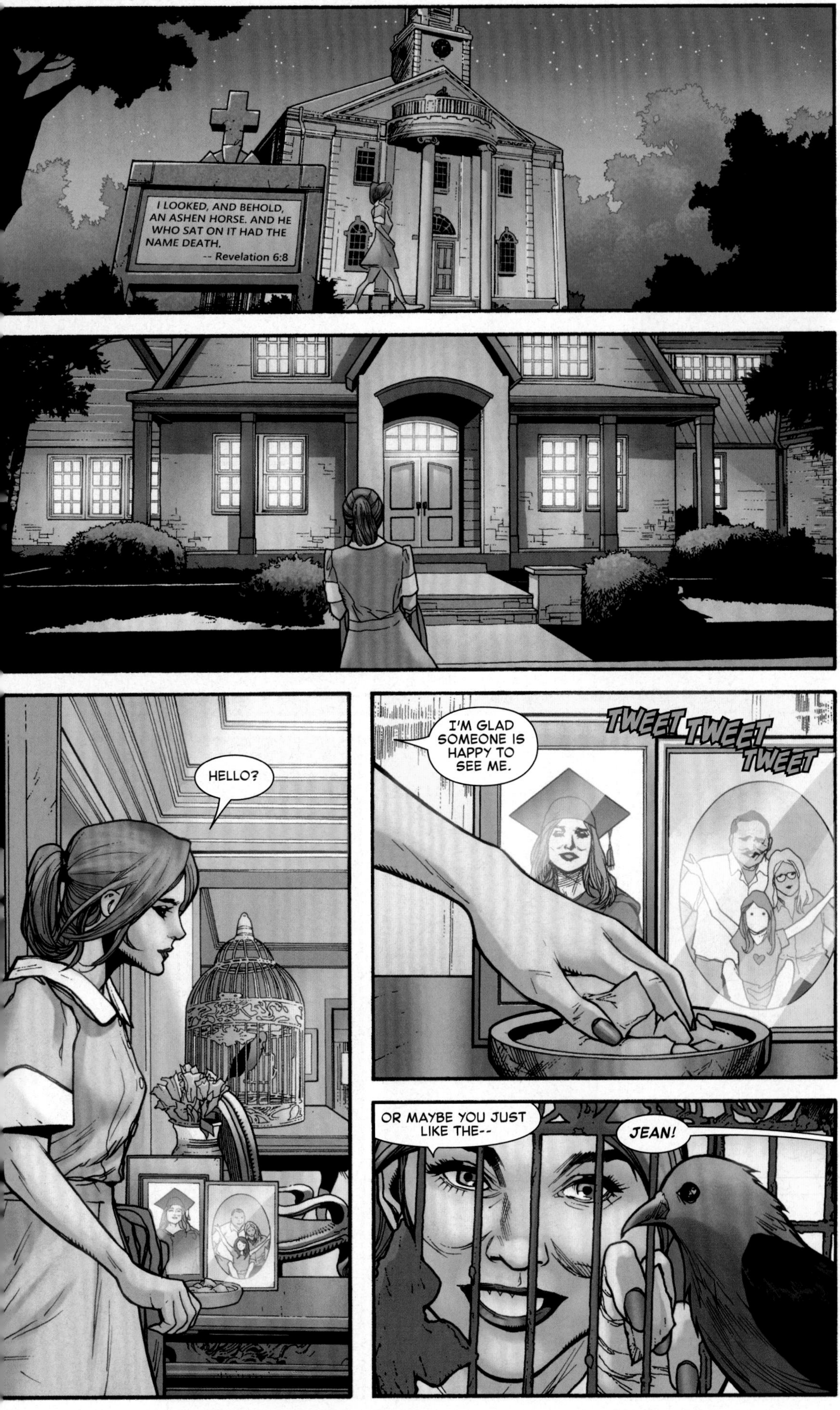
I LOOKED, AND BEHOLD, AN ASHEN HORSE. AND HE WHO SAT ON IT HAD THE NAME DEATH.
-- Revelation 6:8
HELLO?
TWEET TWEET TWEET
I'M GLAD SOMEONE IS HAPPY TO SEE ME.
OR MAYBE YOU JUST LIKE THE--
JEAN!

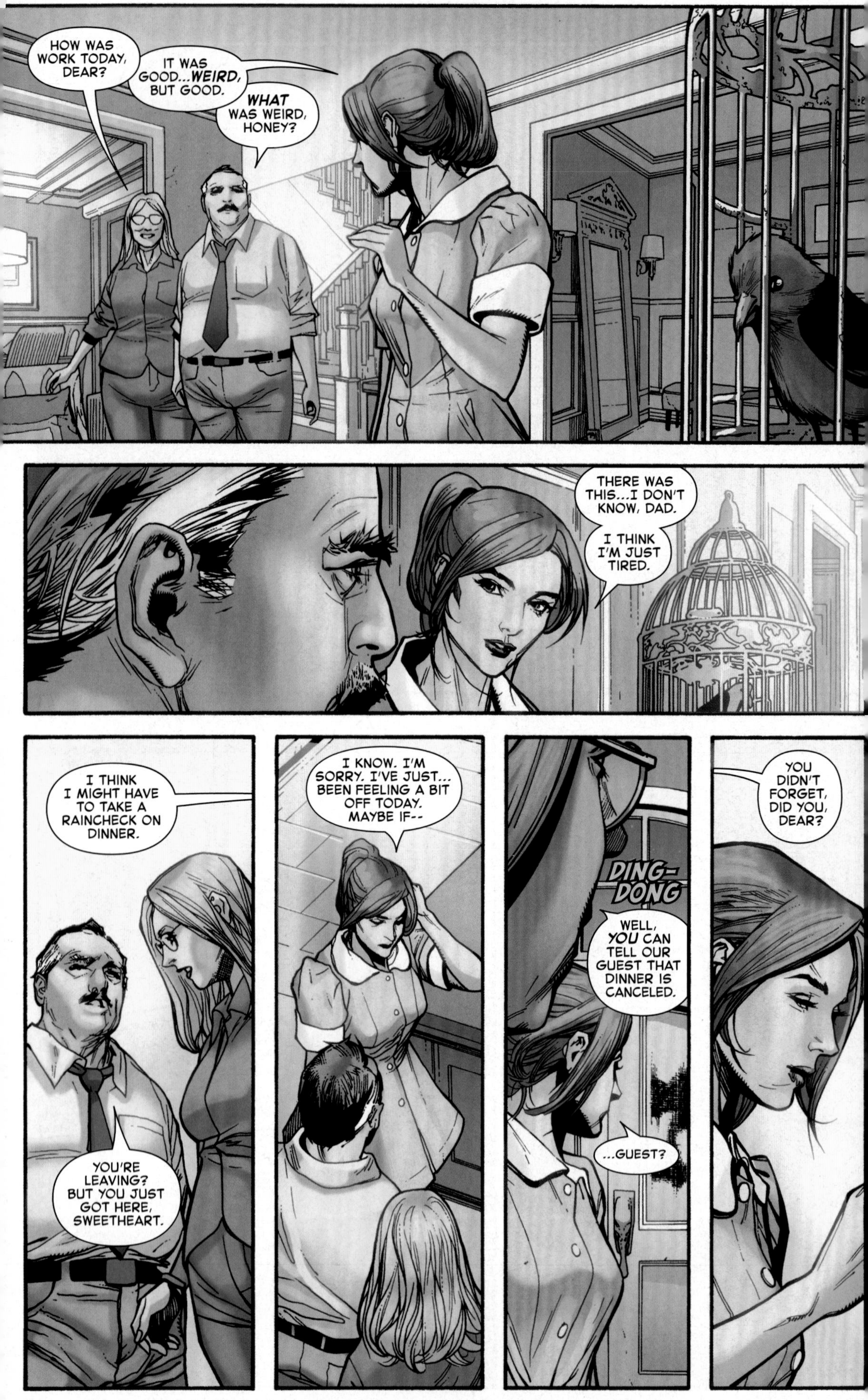

HOW WAS WORK TODAY, DEAR?
IT WAS GOOD...WEIRD, BUT GOOD.
WHAT WAS WEIRD, HONEY?
THERE WAS THIS...I DON'T KNOW, DAD.
I THINK I'M JUST TIRED.
I THINK I MIGHT HAVE TO TAKE A RAINCHECK ON DINNER.
YOU'RE LEAVING? BUT YOU JUST GOT HERE, SWEETHEART.
I KNOW. I'M SORRY. I'VE JUST... BEEN FEELING A BIT OFF TODAY. MAYBE IF--
DING-DONG
WELL, YOU CAN TELL OUR GUEST THAT DINNER IS CANCELED.
...GUEST?
YOU DIDN'T FORGET, DID YOU, DEAR?

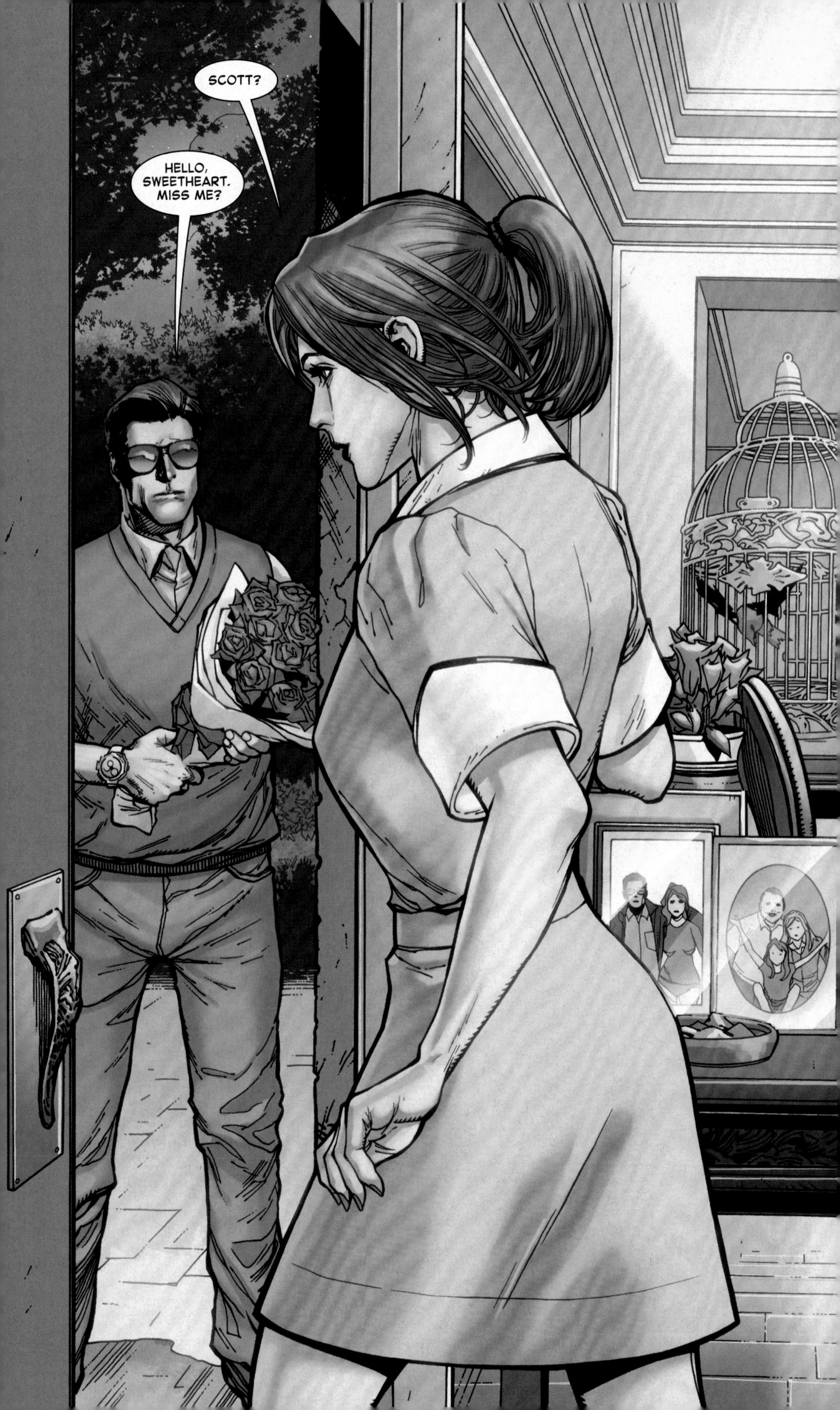
SCOTT?
HELLO, SWEETHEART. MISS ME?

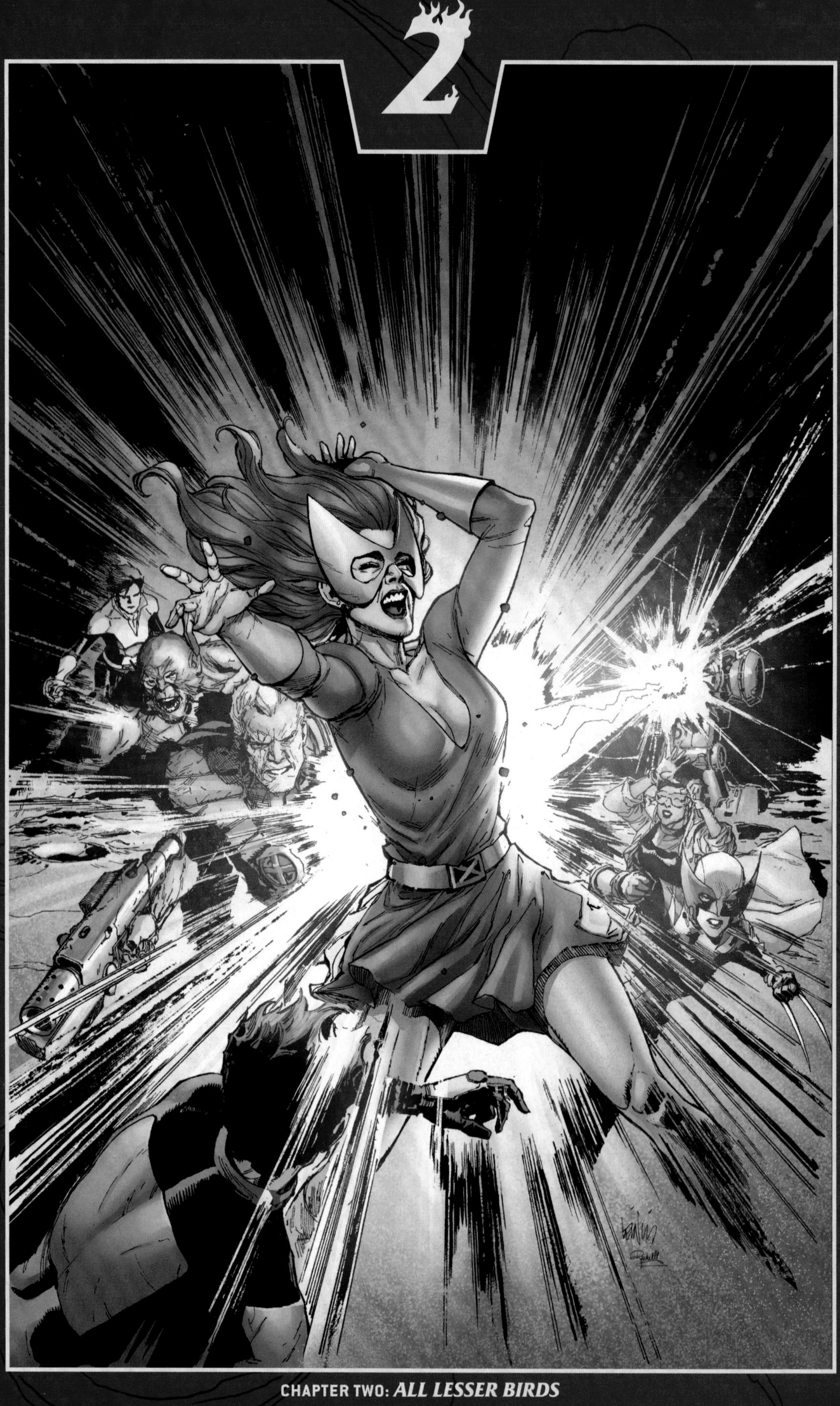

CHAPTER TWO: ***ALL LESSER BIRDS***

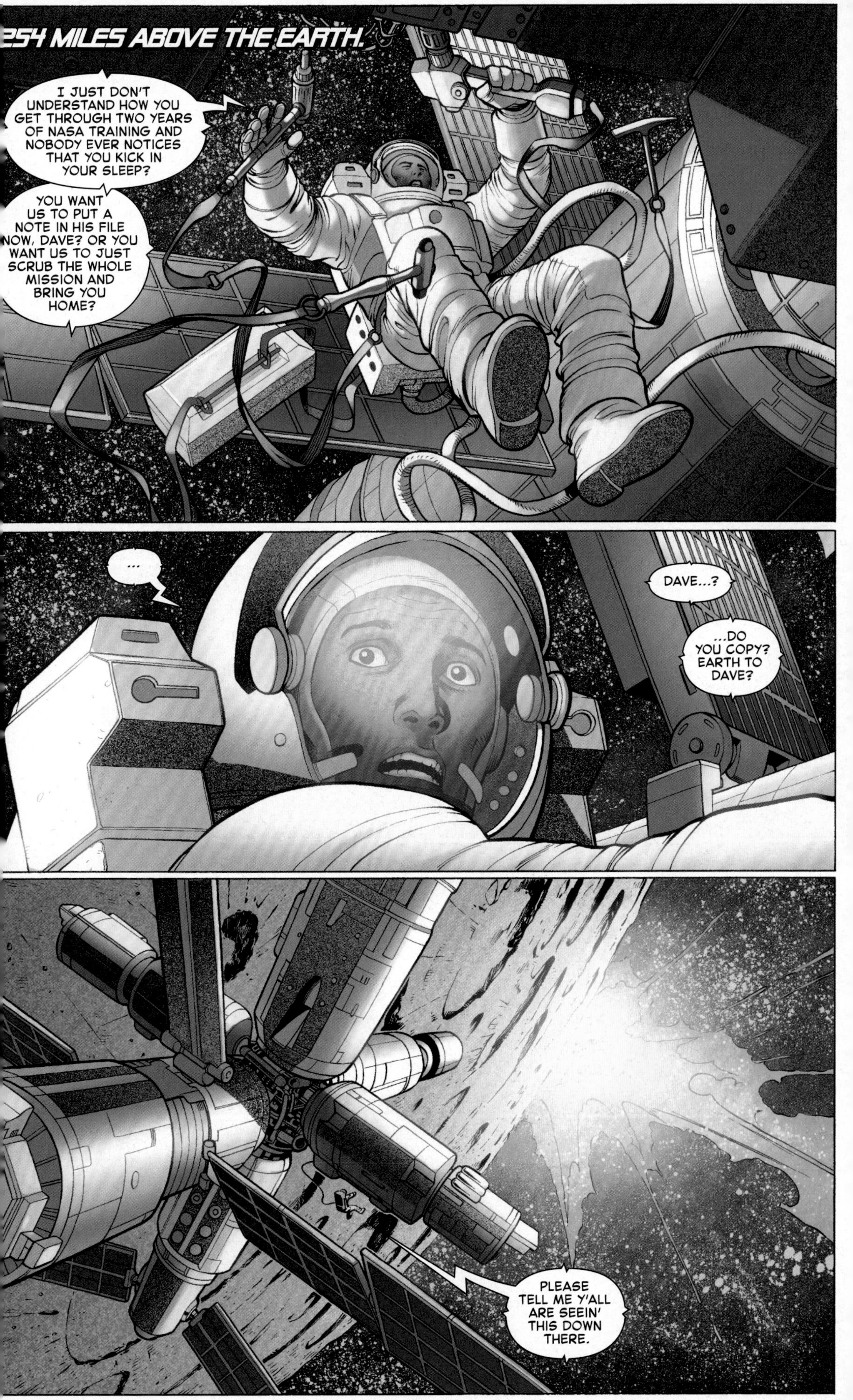
254 MILES ABOVE THE EARTH.
I JUST DON'T UNDERSTAND HOW YOU GET THROUGH TWO YEARS OF NASA TRAINING AND NOBODY EVER NOTICES THAT YOU KICK IN YOUR SLEEP?
YOU WANT US TO PUT A NOTE IN HIS FILE NOW, DAVE? OR YOU WANT US TO JUST SCRUB THE WHOLE MISSION AND BRING YOU HOME?
...
DAVE...?
...DO YOU COPY? EARTH TO DAVE?
PLEASE TELL ME Y'ALL ARE SEEIN' THIS DOWN THERE.

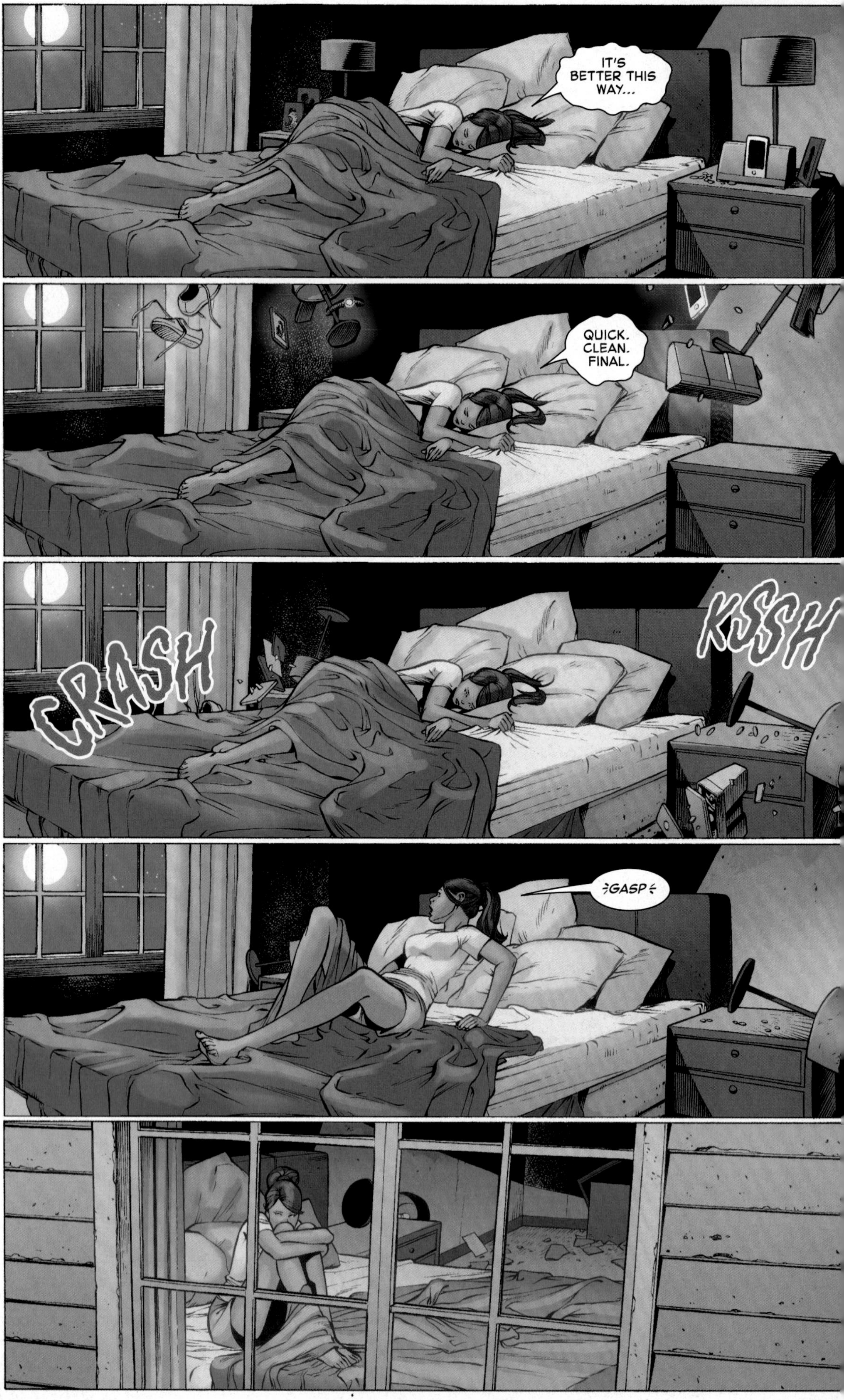
IT'S BETTER THIS WAY...
QUICK. CLEAN. FINAL.
CRASH
KSSH
GASP

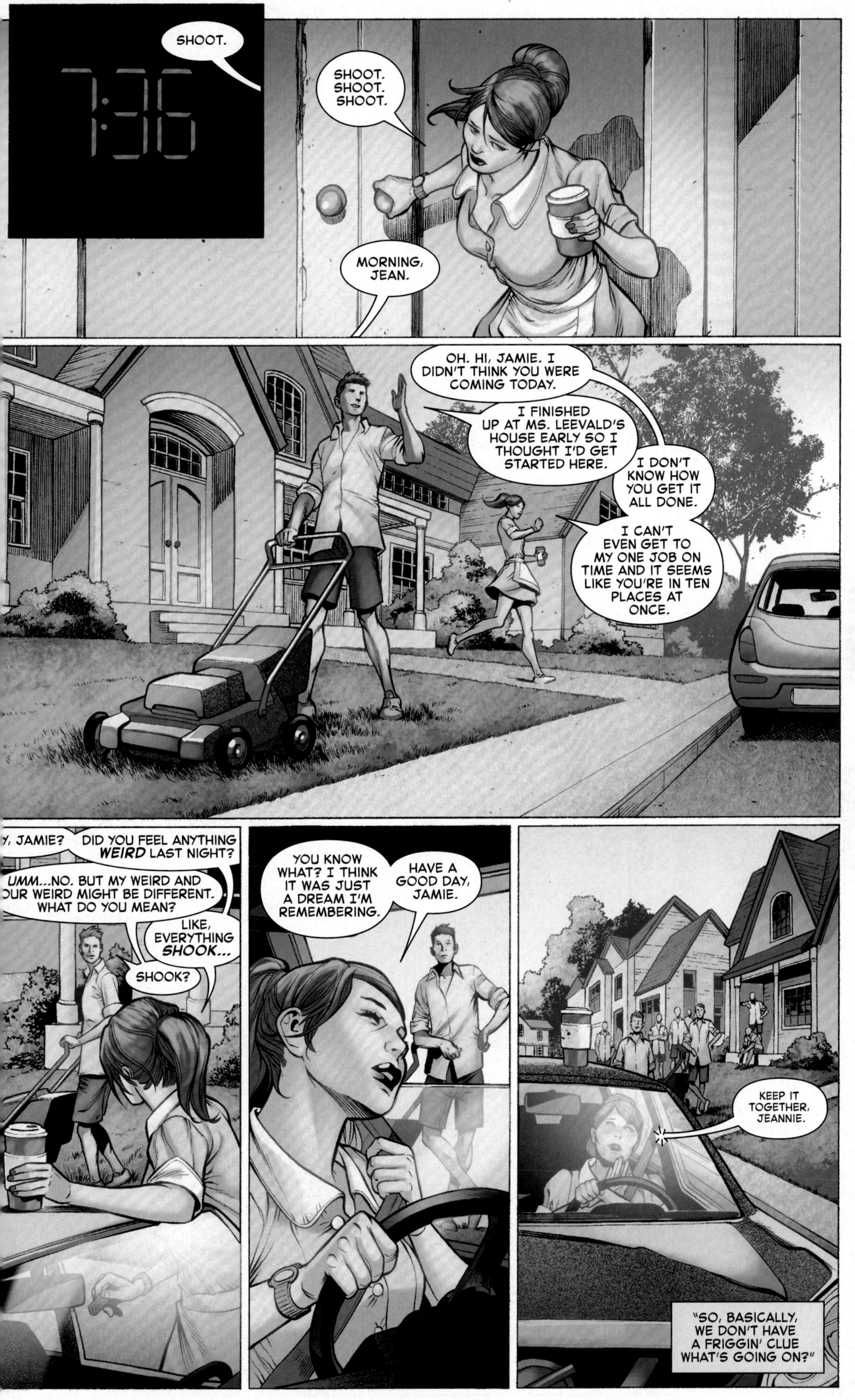

7:36
SHOOT.
SHOOT. SHOOT. SHOOT.
MORNING, JEAN.
OH. HI, JAMIE. I DIDN'T THINK YOU WERE COMING TODAY.
I FINISHED UP AT MS. LEEVALD'S HOUSE EARLY SO I THOUGHT I'D GET STARTED HERE.
I DON'T KNOW HOW YOU GET IT ALL DONE.
I CAN'T EVEN GET TO MY ONE JOB ON TIME AND IT SEEMS LIKE YOU'RE IN TEN PLACES AT ONCE.
Y, JAMIE?
DID YOU FEEL ANYTHING WEIRD LAST NIGHT?
UMM...NO. BUT MY WEIRD AND OUR WEIRD MIGHT BE DIFFERENT. WHAT DO YOU MEAN?
LIKE, EVERYTHING SHOOK...
SHOOK?
YOU KNOW WHAT? I THINK IT WAS JUST A DREAM I'M REMEMBERING.
HAVE A GOOD DAY, JAMIE.
KEEP IT TOGETHER, JEANNIE.
"SO, BASICALLY, WE DON'T HAVE A FRIGGIN' CLUE WHAT'S GOING ON?"

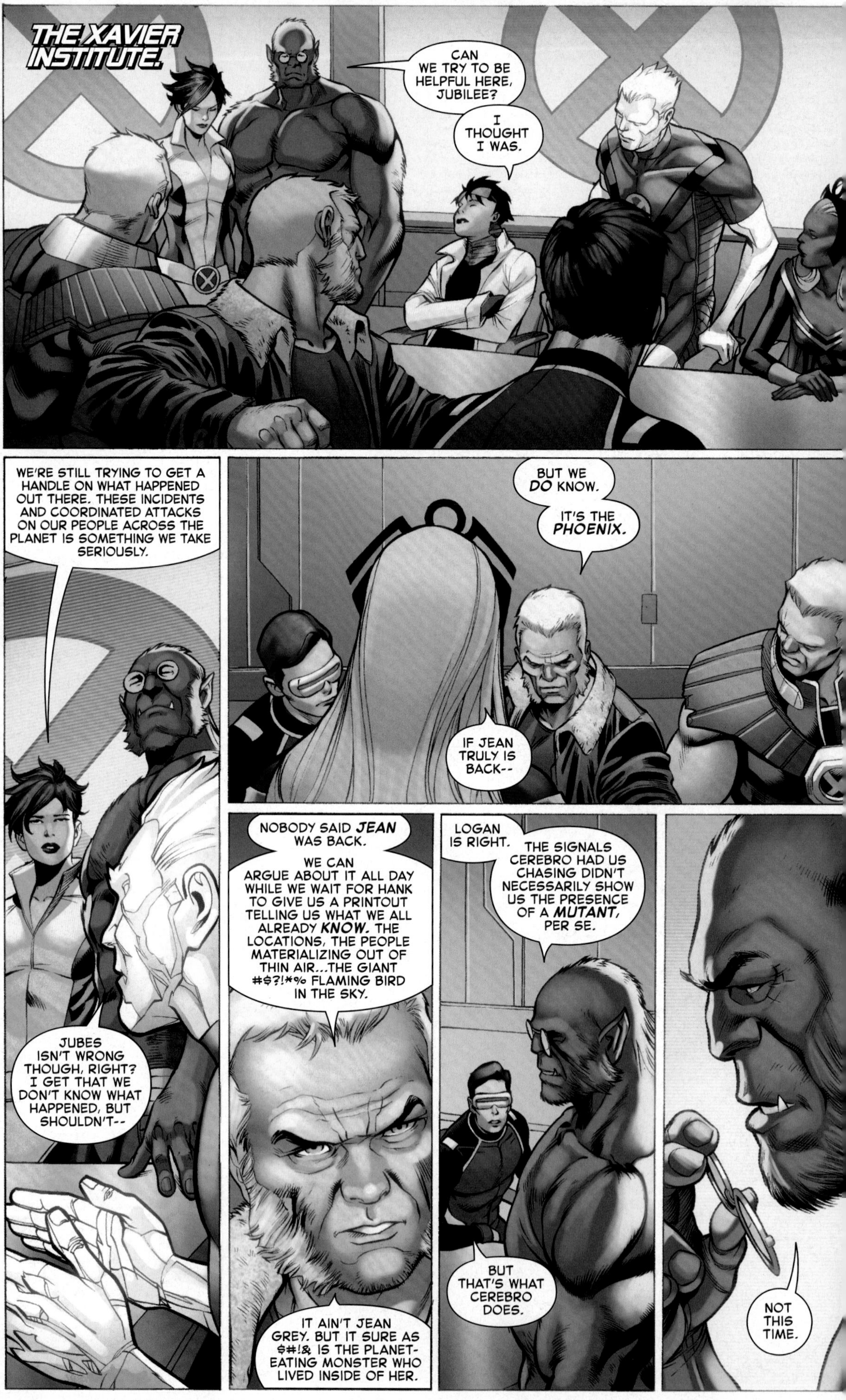
THE XAVIER INSTITUTE.
CAN WE TRY TO BE HELPFUL HERE, JUBILEE?
I THOUGHT I WAS.
WE'RE STILL TRYING TO GET A HANDLE ON WHAT HAPPENED OUT THERE. THESE INCIDENTS AND COORDINATED ATTACKS ON OUR PEOPLE ACROSS THE PLANET IS SOMETHING WE TAKE SERIOUSLY.
JUBES ISN'T WRONG THOUGH, RIGHT? I GET THAT WE DON'T KNOW WHAT HAPPENED, BUT SHOULDN'T--
BUT WE DO KNOW.
IT'S THE PHOENIX.
IF JEAN TRULY IS BACK--
NOBODY SAID JEAN WAS BACK.
WE CAN ARGUE ABOUT IT ALL DAY WHILE WE WAIT FOR HANK TO GIVE US A PRINTOUT TELLING US WHAT WE ALL ALREADY KNOW. THE LOCATIONS, THE PEOPLE MATERIALIZING OUT OF THIN AIR...THE GIANT #$?!*% FLAMING BIRD IN THE SKY.
IT AIN'T JEAN GREY. BUT IT SURE AS $#!& IS THE PLANET-EATING MONSTER WHO LIVED INSIDE OF HER.
LOGAN IS RIGHT.
THE SIGNALS CEREBRO HAD US CHASING DIDN'T NECESSARILY SHOW US THE PRESENCE OF A MUTANT, PER SE.
BUT THAT'S WHAT CEREBRO DOES.
NOT THIS TIME.

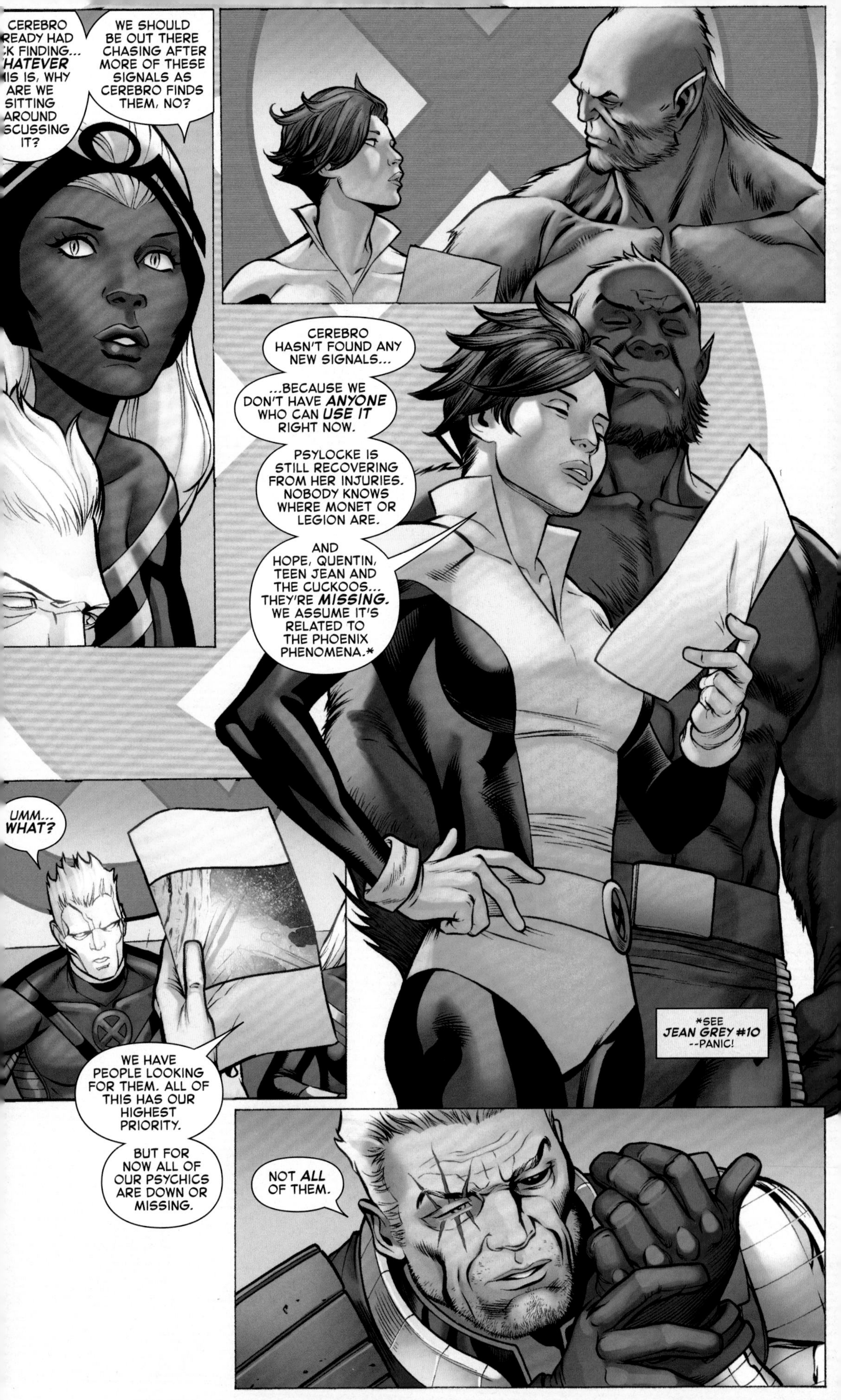
CEREBRO ...READY HAD ...CK FINDING... ...HATEVER ...IS IS, WHY ARE WE SITTING AROUND ...SCUSSING IT?
WE SHOULD BE OUT THERE CHASING AFTER MORE OF THESE SIGNALS AS CEREBRO FINDS THEM, NO?
CEREBRO HASN'T FOUND ANY NEW SIGNALS...
...BECAUSE WE DON'T HAVE ANYONE WHO CAN USE IT RIGHT NOW.
PSYLOCKE IS STILL RECOVERING FROM HER INJURIES. NOBODY KNOWS WHERE MONET OR LEGION ARE.
AND HOPE, QUENTIN, TEEN JEAN AND THE CUCKOOS... THEY'RE MISSING. WE ASSUME IT'S RELATED TO THE PHOENIX PHENOMENA.*
*SEE JEAN GREY #10 --PANIC!
UMM... WHAT?
WE HAVE PEOPLE LOOKING FOR THEM. ALL OF THIS HAS OUR HIGHEST PRIORITY.
BUT FOR NOW ALL OF OUR PSYCHICS ARE DOWN OR MISSING.
NOT ALL OF THEM.

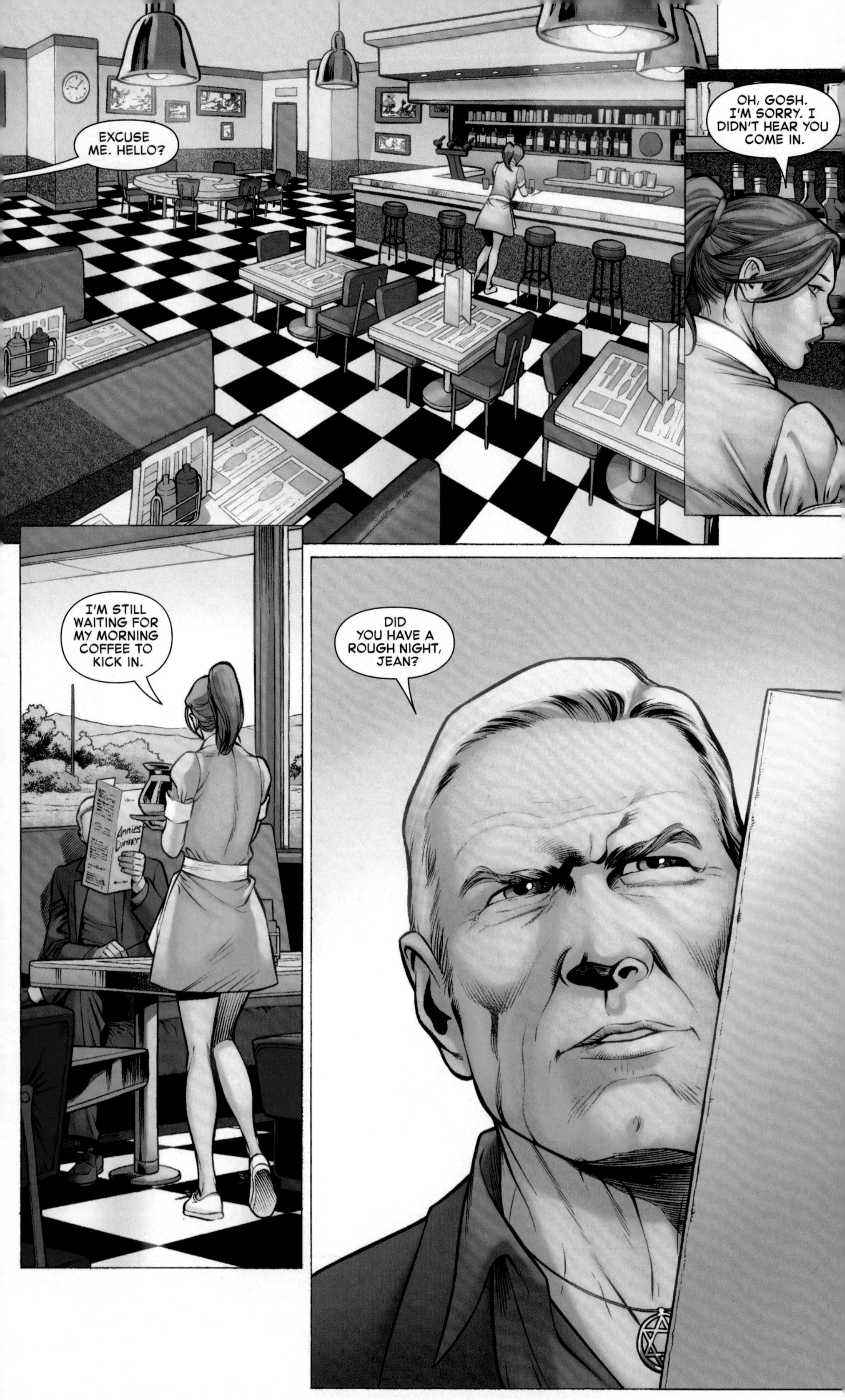
EXCUSE ME. HELLO?
OH, GOSH. I'M SORRY. I DIDN'T HEAR YOU COME IN.
I'M STILL WAITING FOR MY MORNING COFFEE TO KICK IN.
Annies Dinner
DID YOU HAVE A ROUGH NIGHT, JEAN?

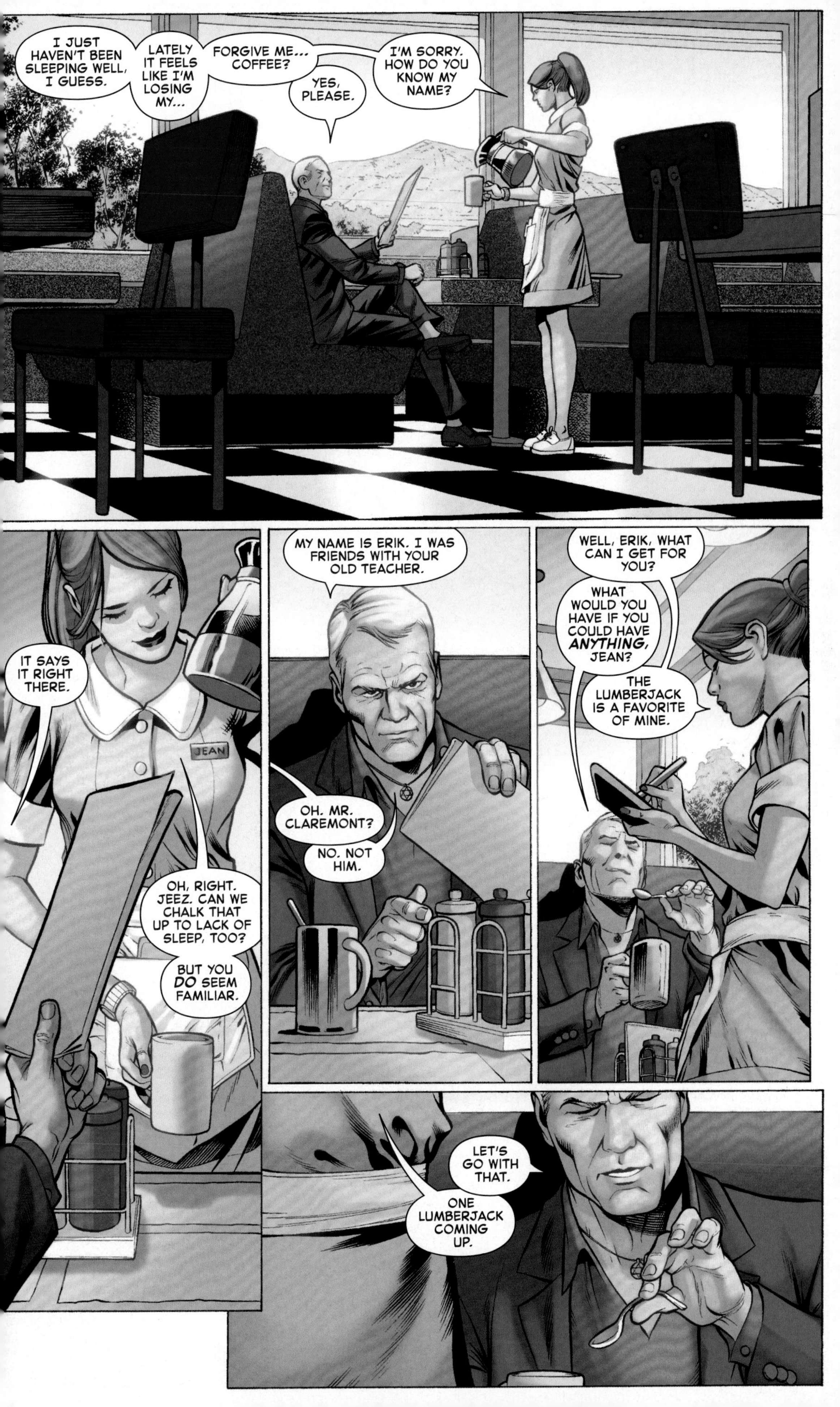

I JUST HAVEN'T BEEN SLEEPING WELL, I GUESS.
LATELY IT FEELS LIKE I'M LOSING MY...
FORGIVE ME... COFFEE?
YES, PLEASE.
I'M SORRY. HOW DO YOU KNOW MY NAME?
IT SAYS IT RIGHT THERE.
JEAN
OH, RIGHT. JEEZ. CAN WE CHALK THAT UP TO LACK OF SLEEP, TOO?
BUT YOU DO SEEM FAMILIAR.
MY NAME IS ERIK. I WAS FRIENDS WITH YOUR OLD TEACHER.
OH. MR. CLAREMONT?
NO. NOT HIM.
WELL, ERIK, WHAT CAN I GET FOR YOU?
WHAT WOULD YOU HAVE IF YOU COULD HAVE ANYTHING, JEAN?
THE LUMBERJACK IS A FAVORITE OF MINE.
LET'S GO WITH THAT.
ONE LUMBERJACK COMING UP.

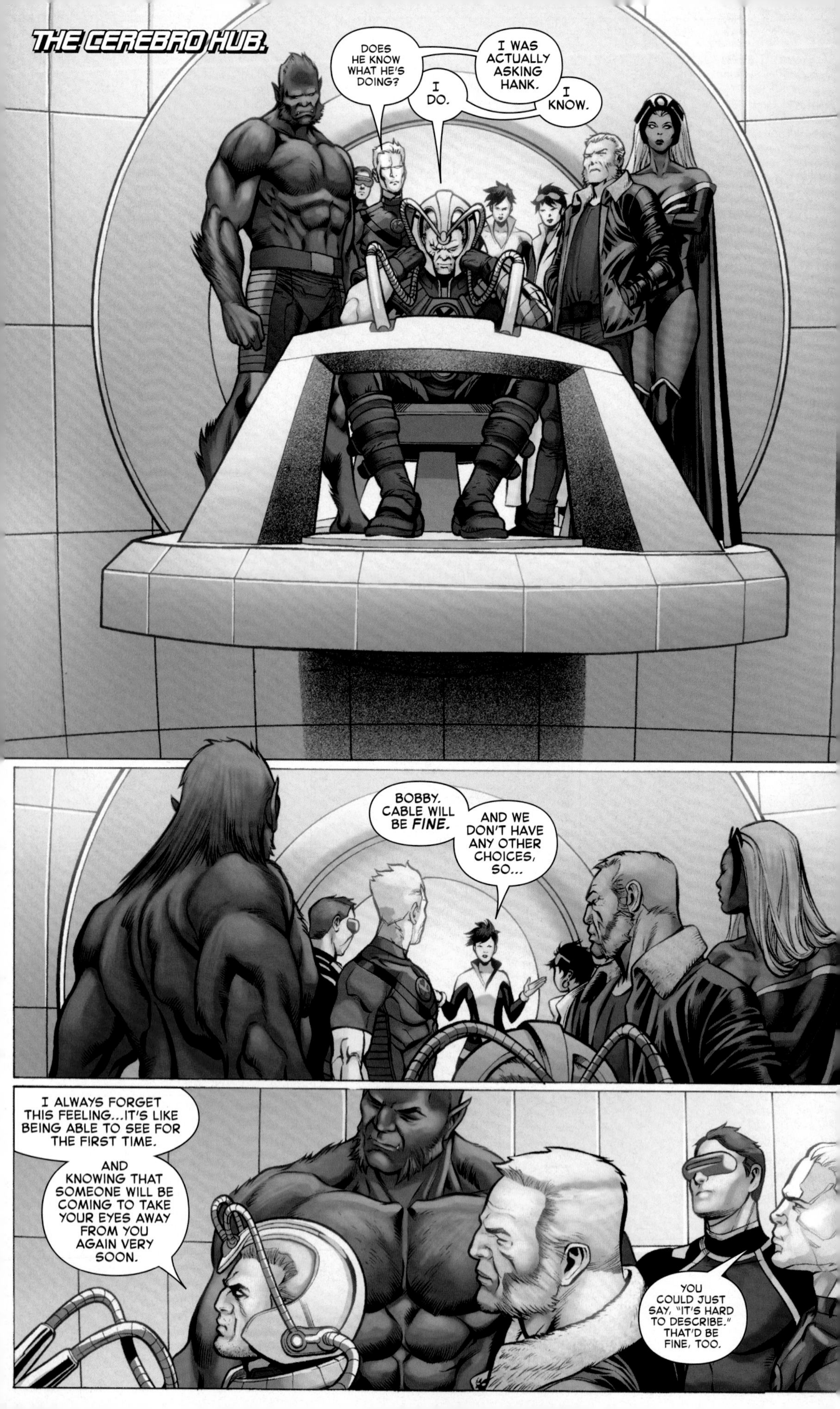
THE CEREBRO HUB.
DOES HE KNOW WHAT HE'S DOING?
I DO.
I WAS ACTUALLY ASKING HANK.
I KNOW.
BOBBY. CABLE WILL BE FINE.
AND WE DON'T HAVE ANY OTHER CHOICES, SO...
I ALWAYS FORGET THIS FEELING...IT'S LIKE BEING ABLE TO SEE FOR THE FIRST TIME.
AND KNOWING THAT SOMEONE WILL BE COMING TO TAKE YOUR EYES AWAY FROM YOU AGAIN VERY SOON.
YOU COULD JUST SAY, "IT'S HARD TO DESCRIBE." THAT'D BE FINE, TOO.

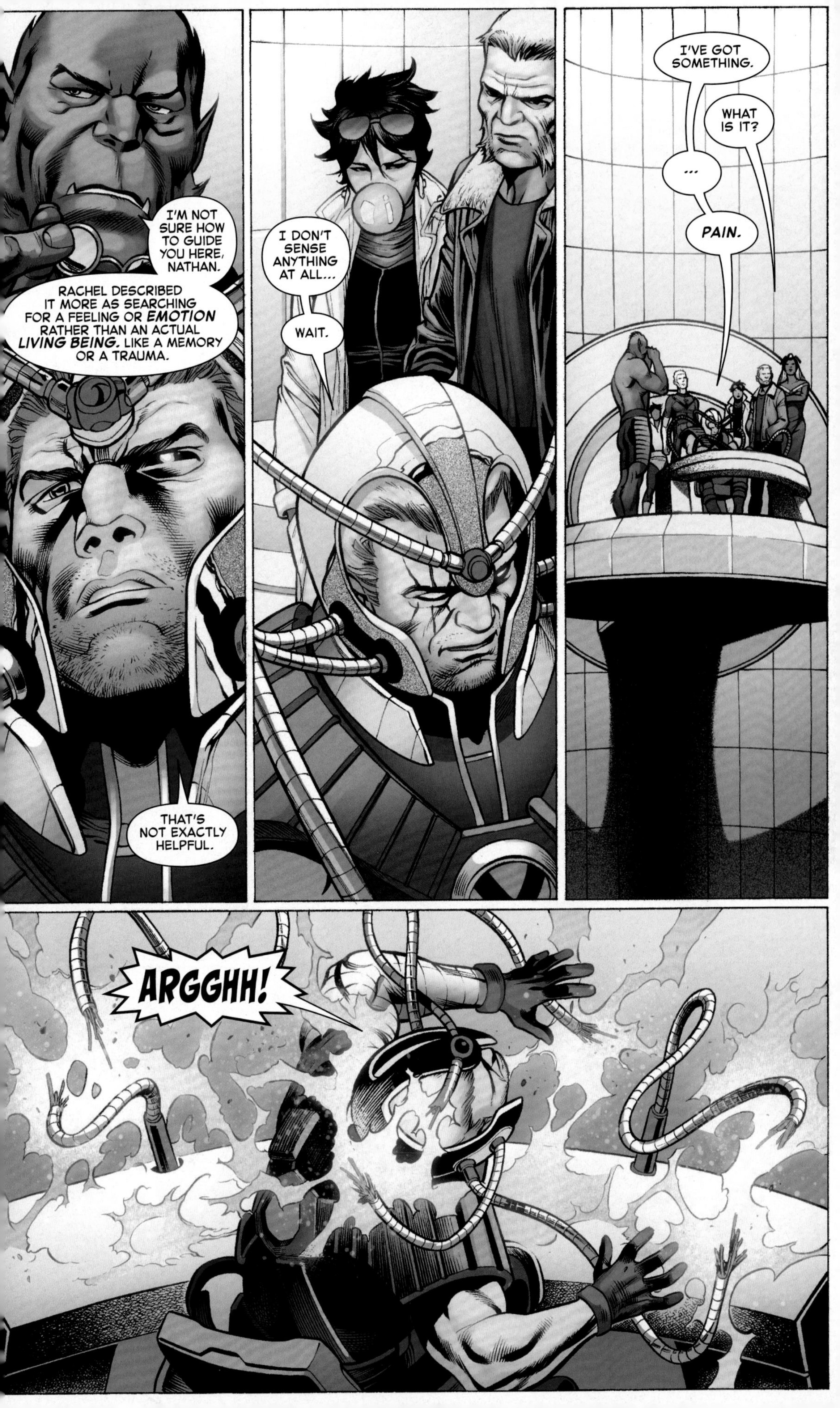
I'M NOT SURE HOW TO GUIDE YOU HERE, NATHAN.
RACHEL DESCRIBED IT MORE AS SEARCHING FOR A FEELING OR EMOTION RATHER THAN AN ACTUAL LIVING BEING. LIKE A MEMORY OR A TRAUMA.
THAT'S NOT EXACTLY HELPFUL.
I DON'T SENSE ANYTHING AT ALL...
WAIT.
I'VE GOT SOMETHING.
WHAT IS IT?
...
PAIN.
ARGGHH!

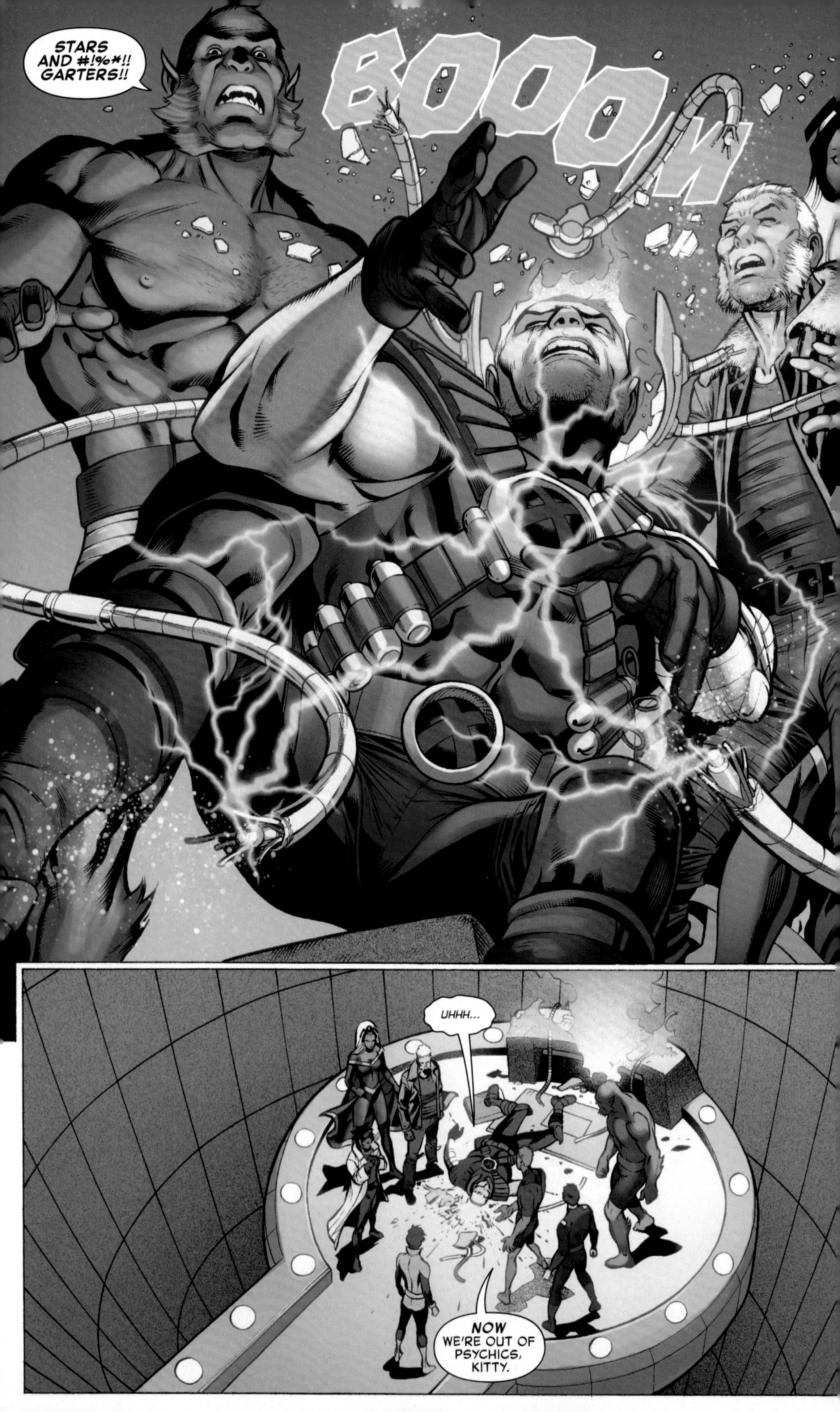
STARS AND #!%*!! GARTERS!!
BOOOOM
UHHH...
NOW WE'RE OUT OF PSYCHICS, KITTY.

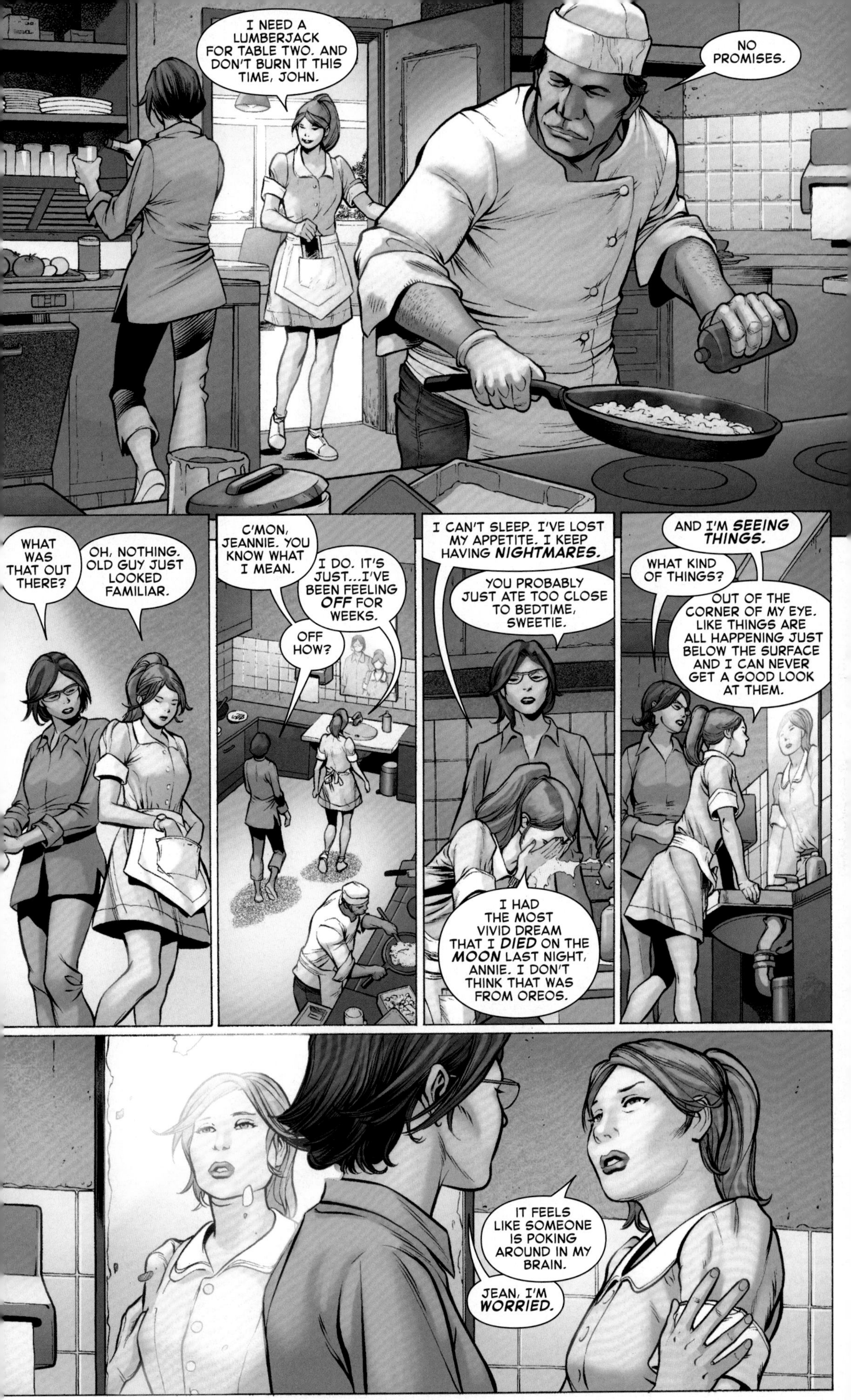
I NEED A LUMBERJACK FOR TABLE TWO. AND DON'T BURN IT THIS TIME, JOHN.
NO PROMISES.
WHAT WAS THAT OUT THERE?
OH, NOTHING. OLD GUY JUST LOOKED FAMILIAR.
C'MON, JEANNIE. YOU KNOW WHAT I MEAN.
I DO. IT'S JUST...I'VE BEEN FEELING OFF FOR WEEKS.
OFF HOW?
I CAN'T SLEEP. I'VE LOST MY APPETITE. I KEEP HAVING NIGHTMARES.
YOU PROBABLY JUST ATE TOO CLOSE TO BEDTIME, SWEETIE.
I HAD THE MOST VIVID DREAM THAT I DIED ON THE MOON LAST NIGHT, ANNIE. I DON'T THINK THAT WAS FROM OREOS.
AND I'M SEEING THINGS.
WHAT KIND OF THINGS?
OUT OF THE CORNER OF MY EYE. LIKE THINGS ARE ALL HAPPENING JUST BELOW THE SURFACE AND I CAN NEVER GET A GOOD LOOK AT THEM.
IT FEELS LIKE SOMEONE IS POKING AROUND IN MY BRAIN.
JEAN, I'M WORRIED.

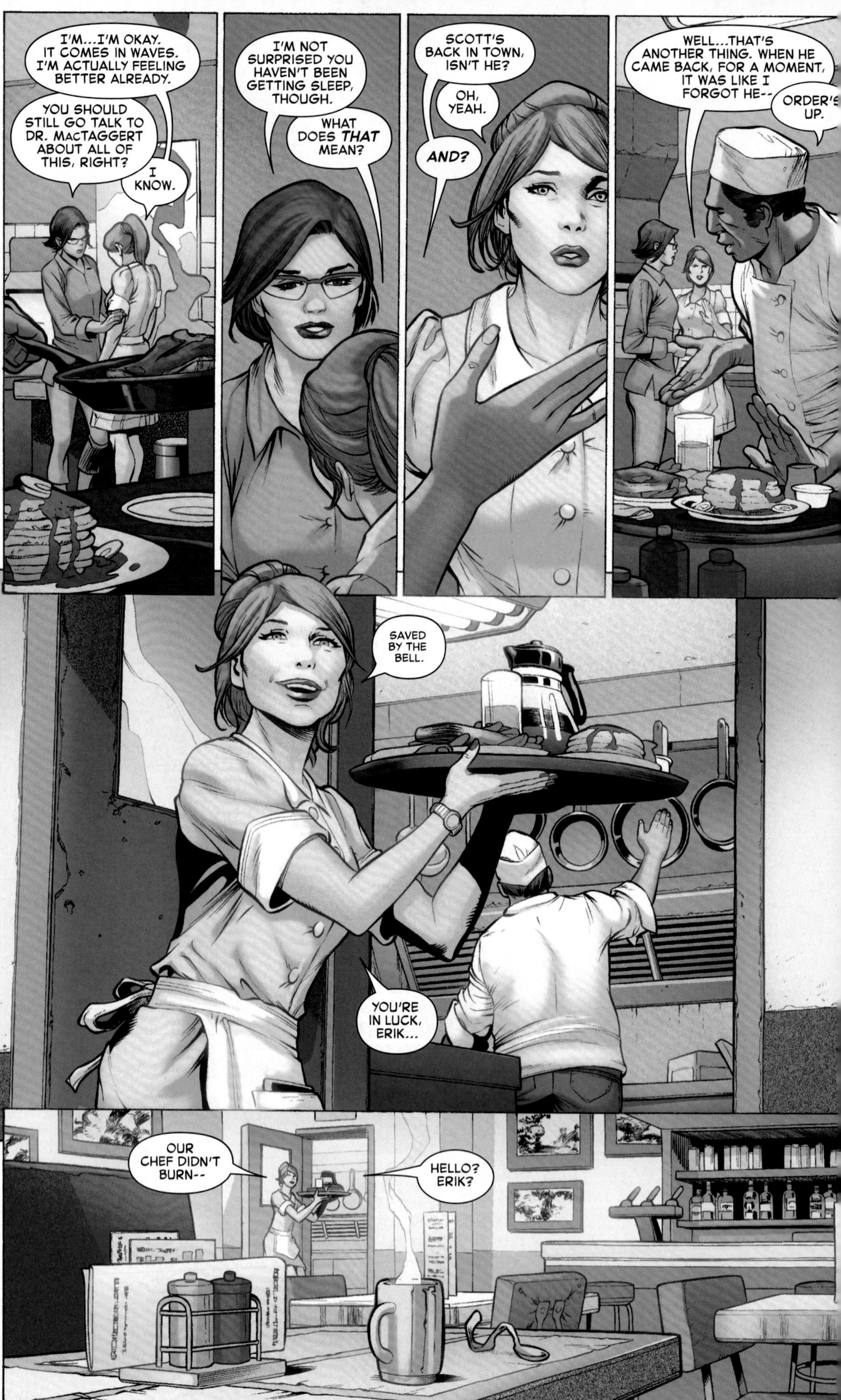

I'M...I'M OKAY. IT COMES IN WAVES. I'M ACTUALLY FEELING BETTER ALREADY.
YOU SHOULD STILL GO TALK TO DR. MacTAGGERT ABOUT ALL OF THIS, RIGHT?
I KNOW.
I'M NOT SURPRISED YOU HAVEN'T BEEN GETTING SLEEP, THOUGH.
WHAT DOES *THAT* MEAN?
SCOTT'S BACK IN TOWN, ISN'T HE?
OH, YEAH.
AND?
WELL...THAT'S ANOTHER THING. WHEN HE CAME BACK, FOR A MOMENT, IT WAS LIKE I FORGOT HE--
ORDER'S UP.
SAVED BY THE BELL.
YOU'RE IN LUCK, ERIK...
OUR CHEF DIDN'T BURN--
HELLO? ERIK?

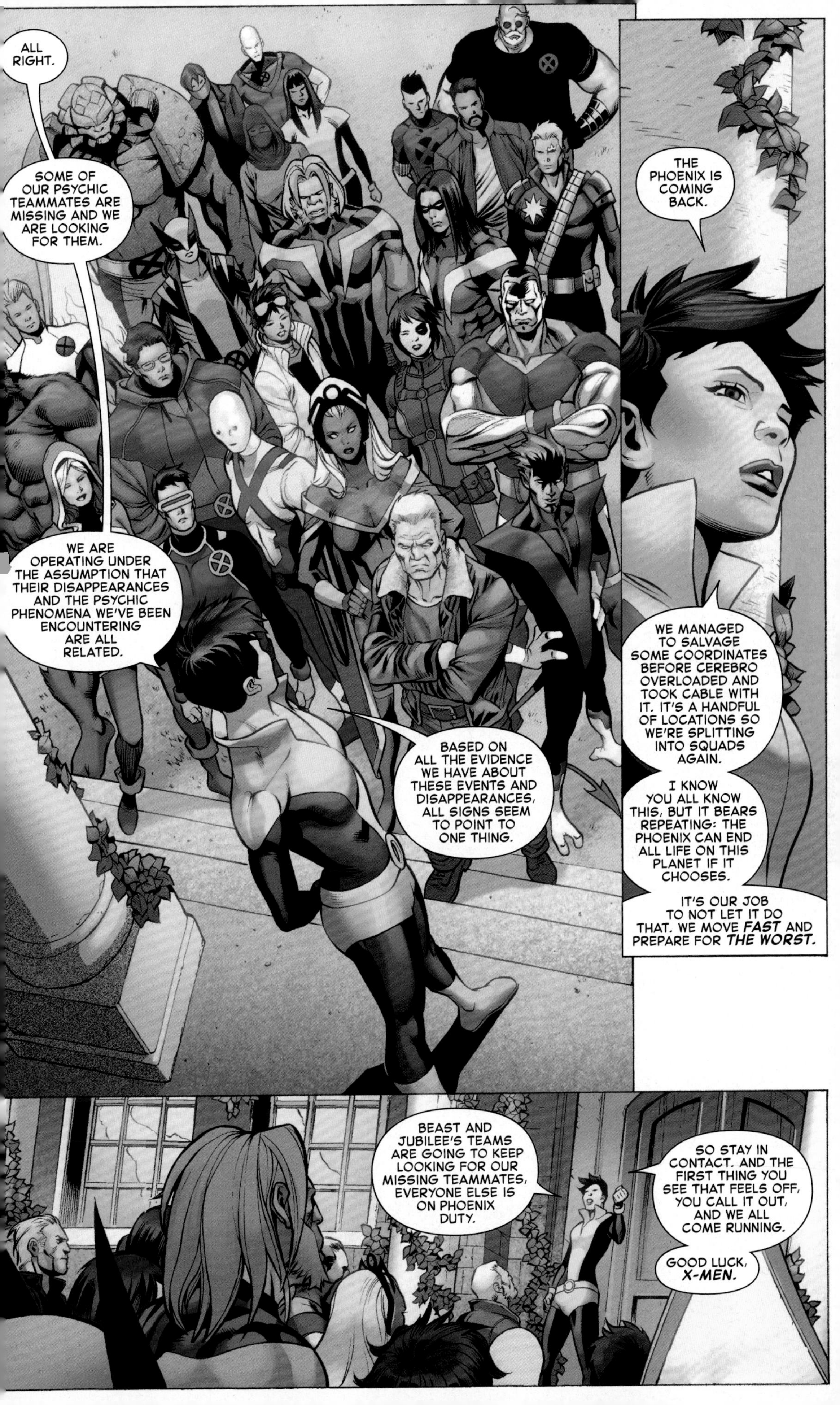
ALL RIGHT.
SOME OF OUR PSYCHIC TEAMMATES ARE MISSING AND WE ARE LOOKING FOR THEM.
WE ARE OPERATING UNDER THE ASSUMPTION THAT THEIR DISAPPEARANCES AND THE PSYCHIC PHENOMENA WE'VE BEEN ENCOUNTERING ARE ALL RELATED.
BASED ON ALL THE EVIDENCE WE HAVE ABOUT THESE EVENTS AND DISAPPEARANCES, ALL SIGNS SEEM TO POINT TO ONE THING.
THE PHOENIX IS COMING BACK.
WE MANAGED TO SALVAGE SOME COORDINATES BEFORE CEREBRO OVERLOADED AND TOOK CABLE WITH IT. IT'S A HANDFUL OF LOCATIONS SO WE'RE SPLITTING INTO SQUADS AGAIN.
I KNOW YOU ALL KNOW THIS, BUT IT BEARS REPEATING: THE PHOENIX CAN END ALL LIFE ON THIS PLANET IF IT CHOOSES.
IT'S OUR JOB TO NOT LET IT DO THAT. WE MOVE ***FAST*** AND PREPARE FOR ***THE WORST.***
BEAST AND JUBILEE'S TEAMS ARE GOING TO KEEP LOOKING FOR OUR MISSING TEAMMATES, EVERYONE ELSE IS ON PHOENIX DUTY.
SO STAY IN CONTACT. AND THE FIRST THING YOU SEE THAT FEELS OFF, YOU CALL IT OUT, AND WE ALL COME RUNNING.
GOOD LUCK, ***X-MEN.***

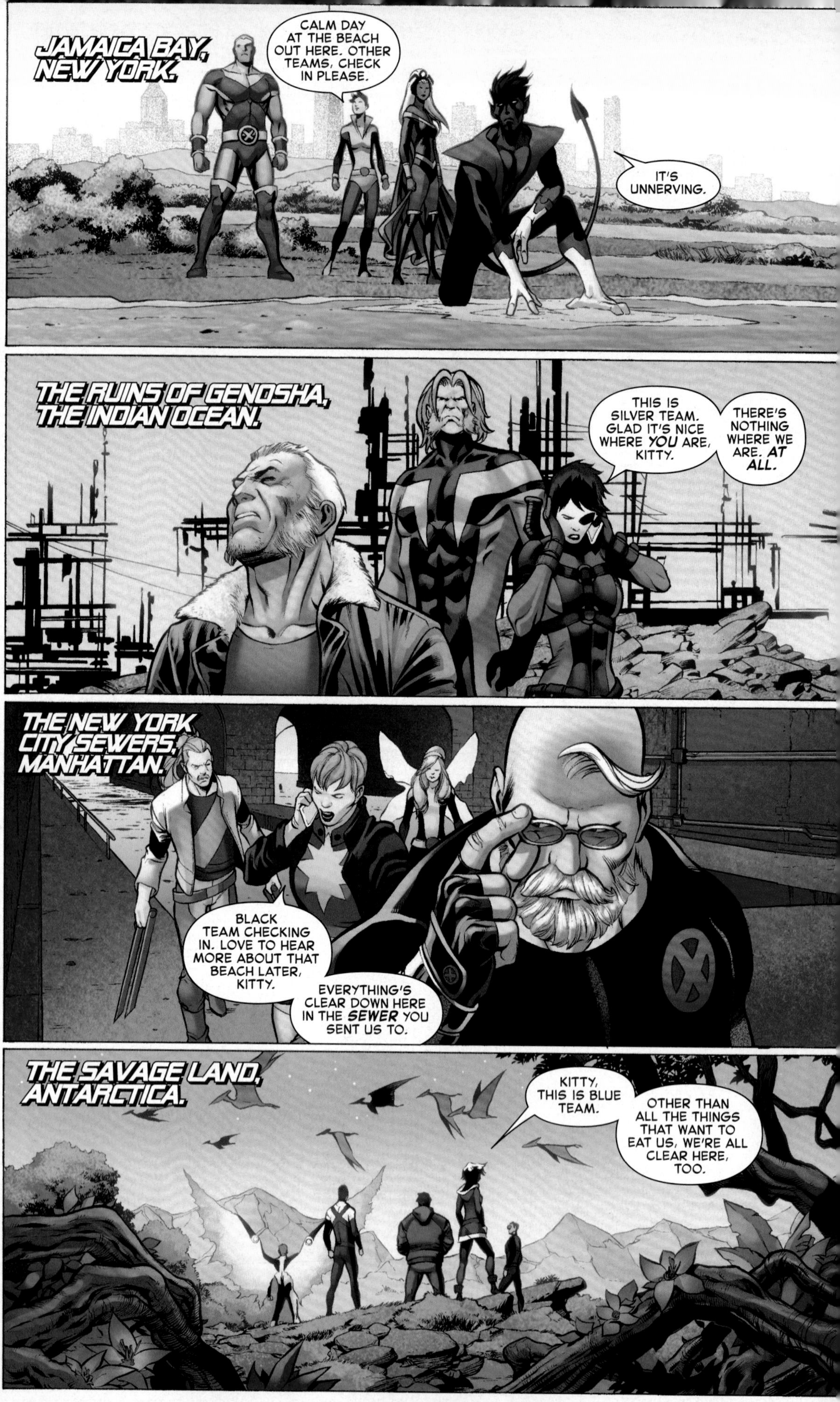
JAMAICA BAY, NEW YORK.
CALM DAY AT THE BEACH OUT HERE. OTHER TEAMS, CHECK IN PLEASE.
IT'S UNNERVING.
THE RUINS OF GENOSHA, THE INDIAN OCEAN.
THIS IS SILVER TEAM. GLAD IT'S NICE WHERE YOU ARE, KITTY.
THERE'S NOTHING WHERE WE ARE. AT ALL.
THE NEW YORK CITY SEWERS, MANHATTAN.
BLACK TEAM CHECKING IN. LOVE TO HEAR MORE ABOUT THAT BEACH LATER, KITTY.
EVERYTHING'S CLEAR DOWN HERE IN THE SEWER YOU SENT US TO.
THE SAVAGE LAND, ANTARCTICA.
KITTY, THIS IS BLUE TEAM.
OTHER THAN ALL THE THINGS THAT WANT TO EAT US, WE'RE ALL CLEAR HERE, TOO.

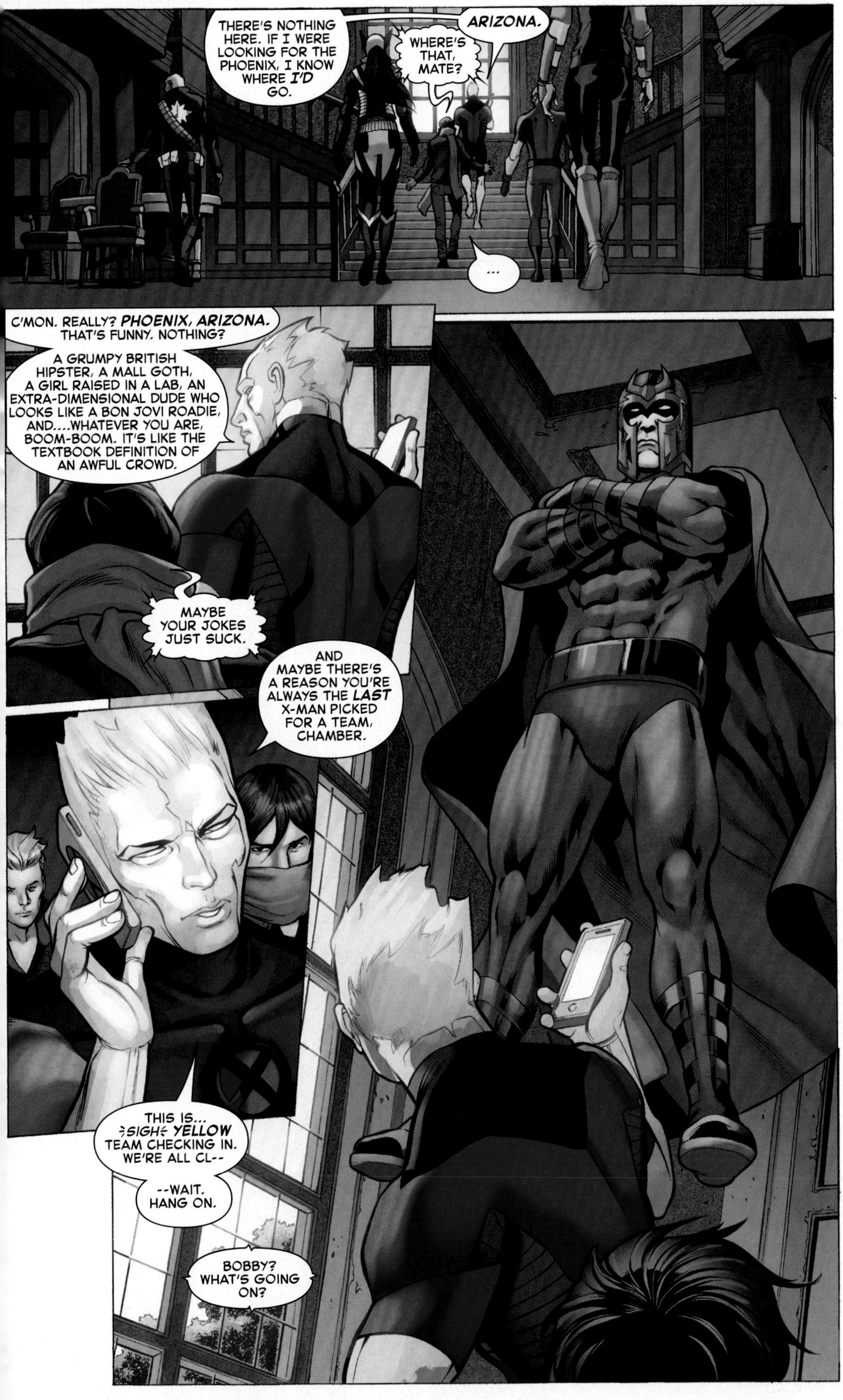
THERE'S NOTHING HERE. IF I WERE LOOKING FOR THE PHOENIX, I KNOW WHERE I'D GO.
ARIZONA.
WHERE'S THAT, MATE?
...
C'MON. REALLY? PHOENIX, ARIZONA. THAT'S FUNNY. NOTHING?
A GRUMPY BRITISH HIPSTER, A MALL GOTH, A GIRL RAISED IN A LAB, AN EXTRA-DIMENSIONAL DUDE WHO LOOKS LIKE A BON JOVI ROADIE, AND....WHATEVER YOU ARE, BOOM-BOOM. IT'S LIKE THE TEXTBOOK DEFINITION OF AN AWFUL CROWD.
MAYBE YOUR JOKES JUST SUCK.
AND MAYBE THERE'S A REASON YOU'RE ALWAYS THE LAST X-MAN PICKED FOR A TEAM, CHAMBER.
THIS IS... SIGH YELLOW TEAM CHECKING IN. WE'RE ALL CL--
--WAIT. HANG ON.
BOBBY? WHAT'S GOING ON?

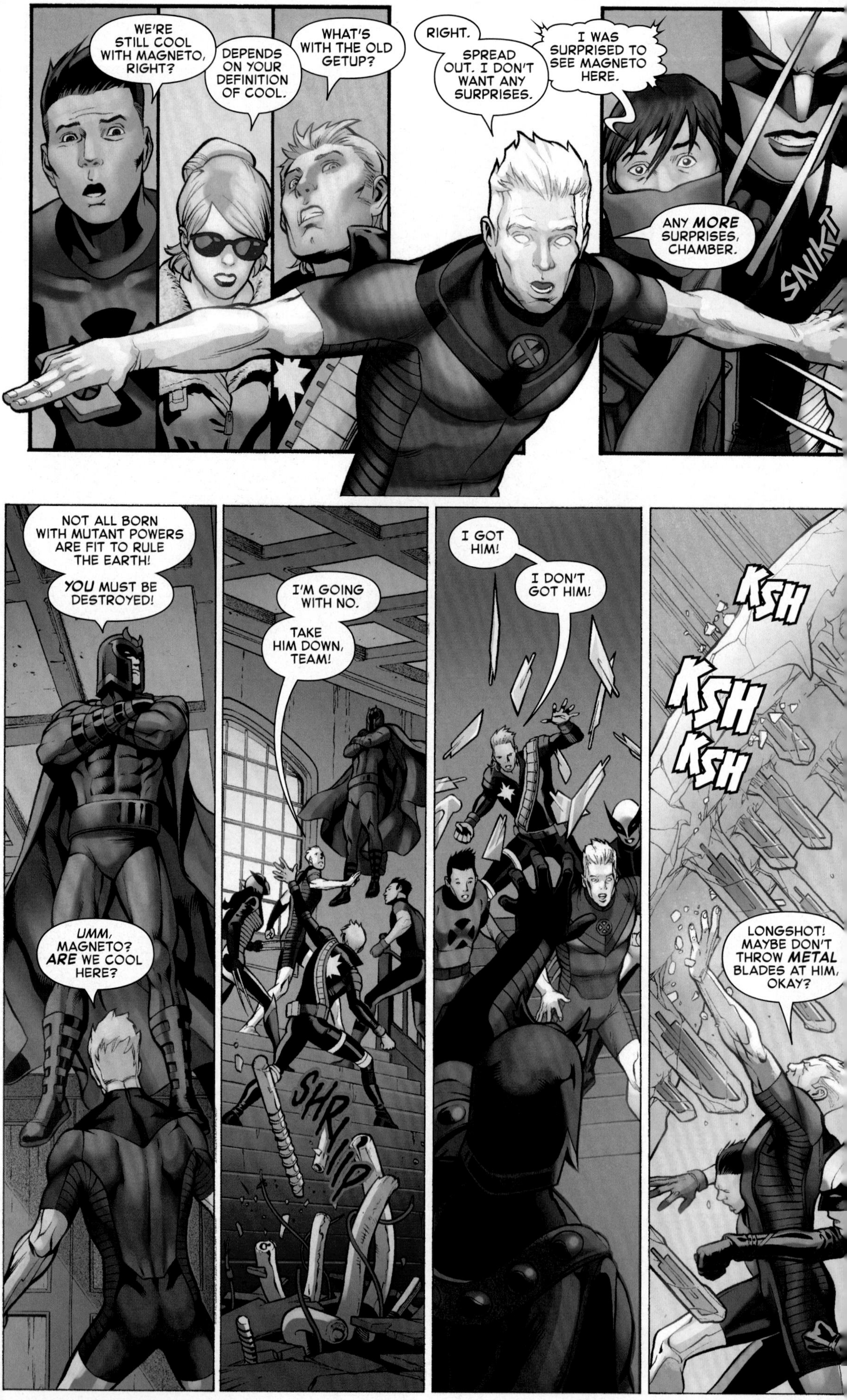

WE'RE STILL COOL WITH MAGNETO, RIGHT?
DEPENDS ON YOUR DEFINITION OF COOL.
WHAT'S WITH THE OLD GETUP?
RIGHT.
SPREAD OUT. I DON'T WANT ANY SURPRISES.
I WAS SURPRISED TO SEE MAGNETO HERE.
ANY MORE SURPRISES, CHAMBER.
SNIKT
NOT ALL BORN WITH MUTANT POWERS ARE FIT TO RULE THE EARTH!
YOU MUST BE DESTROYED!
UMM, MAGNETO? ARE WE COOL HERE?
I'M GOING WITH NO.
TAKE HIM DOWN, TEAM!
SHRIIIP
I GOT HIM!
I DON'T GOT HIM!
KSH
KSH
KSH
LONGSHOT! MAYBE DON'T THROW METAL BLADES AT HIM, OKAY?

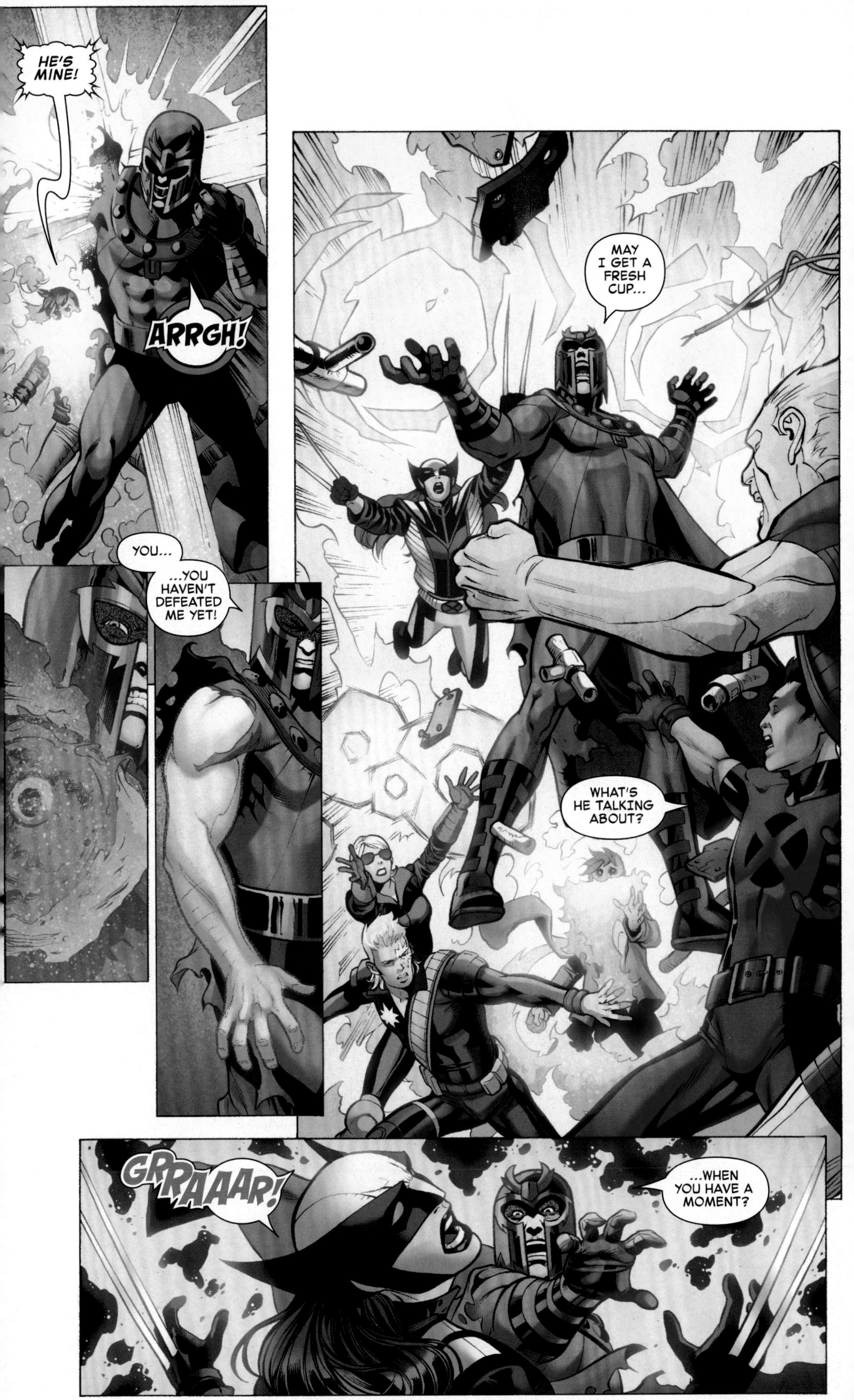

HE'S MINE!
ARRGH!
YOU...
...YOU HAVEN'T DEFEATED ME YET!
MAY I GET A FRESH CUP...
WHAT'S HE TALKING ABOUT?
GRRAAAR!
...WHEN YOU HAVE A MOMENT?

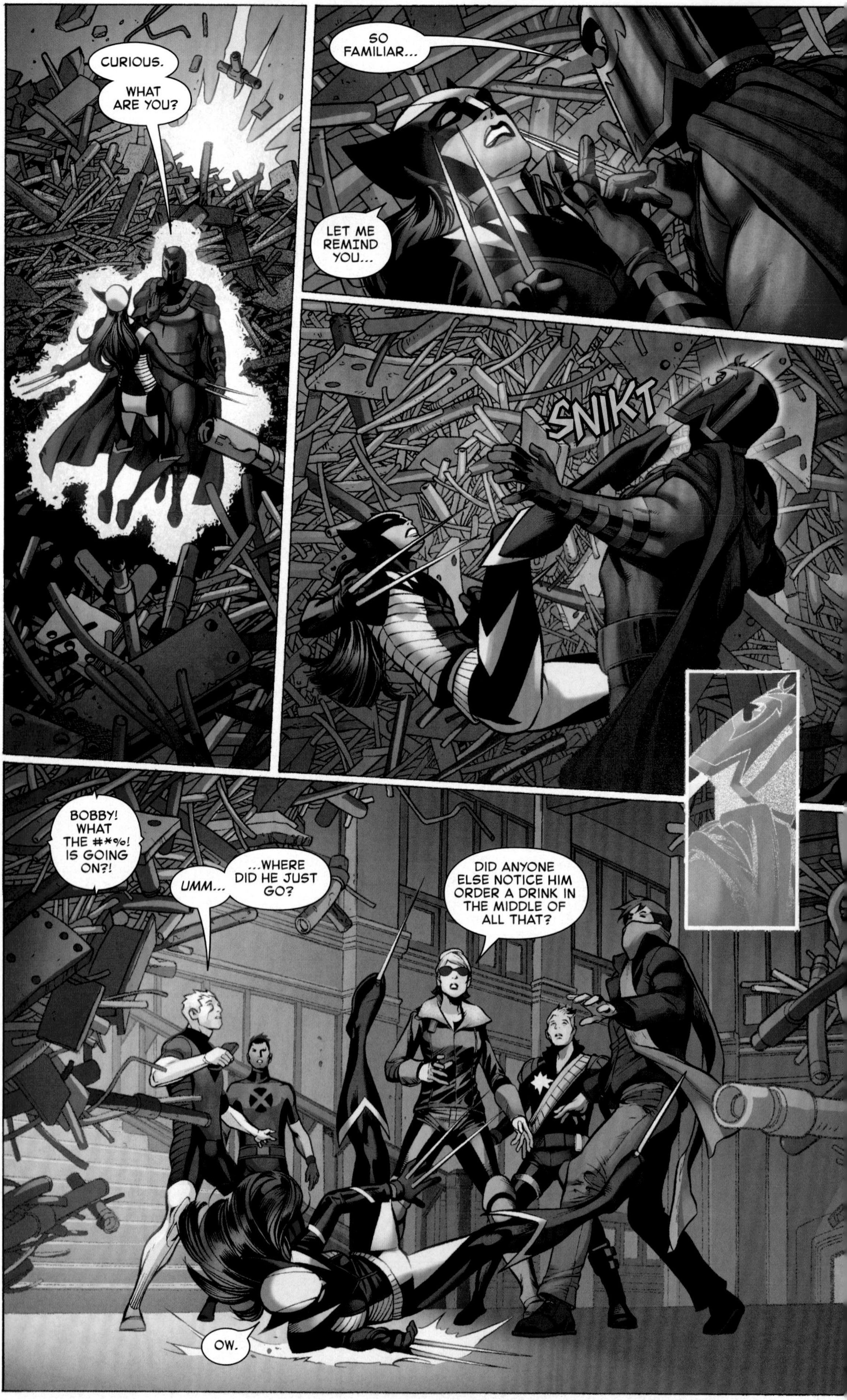

CURIOUS.
WHAT ARE YOU?
SO FAMILIAR...
LET ME REMIND YOU...
SNIKT
BOBBY! WHAT THE #*%! IS GOING ON?!
UMM...
...WHERE DID HE JUST GO?
DID ANYONE ELSE NOTICE HIM ORDER A DRINK IN THE MIDDLE OF ALL THAT?
OW.

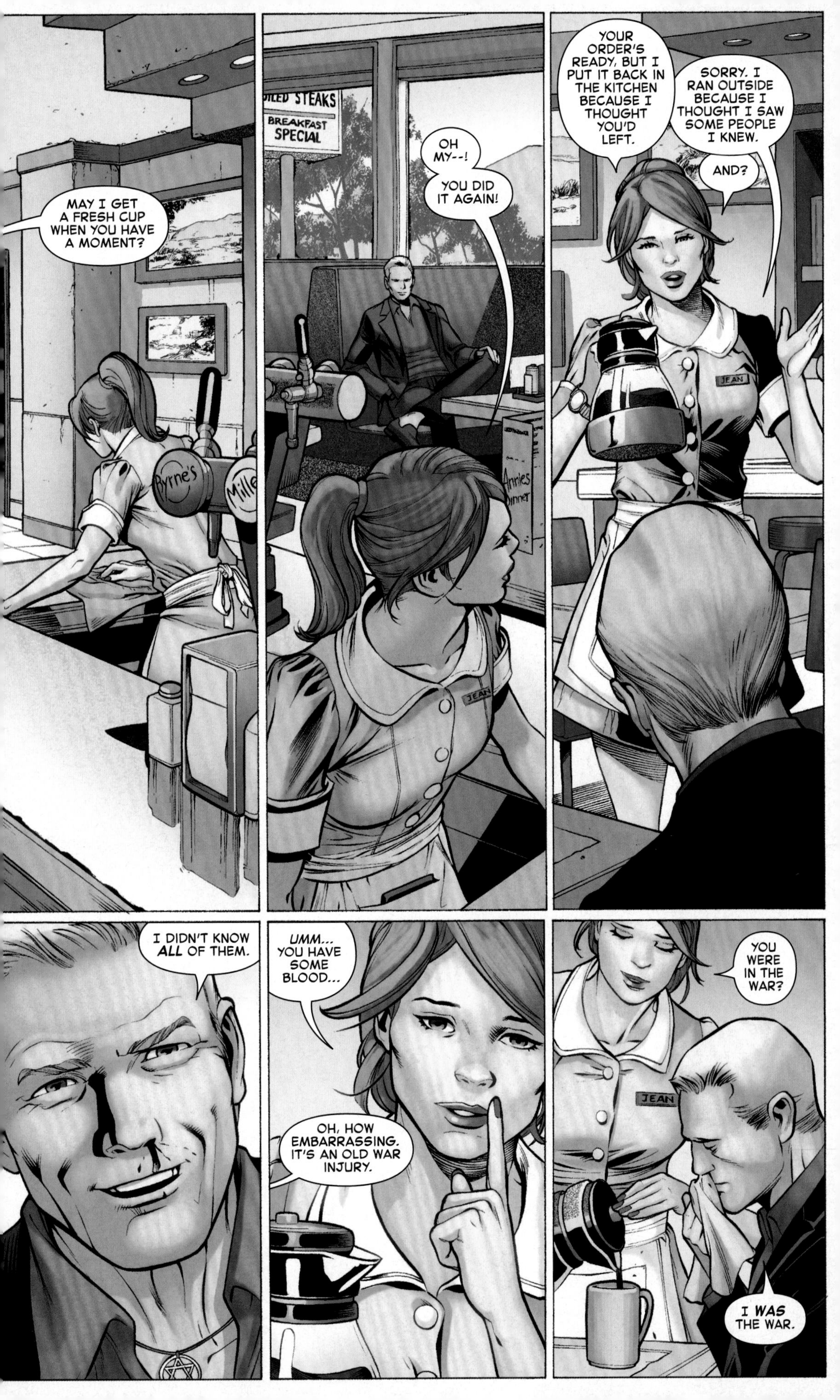
MAY I GET A FRESH CUP WHEN YOU HAVE A MOMENT?
Byrne's
Mille
OILED STEAKS
BREAKFAST SPECIAL
OH MY--!
YOU DID IT AGAIN!
Annies Dinner
JEAN
YOUR ORDER'S READY, BUT I PUT IT BACK IN THE KITCHEN BECAUSE I THOUGHT YOU'D LEFT.
SORRY. I RAN OUTSIDE BECAUSE I THOUGHT I SAW SOME PEOPLE I KNEW.
AND?
JEAN
I DIDN'T KNOW ALL OF THEM.
UMM... YOU HAVE SOME BLOOD...
OH, HOW EMBARRASSING. IT'S AN OLD WAR INJURY.
YOU WERE IN THE WAR?
JEAN
I WAS THE WAR.

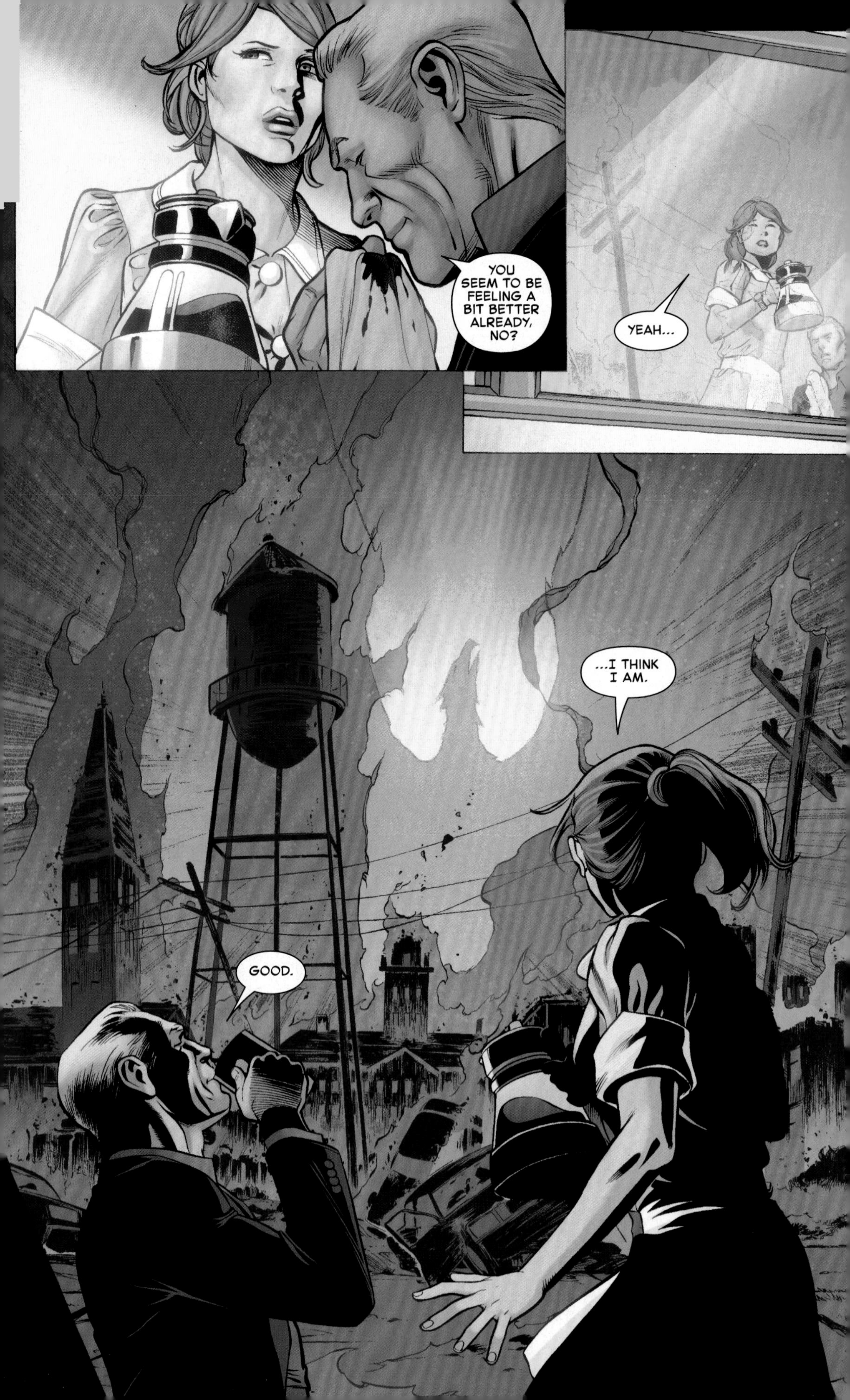
YOU SEEM TO BE FEELING A BIT BETTER ALREADY, NO?
YEAH...
...I THINK I AM.
GOOD.

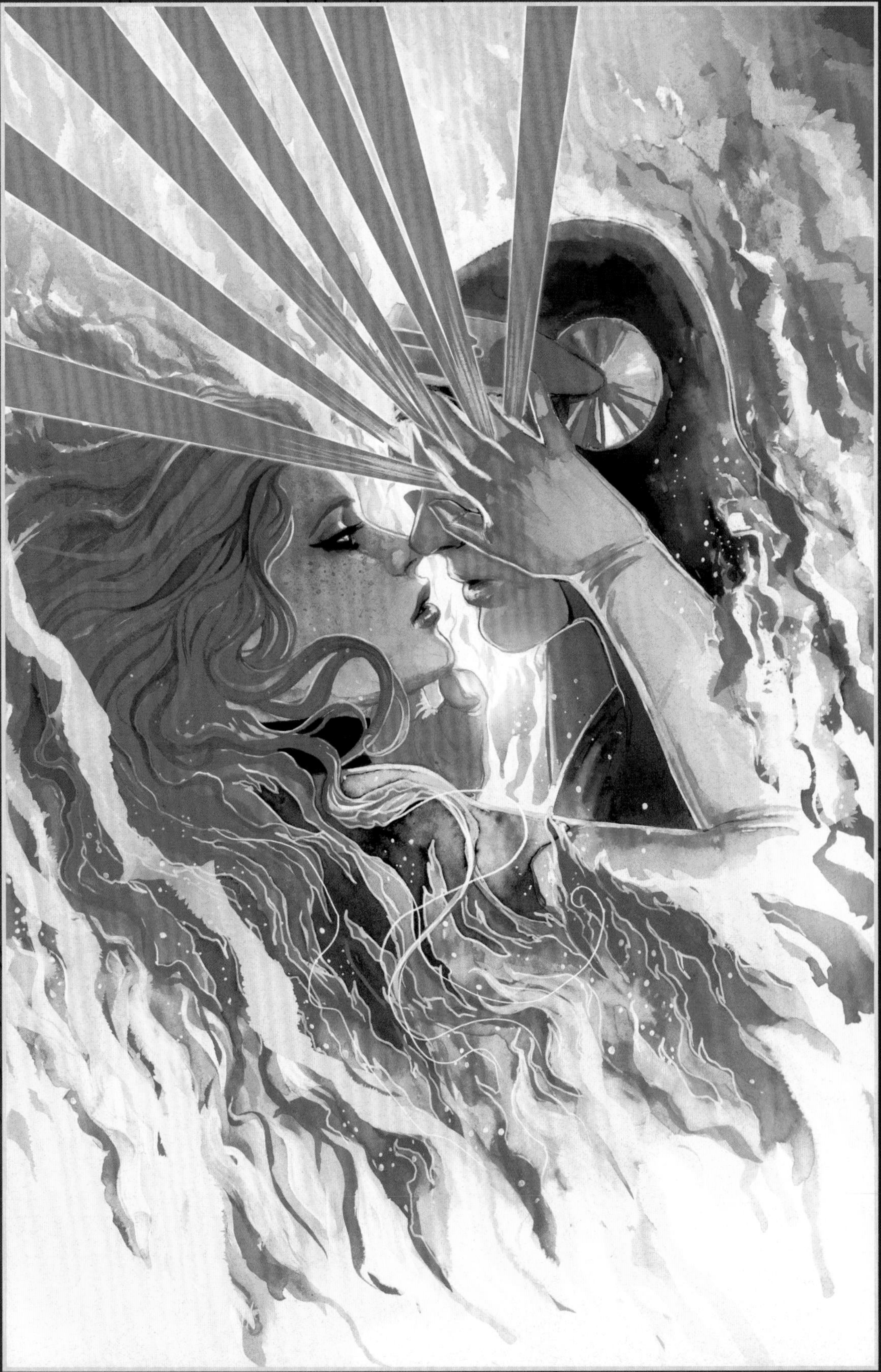

#3 VARIANT BY *STEPHANIE HANS*

3

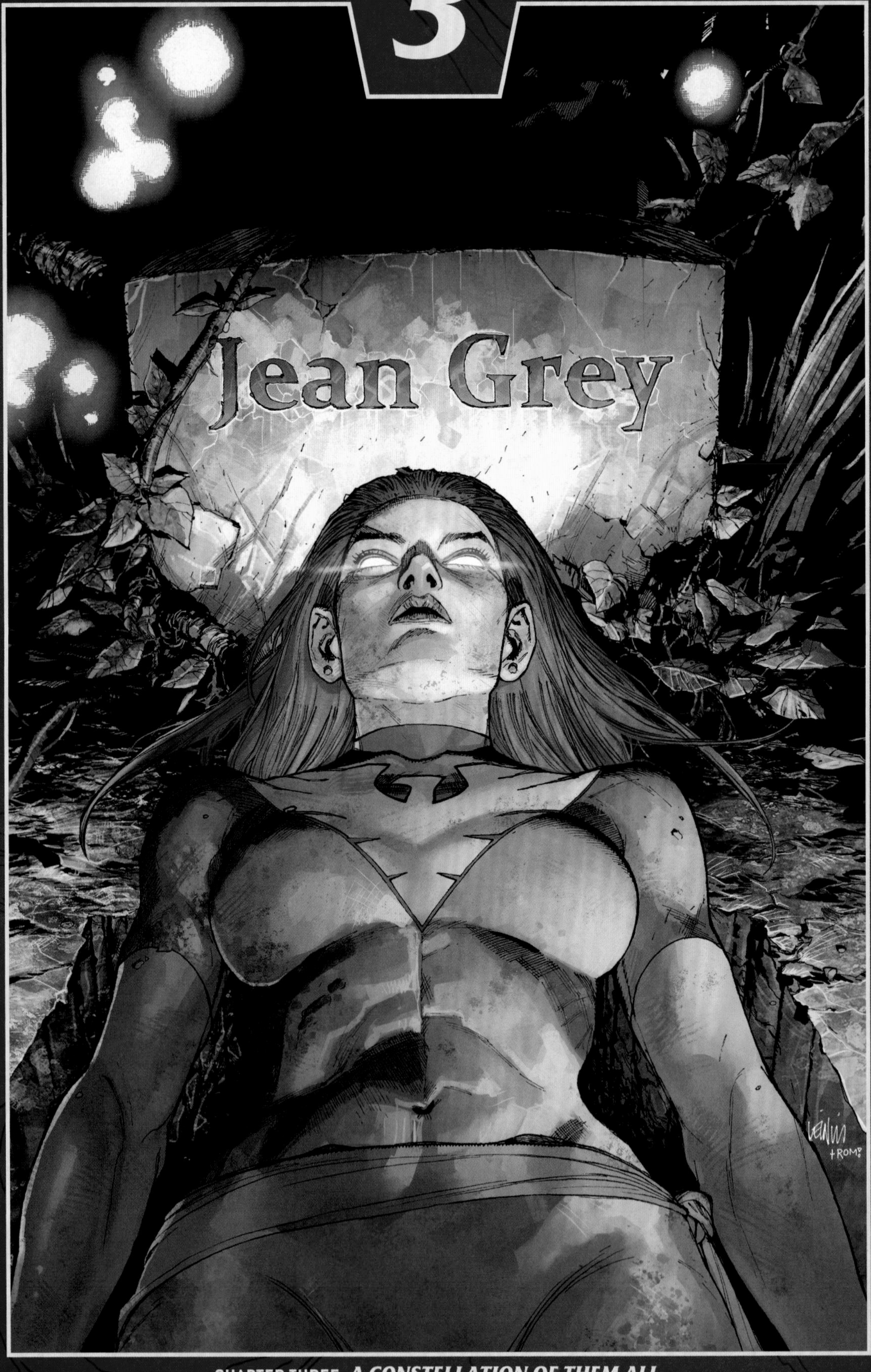
Jean Grey

CHAPTER THREE: ***A CONSTELLATION OF THEM ALL***

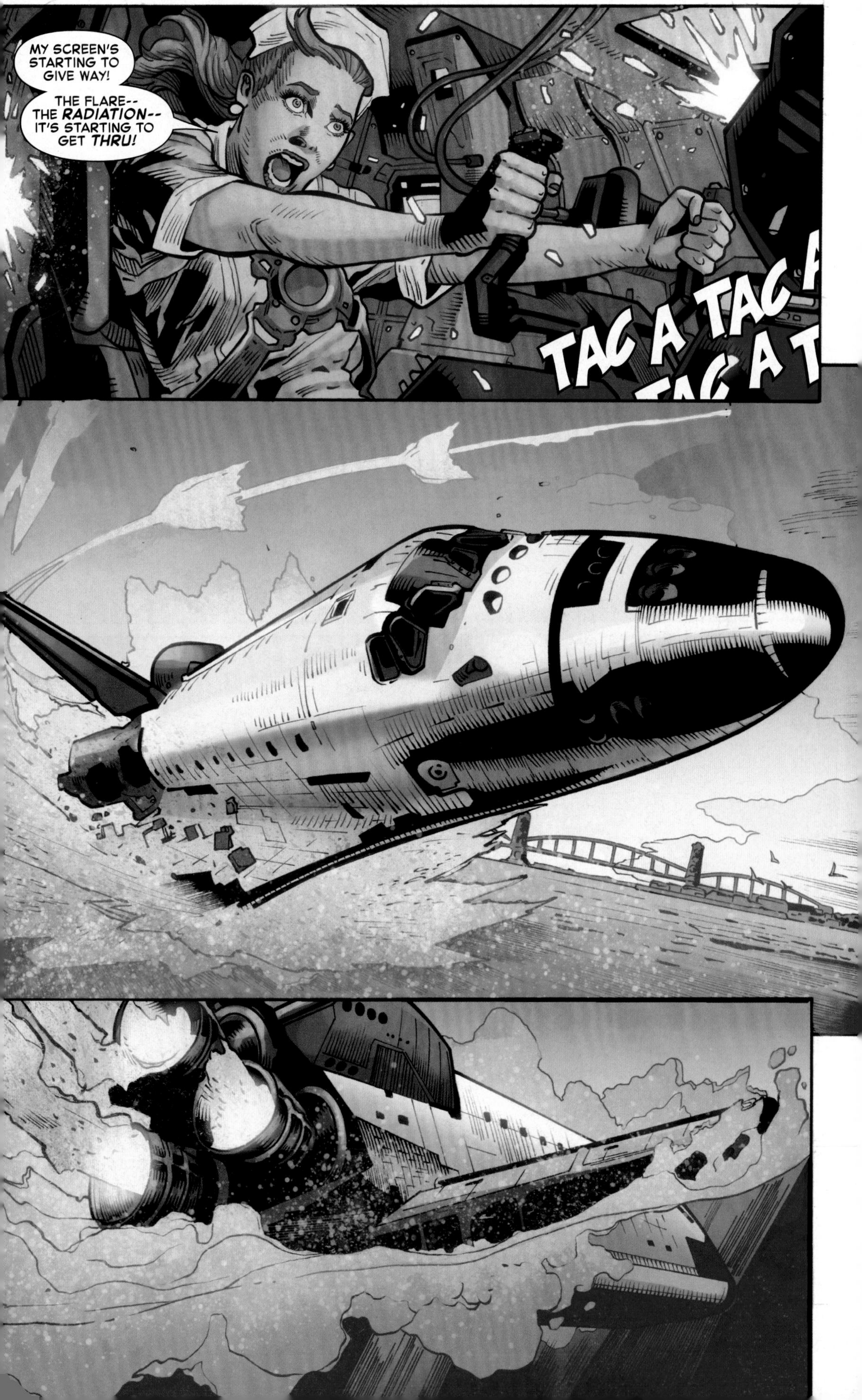
MY SCREEN'S STARTING TO GIVE WAY!
THE FLARE-- THE RADIATION-- IT'S STARTING TO GET THRU!
TAC A TAC A
TAC A T

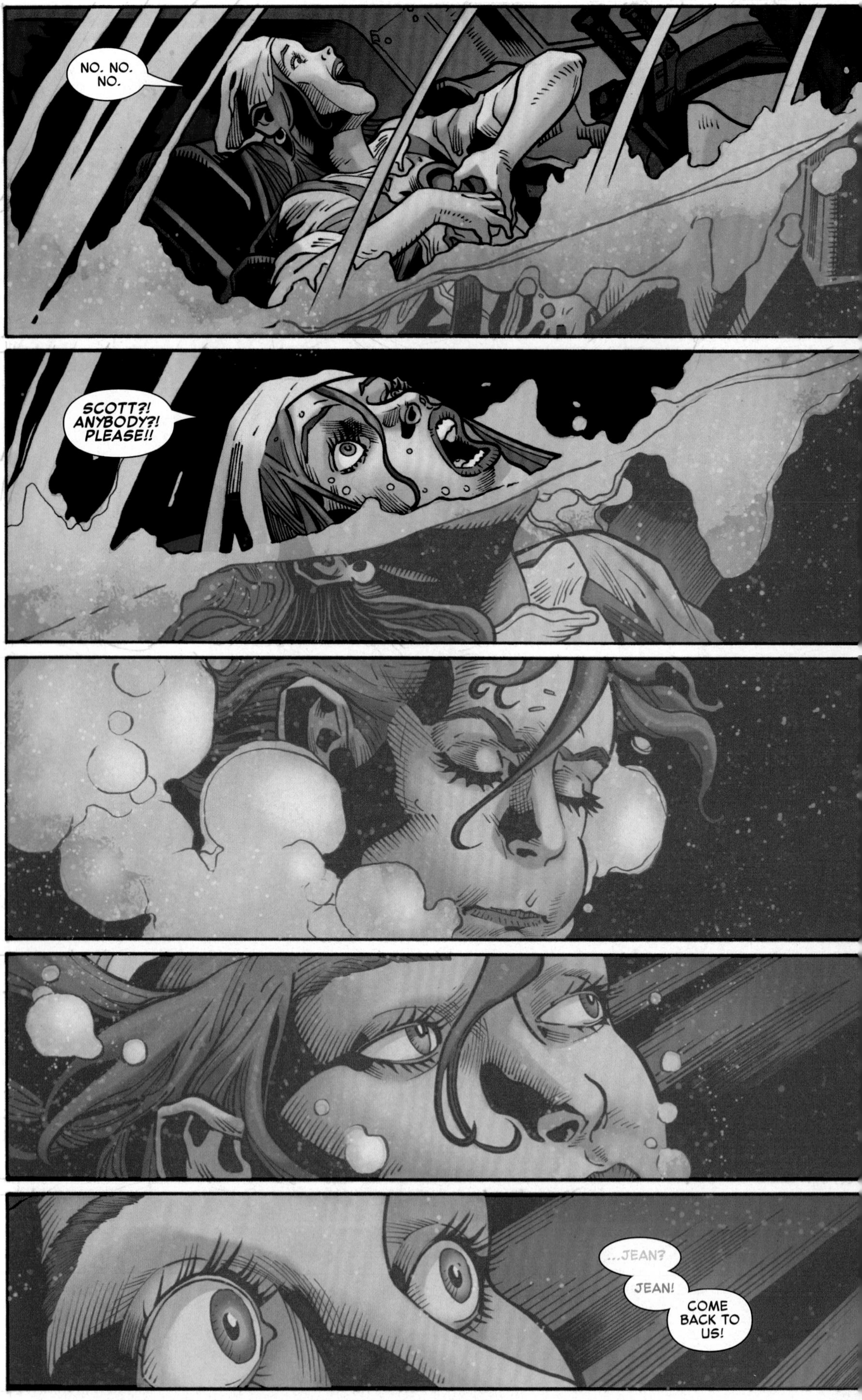

NO. NO. NO.
SCOTT?! ANYBODY?! PLEASE!!
...JEAN?
JEAN!
COME BACK TO US!

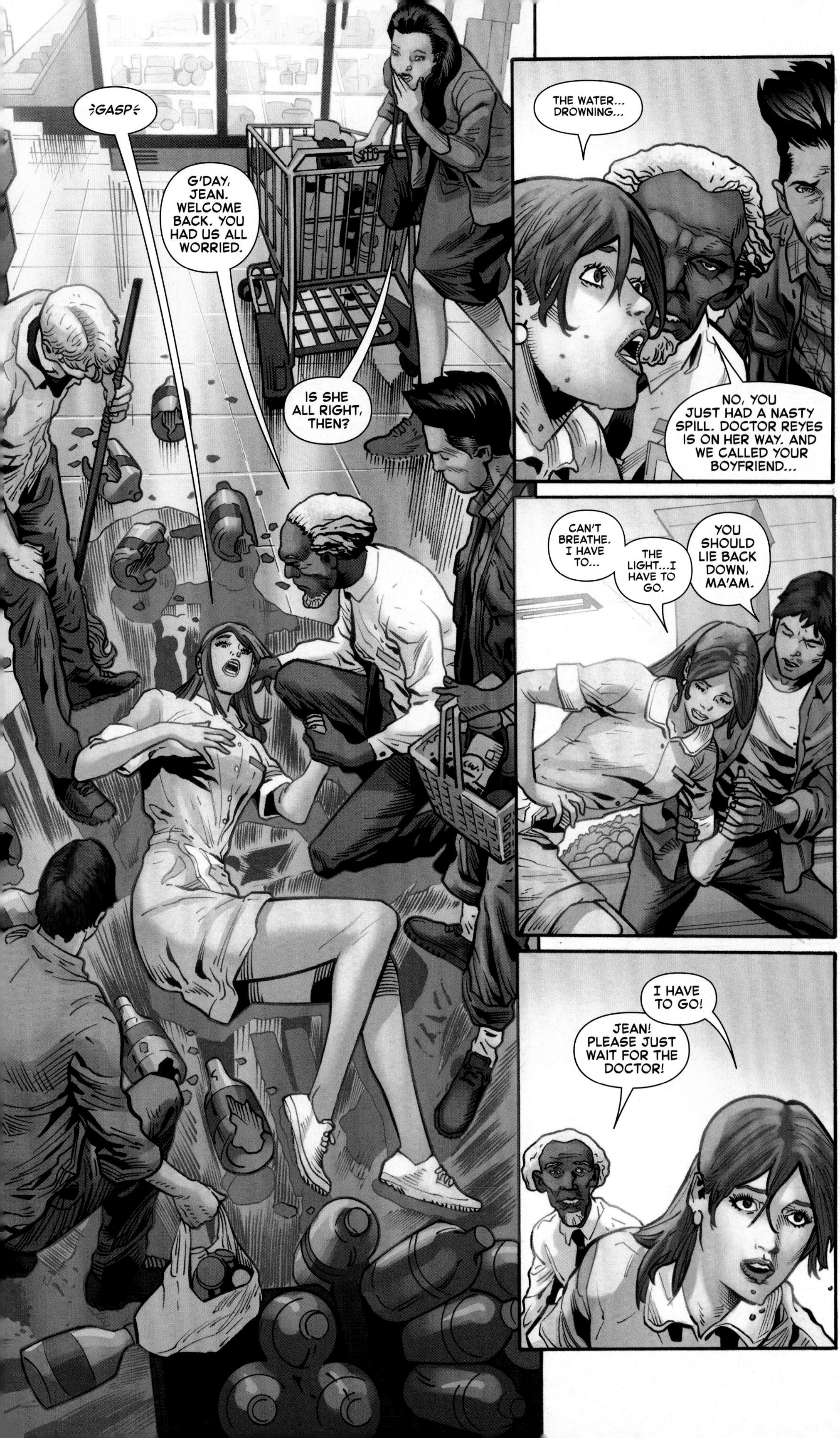

⊰GASP⊱
G'DAY, JEAN. WELCOME BACK. YOU HAD US ALL WORRIED.
IS SHE ALL RIGHT, THEN?
THE WATER... DROWNING...
NO, YOU JUST HAD A NASTY SPILL. DOCTOR REYES IS ON HER WAY. AND WE CALLED YOUR BOYFRIEND...
CAN'T BREATHE. I HAVE TO...
THE LIGHT...I HAVE TO GO.
YOU SHOULD LIE BACK DOWN, MA'AM.
I HAVE TO GO!
JEAN! PLEASE JUST WAIT FOR THE DOCTOR!

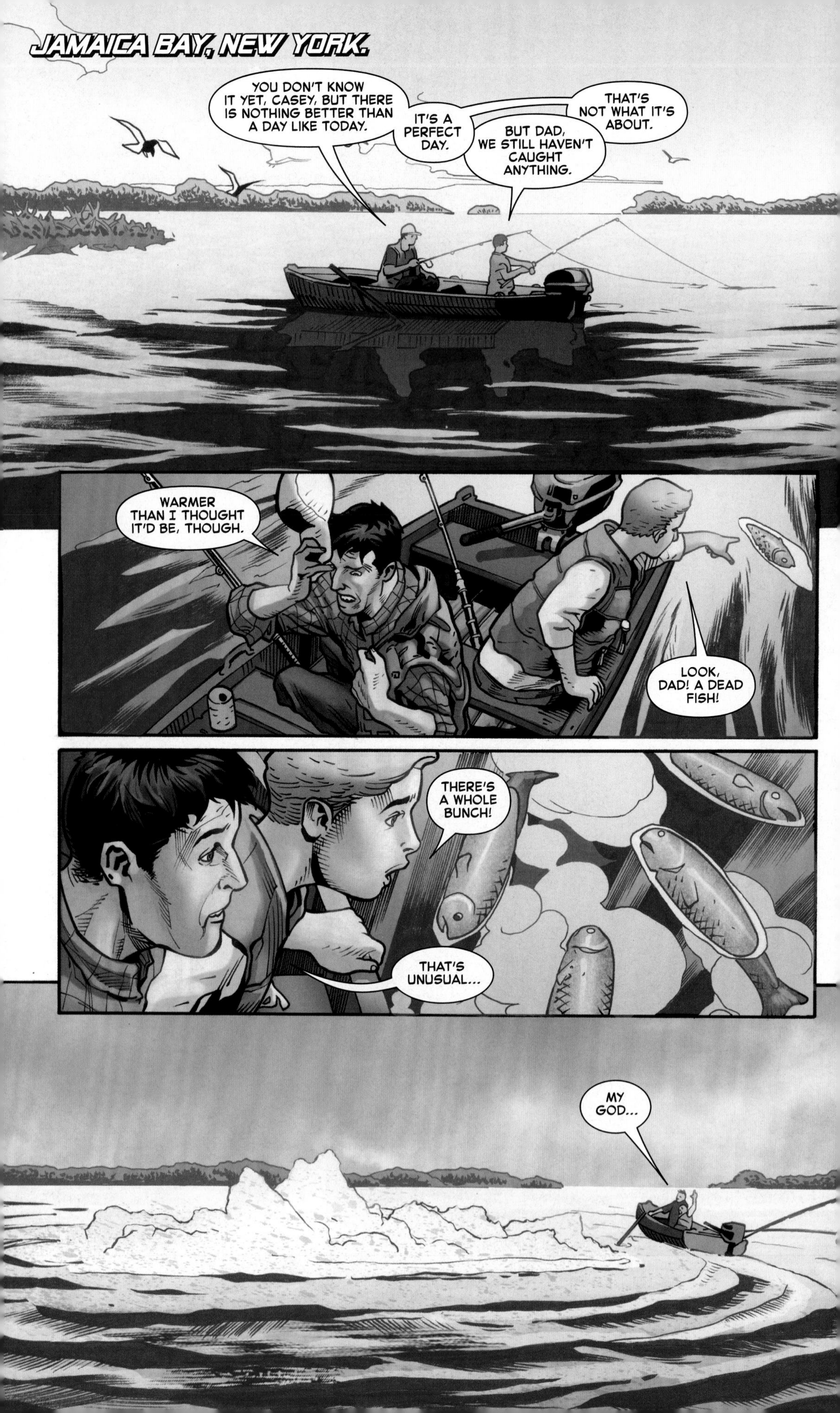
JAMAICA BAY, NEW YORK.
YOU DON'T KNOW IT YET, CASEY, BUT THERE IS NOTHING BETTER THAN A DAY LIKE TODAY.
IT'S A PERFECT DAY.
BUT DAD, WE STILL HAVEN'T CAUGHT ANYTHING.
THAT'S NOT WHAT IT'S ABOUT.
WARMER THAN I THOUGHT IT'D BE, THOUGH.
LOOK, DAD! A DEAD FISH!
THERE'S A WHOLE BUNCH!
THAT'S UNUSUAL...
MY GOD...

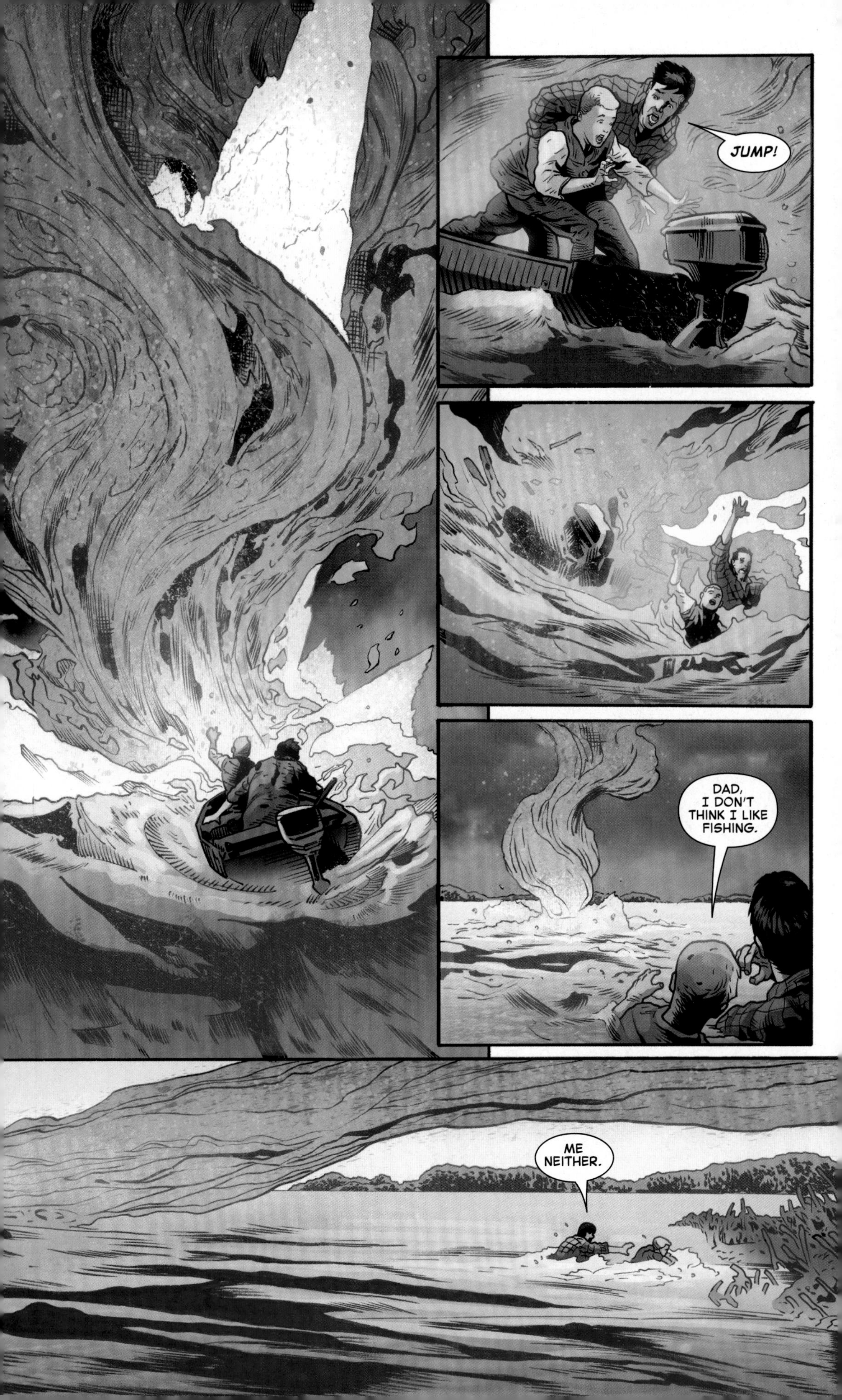
JUMP!
DAD, I DON'T THINK I LIKE FISHING.
ME NEITHER.

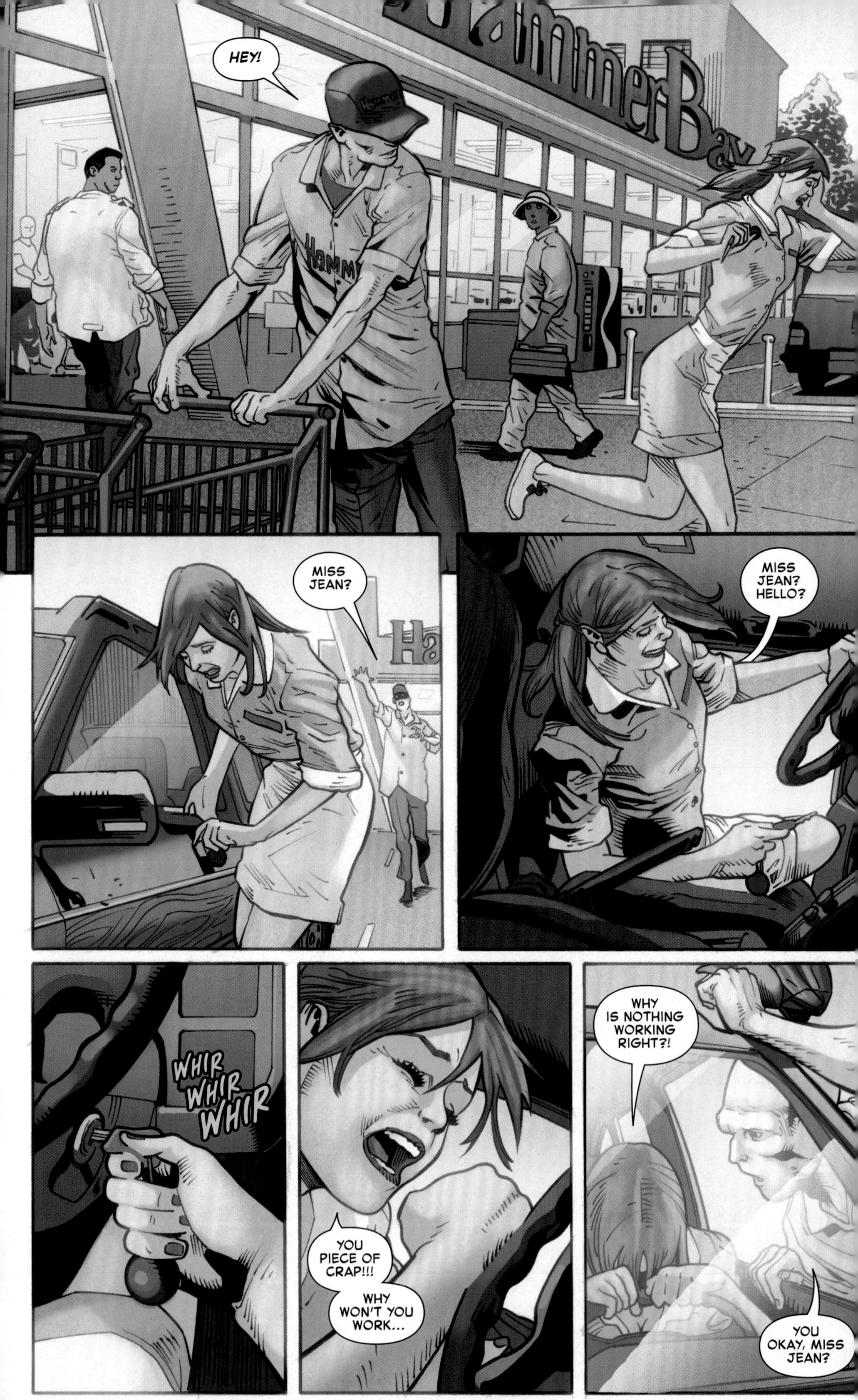

HEY!
MISS JEAN?
MISS JEAN? HELLO?
WHIR WHIR WHIR
YOU PIECE OF CRAP!!!
WHY WON'T YOU WORK...
WHY IS NOTHING WORKING RIGHT?!
YOU OKAY, MISS JEAN?

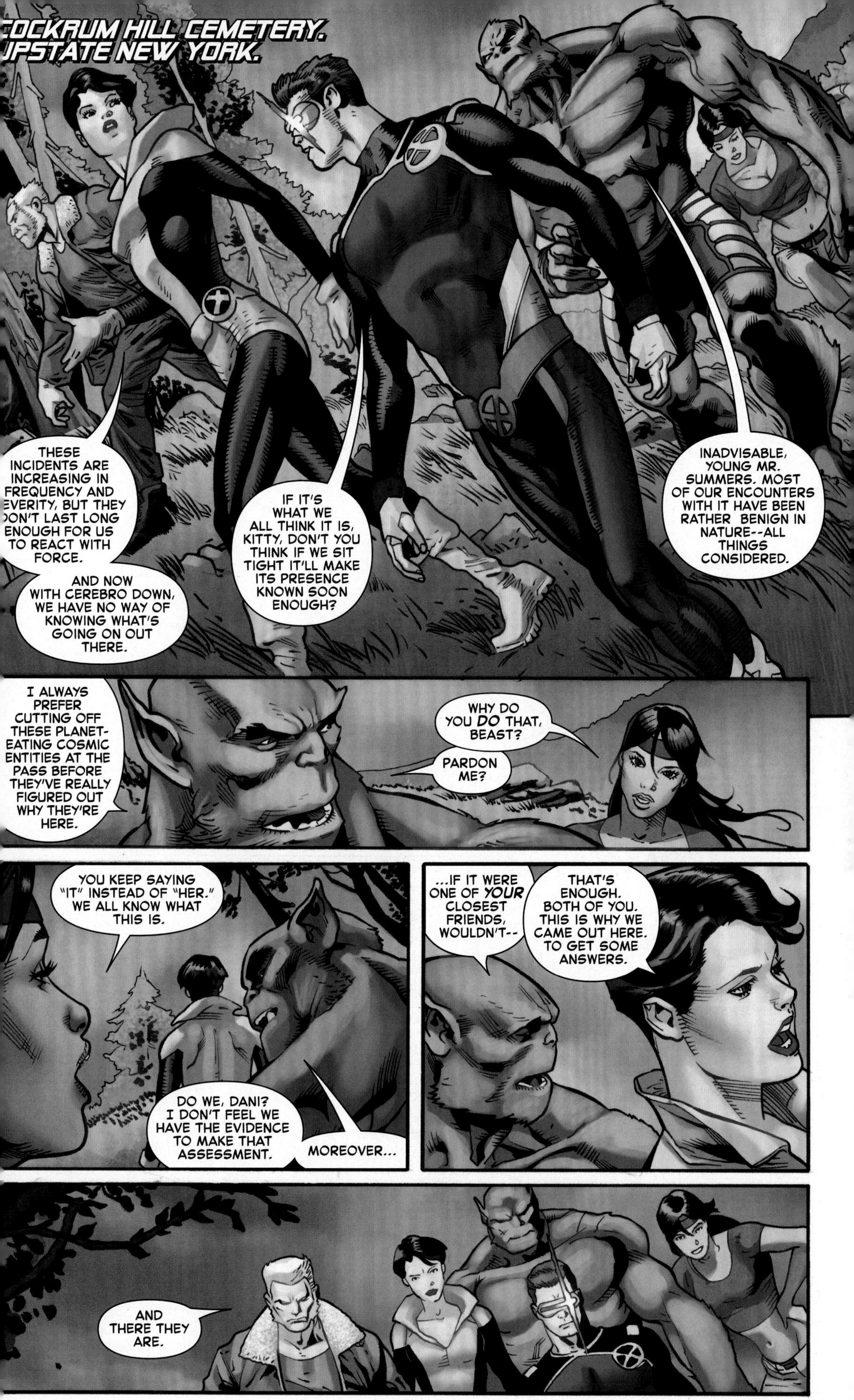
COCKRUM HILL CEMETERY. UPSTATE NEW YORK.
THESE INCIDENTS ARE INCREASING IN FREQUENCY AND SEVERITY, BUT THEY DON'T LAST LONG ENOUGH FOR US TO REACT WITH FORCE.
AND NOW WITH CEREBRO DOWN, WE HAVE NO WAY OF KNOWING WHAT'S GOING ON OUT THERE.
IF IT'S WHAT WE ALL THINK IT IS, KITTY, DON'T YOU THINK IF WE SIT TIGHT IT'LL MAKE ITS PRESENCE KNOWN SOON ENOUGH?
INADVISABLE, YOUNG MR. SUMMERS. MOST OF OUR ENCOUNTERS WITH IT HAVE BEEN RATHER BENIGN IN NATURE--ALL THINGS CONSIDERED.
I ALWAYS PREFER CUTTING OFF THESE PLANET-EATING COSMIC ENTITIES AT THE PASS BEFORE THEY'VE REALLY FIGURED OUT WHY THEY'RE HERE.
WHY DO YOU DO THAT, BEAST?
PARDON ME?
YOU KEEP SAYING "IT" INSTEAD OF "HER." WE ALL KNOW WHAT THIS IS.
DO WE, DANI? I DON'T FEEL WE HAVE THE EVIDENCE TO MAKE THAT ASSESSMENT.
MOREOVER...
...IF IT WERE ONE OF YOUR CLOSEST FRIENDS, WOULDN'T--
THAT'S ENOUGH. BOTH OF YOU. THIS IS WHY WE CAME OUT HERE. TO GET SOME ANSWERS.
AND THERE THEY ARE.

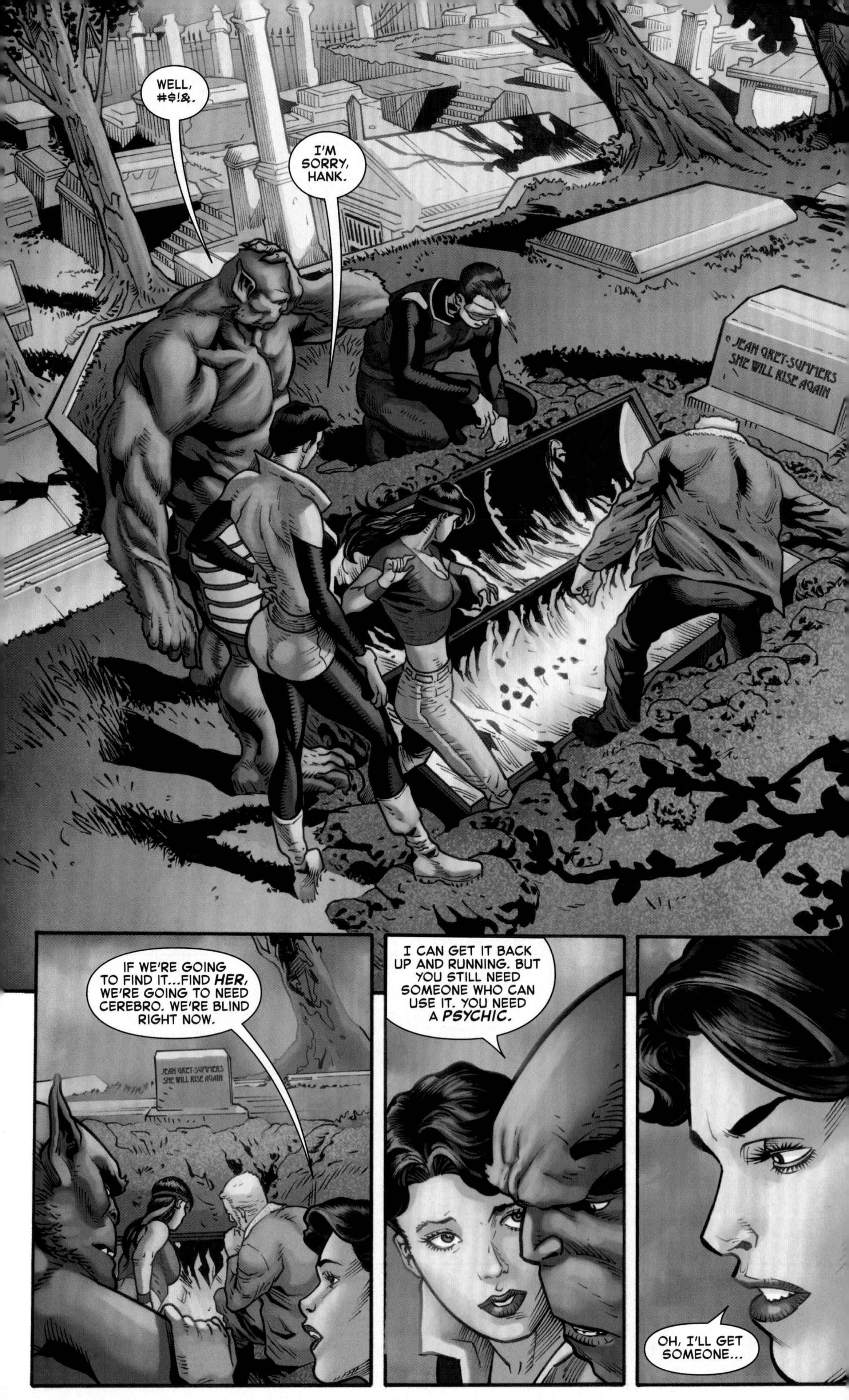

WELL, #$!&.
I'M SORRY, HANK.
JEAN GREY-SUMMERS SHE WILL RISE AGAIN
IF WE'RE GOING TO FIND IT...FIND HER, WE'RE GOING TO NEED CEREBRO. WE'RE BLIND RIGHT NOW.
JEAN GREY-SUMMERS SHE WILL RISE AGAIN
I CAN GET IT BACK UP AND RUNNING. BUT YOU STILL NEED SOMEONE WHO CAN USE IT. YOU NEED A PSYCHIC.
OH, I'LL GET SOMEONE...

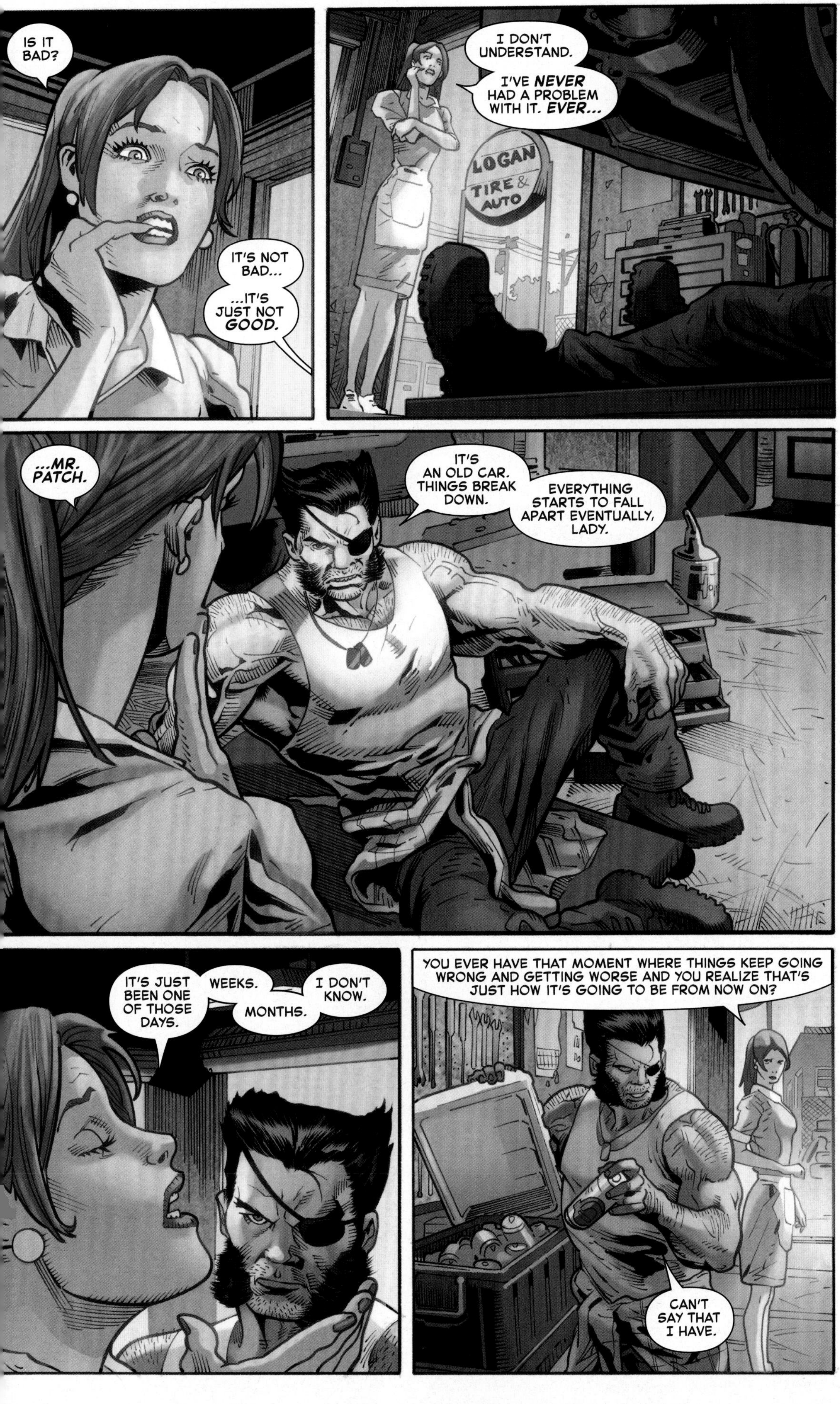
IS IT BAD?
IT'S NOT BAD...
...IT'S JUST NOT GOOD.
I DON'T UNDERSTAND.
I'VE NEVER HAD A PROBLEM WITH IT. EVER...
LOGAN TIRE & AUTO
...MR. PATCH.
IT'S AN OLD CAR. THINGS BREAK DOWN.
EVERYTHING STARTS TO FALL APART EVENTUALLY, LADY.
IT'S JUST BEEN ONE OF THOSE DAYS.
WEEKS.
MONTHS.
I DON'T KNOW.
YOU EVER HAVE THAT MOMENT WHERE THINGS KEEP GOING WRONG AND GETTING WORSE AND YOU REALIZE THAT'S JUST HOW IT'S GOING TO BE FROM NOW ON?
CAN'T SAY THAT I HAVE.

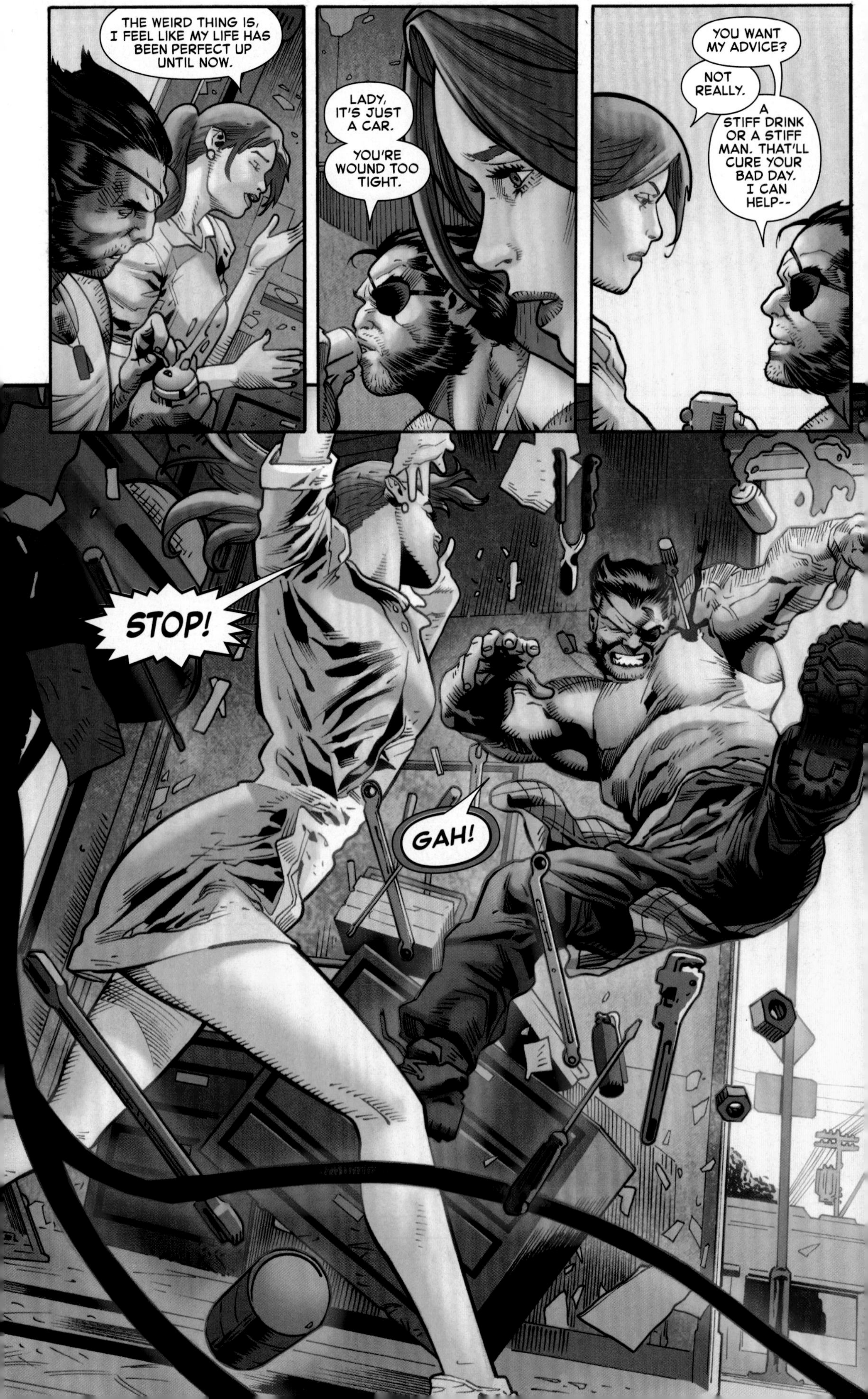
THE WEIRD THING IS, I FEEL LIKE MY LIFE HAS BEEN PERFECT UP UNTIL NOW.
LADY, IT'S JUST A CAR.
YOU'RE WOUND TOO TIGHT.
YOU WANT MY ADVICE?
NOT REALLY.
A STIFF DRINK OR A STIFF MAN. THAT'LL CURE YOUR BAD DAY. I CAN HELP--
STOP!
GAH!

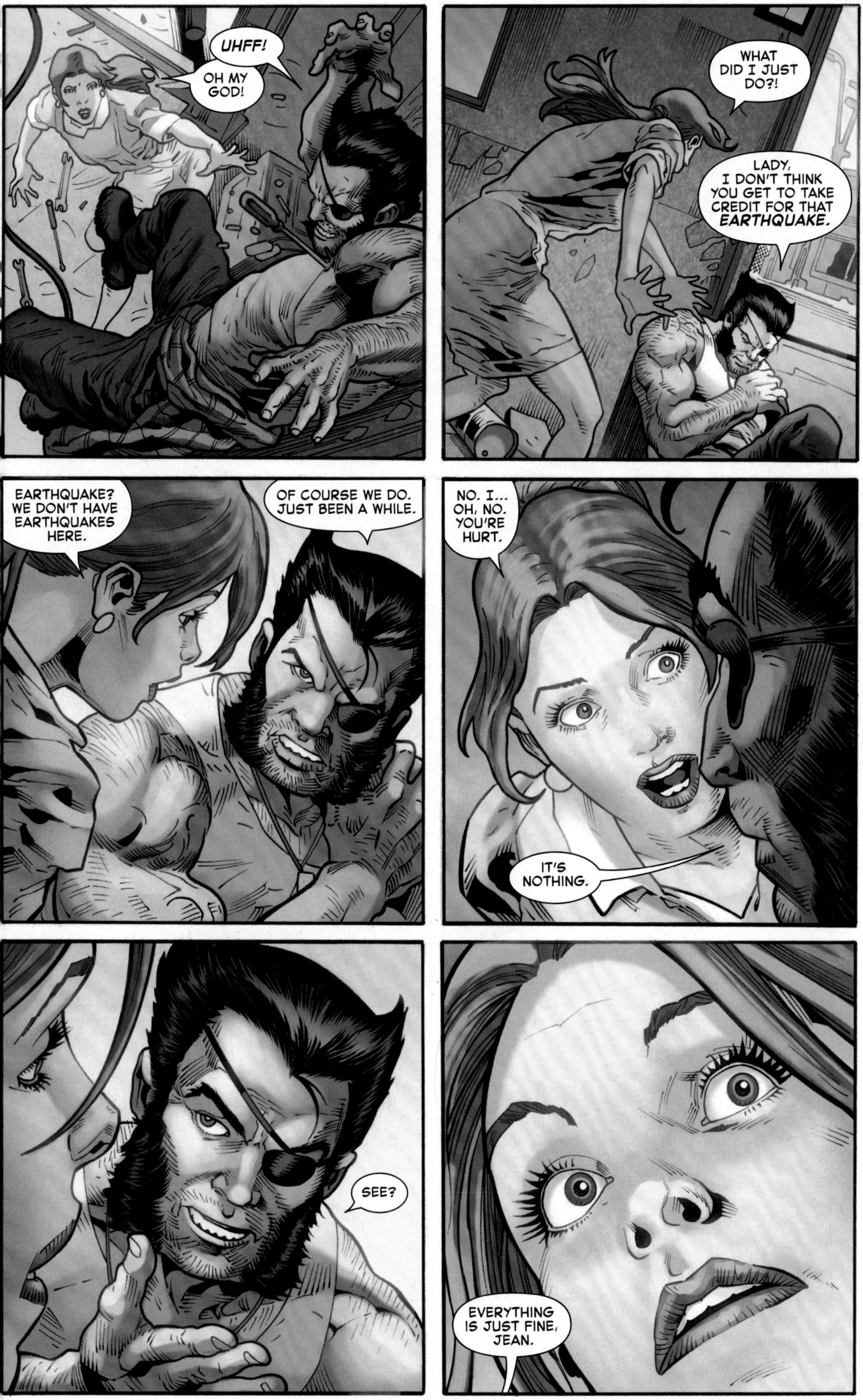
UHFF!
OH MY GOD!
WHAT DID I JUST DO?!
LADY, I DON'T THINK YOU GET TO TAKE CREDIT FOR THAT EARTHQUAKE.
EARTHQUAKE? WE DON'T HAVE EARTHQUAKES HERE.
OF COURSE WE DO. JUST BEEN A WHILE.
NO. I... OH, NO. YOU'RE HURT.
IT'S NOTHING.
SEE?
EVERYTHING IS JUST FINE, JEAN.

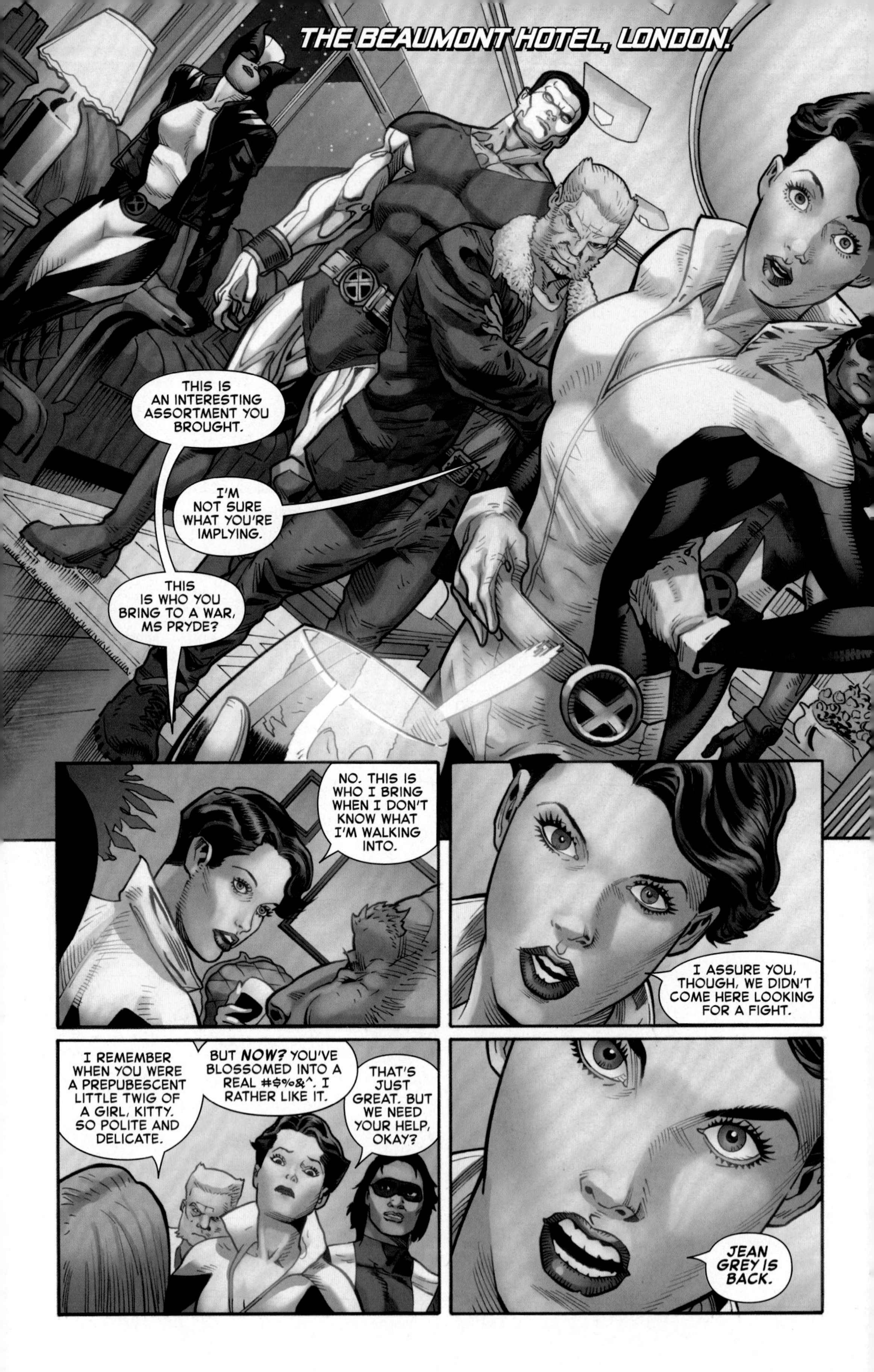
THE BEAUMONT HOTEL, LONDON.
THIS IS AN INTERESTING ASSORTMENT YOU BROUGHT.
I'M NOT SURE WHAT YOU'RE IMPLYING.
THIS IS WHO YOU BRING TO A WAR, MS PRYDE?
NO. THIS IS WHO I BRING WHEN I DON'T KNOW WHAT I'M WALKING INTO.
I ASSURE YOU, THOUGH, WE DIDN'T COME HERE LOOKING FOR A FIGHT.
I REMEMBER WHEN YOU WERE A PREPUBESCENT LITTLE TWIG OF A GIRL, KITTY. SO POLITE AND DELICATE.
BUT NOW? YOU'VE BLOSSOMED INTO A REAL #$%&^. I RATHER LIKE IT.
THAT'S JUST GREAT. BUT WE NEED YOUR HELP, OKAY?
JEAN GREY IS BACK.

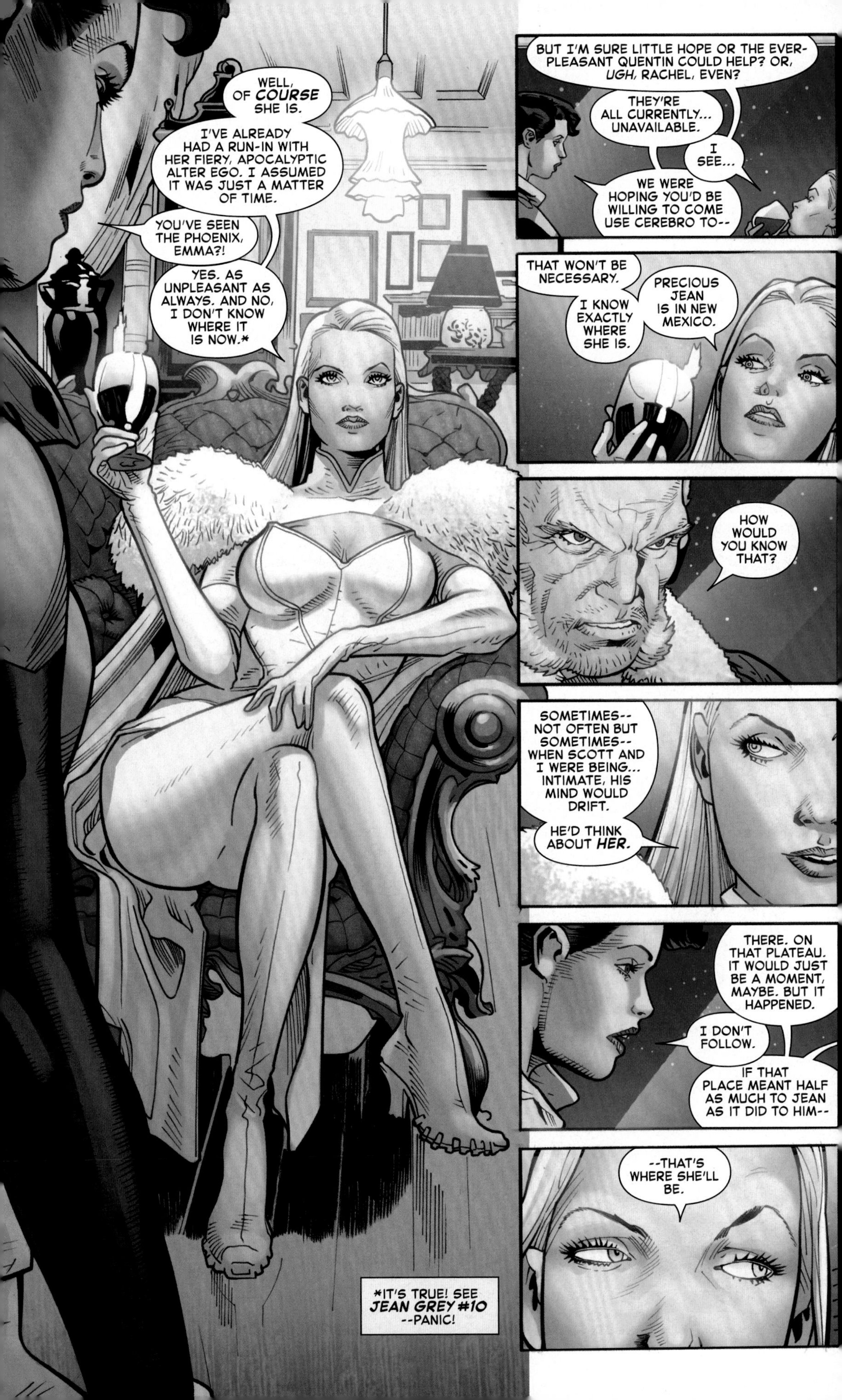
WELL, OF COURSE SHE IS.
I'VE ALREADY HAD A RUN-IN WITH HER FIERY, APOCALYPTIC ALTER EGO. I ASSUMED IT WAS JUST A MATTER OF TIME.
YOU'VE SEEN THE PHOENIX, EMMA?!
YES. AS UNPLEASANT AS ALWAYS. AND NO, I DON'T KNOW WHERE IT IS NOW.*
*IT'S TRUE! SEE JEAN GREY #10 --PANIC!
BUT I'M SURE LITTLE HOPE OR THE EVER-PLEASANT QUENTIN COULD HELP? OR, UGH, RACHEL, EVEN?
THEY'RE ALL CURRENTLY... UNAVAILABLE.
I SEE...
WE WERE HOPING YOU'D BE WILLING TO COME USE CEREBRO TO--
THAT WON'T BE NECESSARY.
I KNOW EXACTLY WHERE SHE IS.
PRECIOUS JEAN IS IN NEW MEXICO.
HOW WOULD YOU KNOW THAT?
SOMETIMES-- NOT OFTEN BUT SOMETIMES-- WHEN SCOTT AND I WERE BEING... INTIMATE, HIS MIND WOULD DRIFT.
HE'D THINK ABOUT HER.
THERE. ON THAT PLATEAU. IT WOULD JUST BE A MOMENT, MAYBE. BUT IT HAPPENED.
I DON'T FOLLOW.
IF THAT PLACE MEANT HALF AS MUCH TO JEAN AS IT DID TO HIM--
--THAT'S WHERE SHE'LL BE.

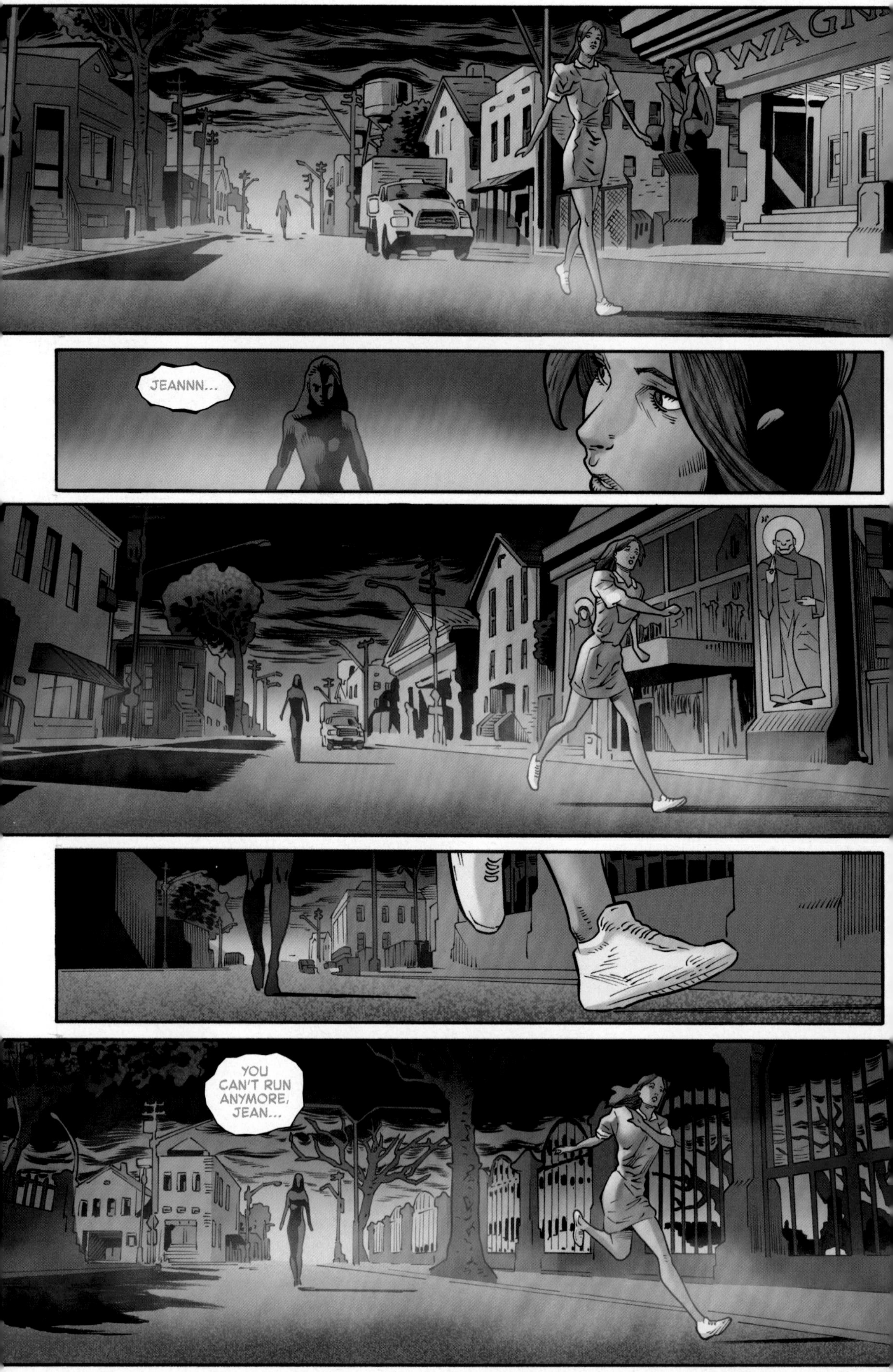
WAGN
JEANNN...
YOU CAN'T RUN ANYMORE, JEAN...

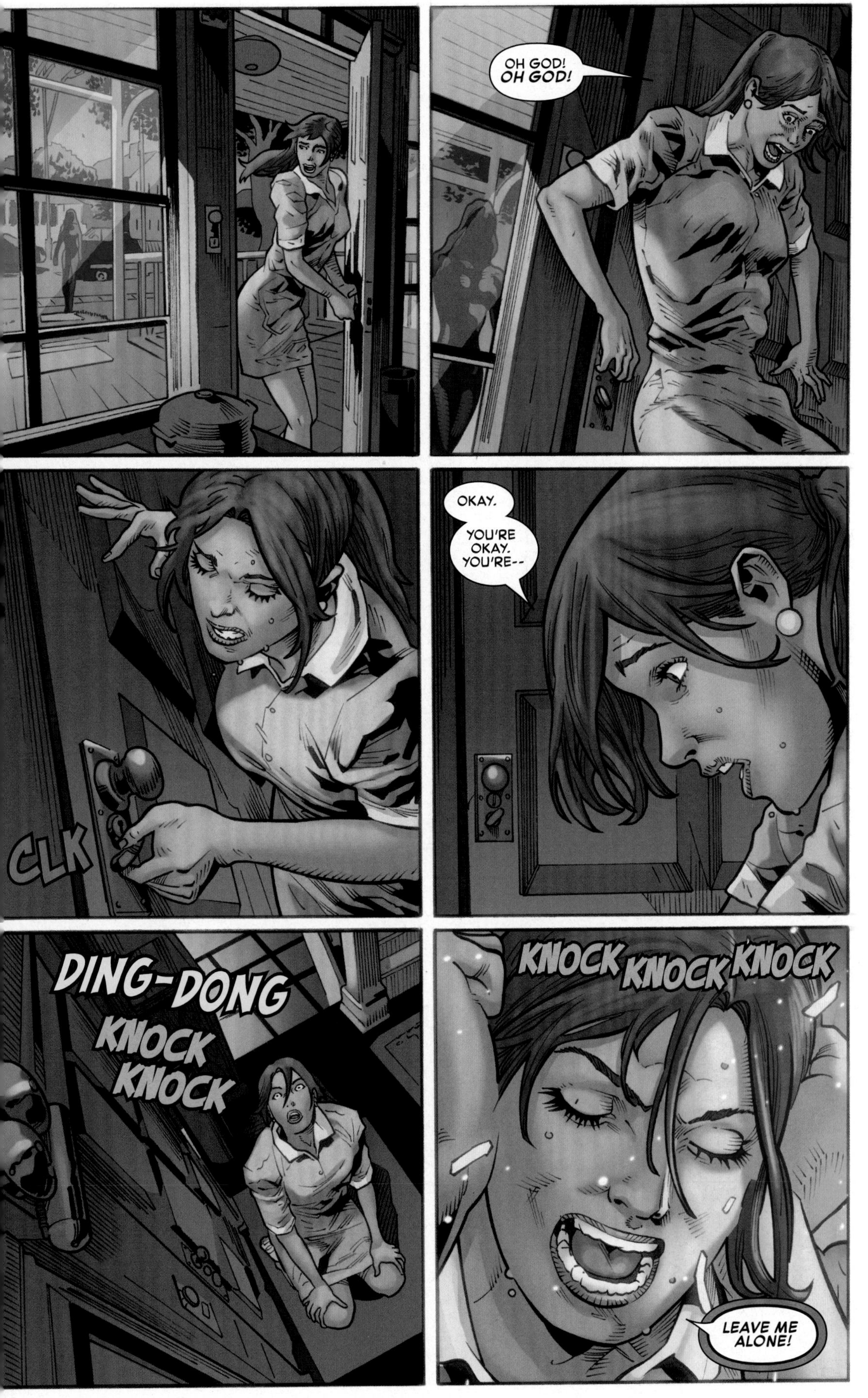
OH GOD! OH GOD!
OKAY.
YOU'RE OKAY. YOU'RE--
CLK
DING-DONG
KNOCK KNOCK
KNOCK KNOCK KNOCK
LEAVE ME ALONE!

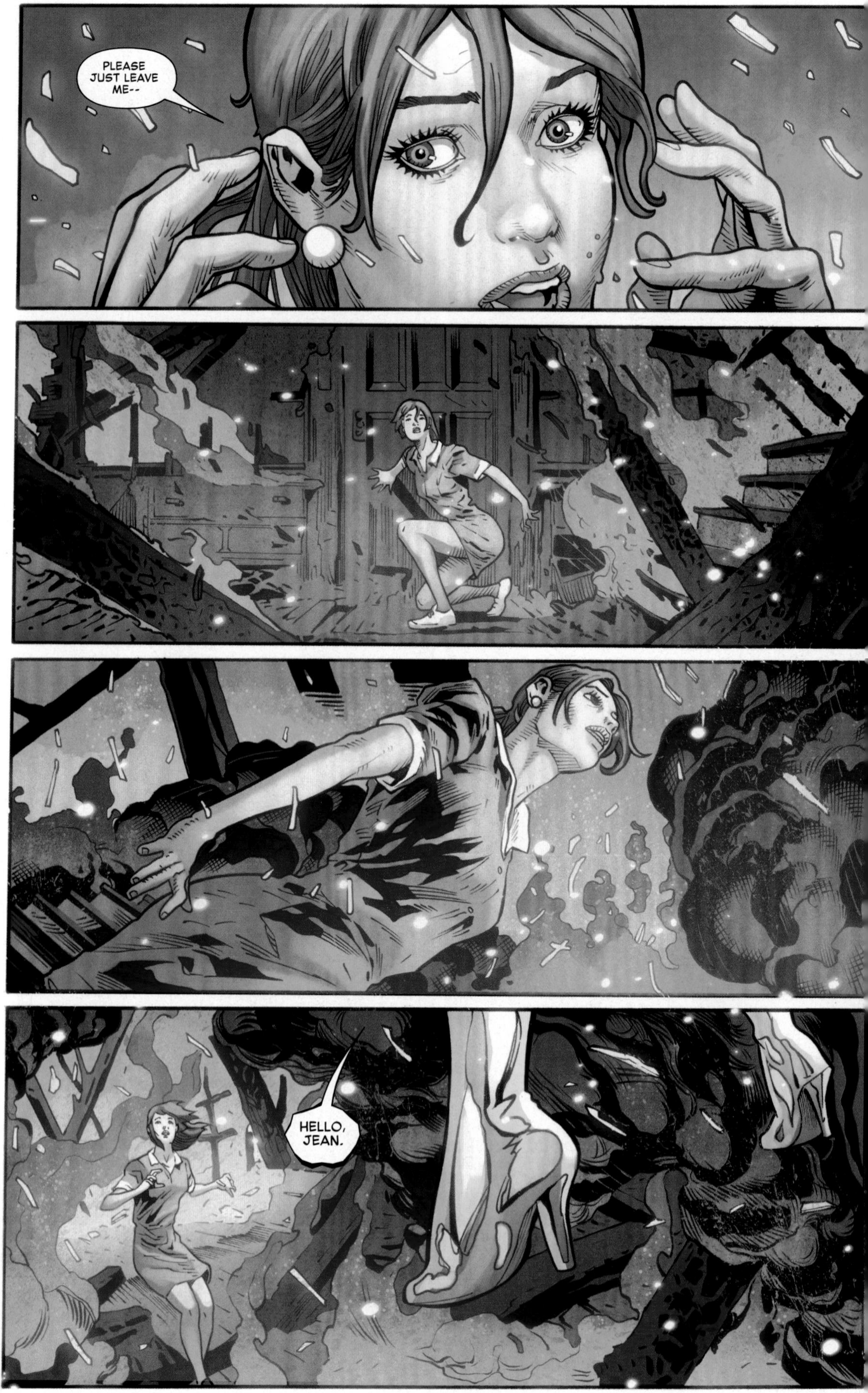
PLEASE JUST LEAVE ME--
HELLO, JEAN.

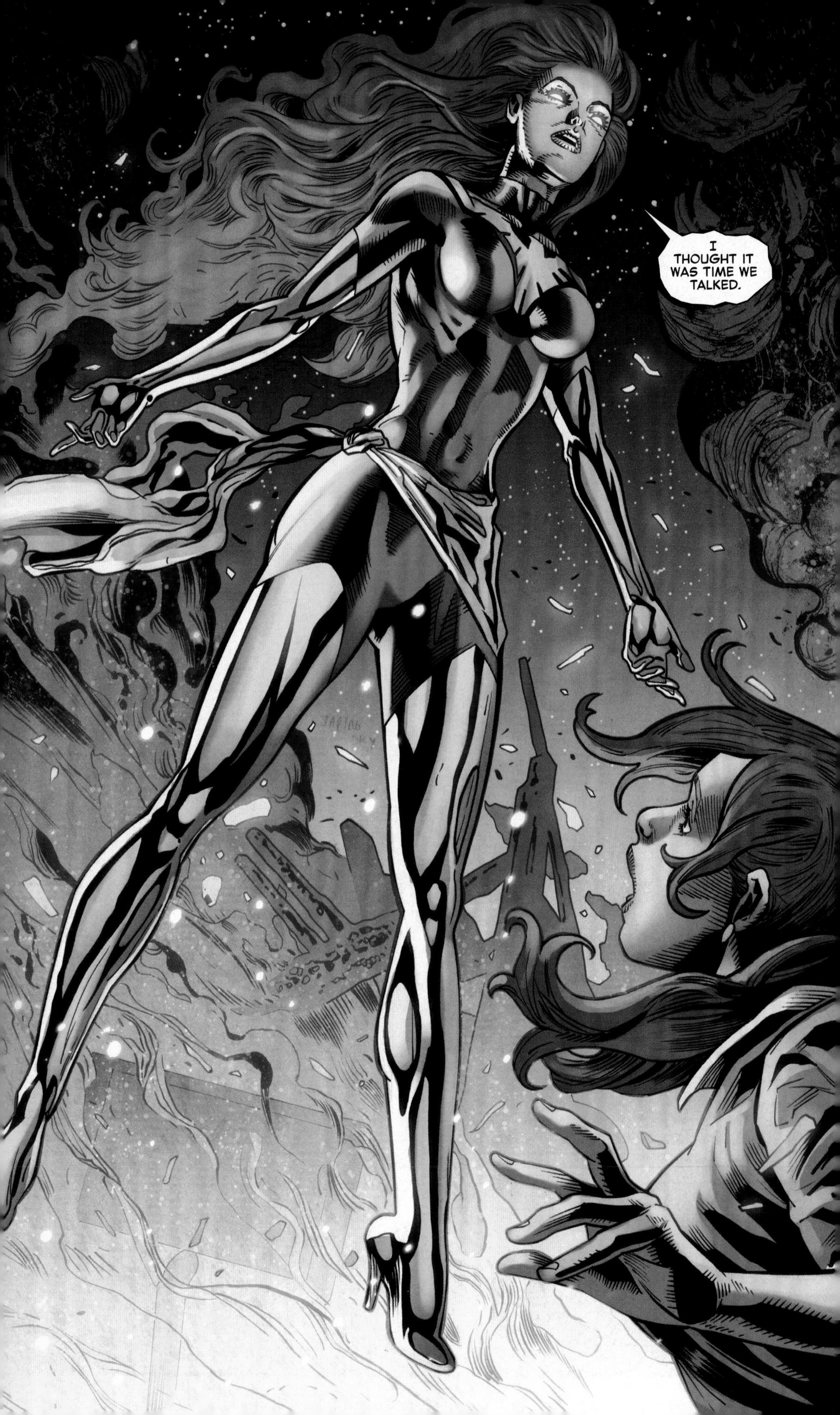
I THOUGHT IT WAS TIME WE TALKED.

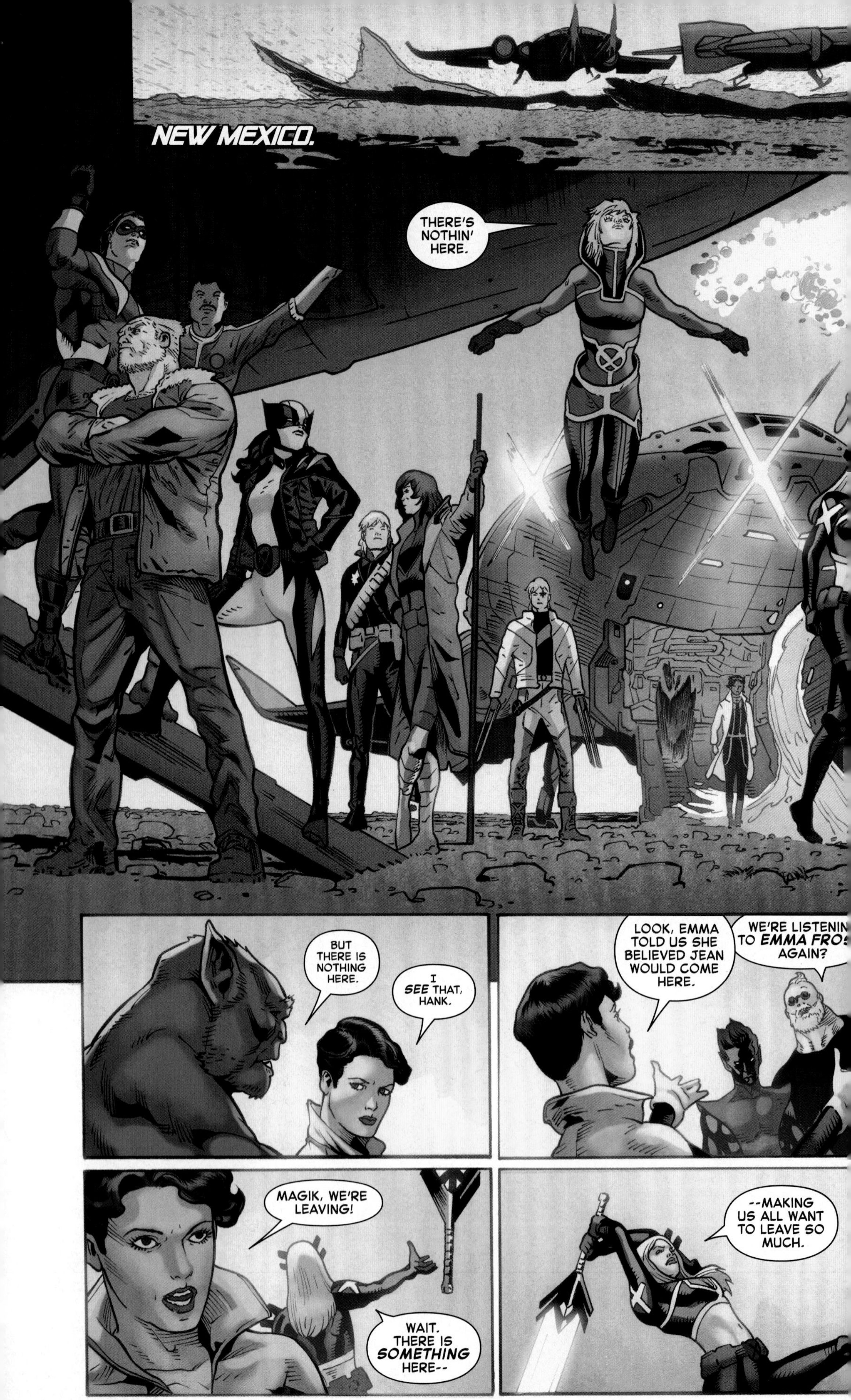
NEW MEXICO.
THERE'S NOTHIN' HERE.
BUT THERE IS NOTHING HERE.
I *SEE* THAT, HANK.
LOOK, EMMA TOLD US SHE BELIEVED JEAN WOULD COME HERE.
WE'RE LISTENIN TO *EMMA FRO* AGAIN?
MAGIK, WE'RE LEAVING!
WAIT. THERE IS *SOMETHING* HERE--
--MAKING US ALL WANT TO LEAVE SO MUCH.

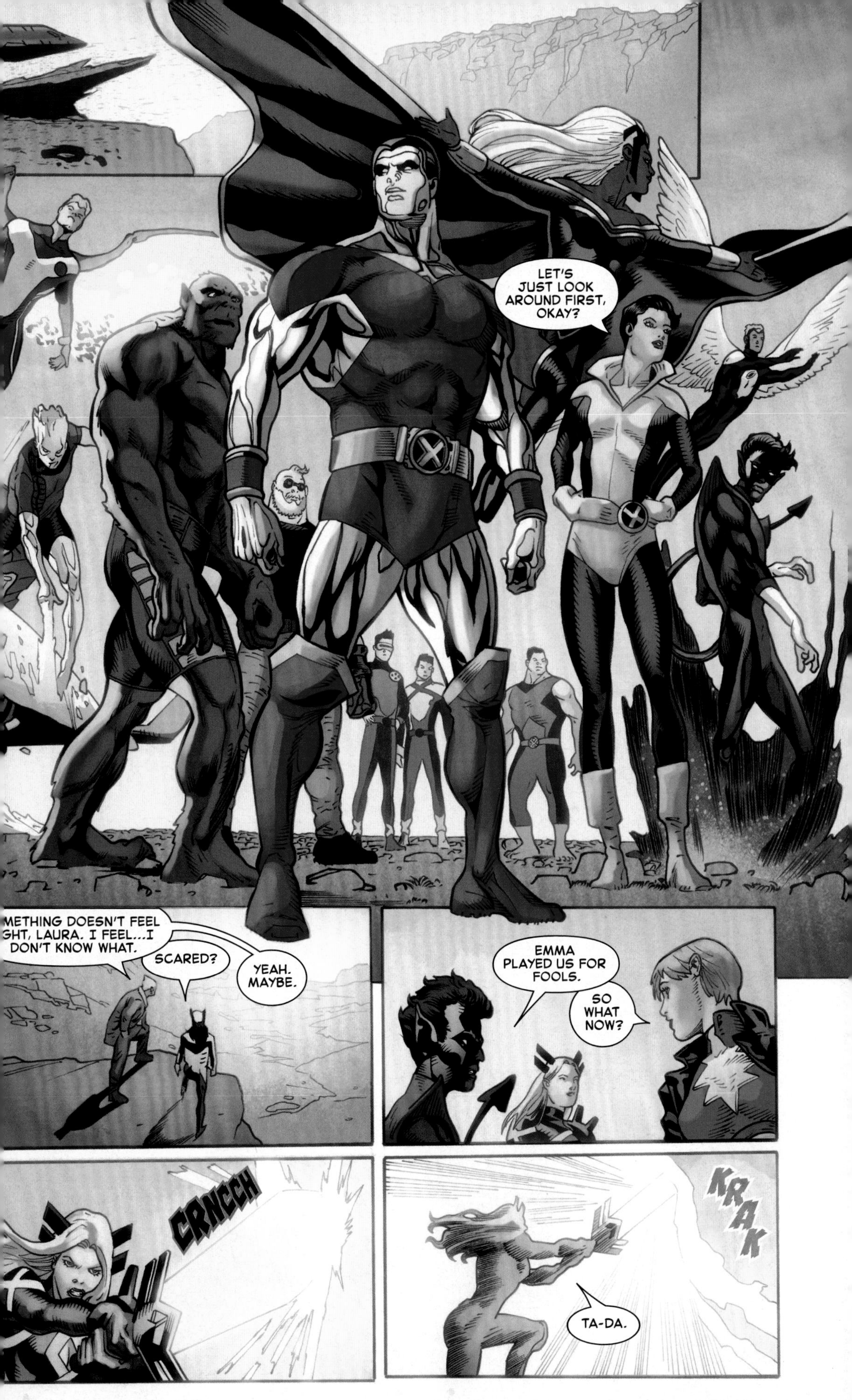

LET'S JUST LOOK AROUND FIRST, OKAY?
METHING DOESN'T FEEL GHT, LAURA. I FEEL...I DON'T KNOW WHAT.
SCARED?
YEAH. MAYBE.
EMMA PLAYED US FOR FOOLS.
SO WHAT NOW?
CRNCCH
KRAK
TA-DA.

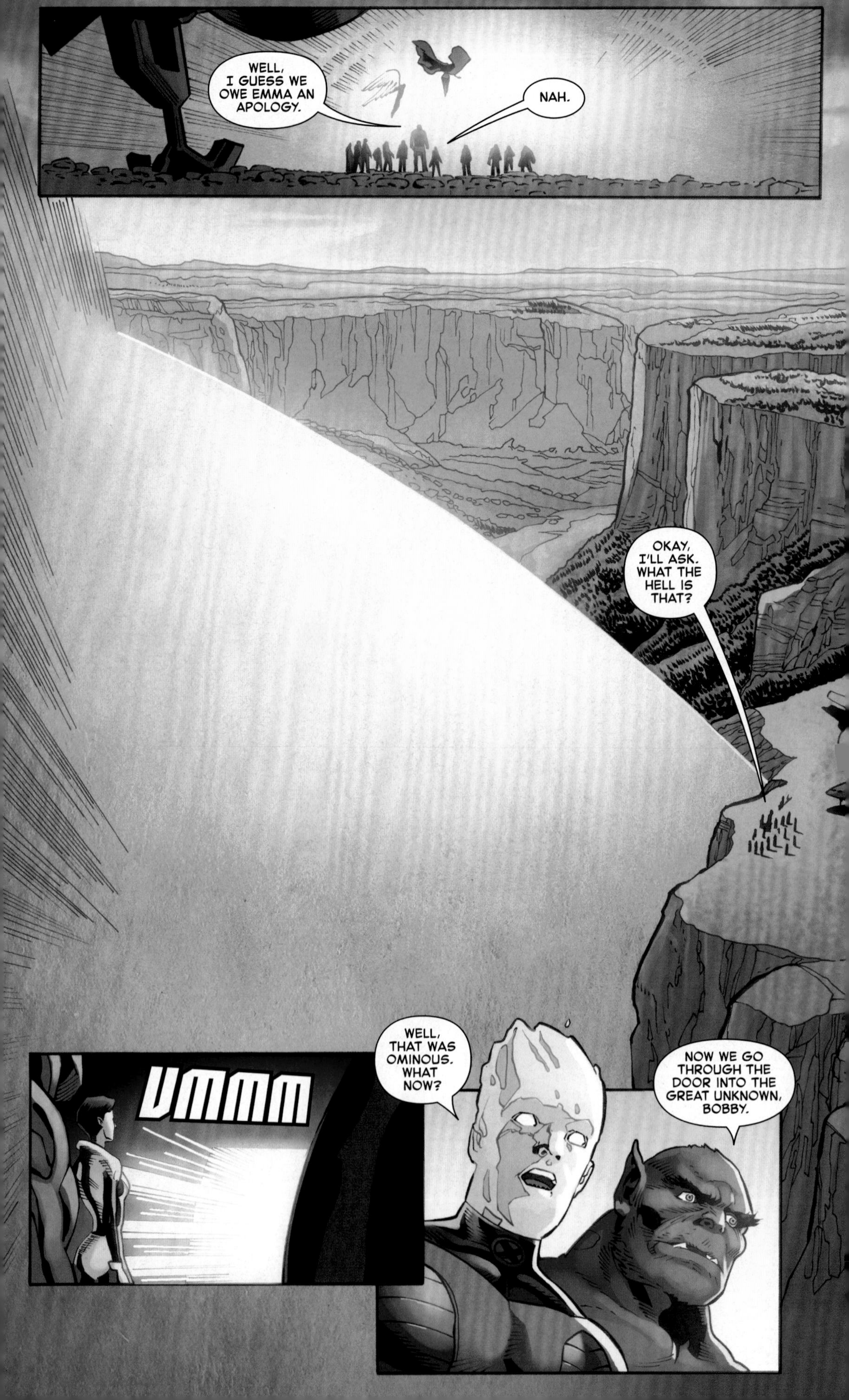
WELL, I GUESS WE OWE EMMA AN APOLOGY.
NAH.
OKAY, I'LL ASK. WHAT THE HELL IS THAT?
VMMM
WELL, THAT WAS OMINOUS. WHAT NOW?
NOW WE GO THROUGH THE DOOR INTO THE GREAT UNKNOWN, BOBBY.

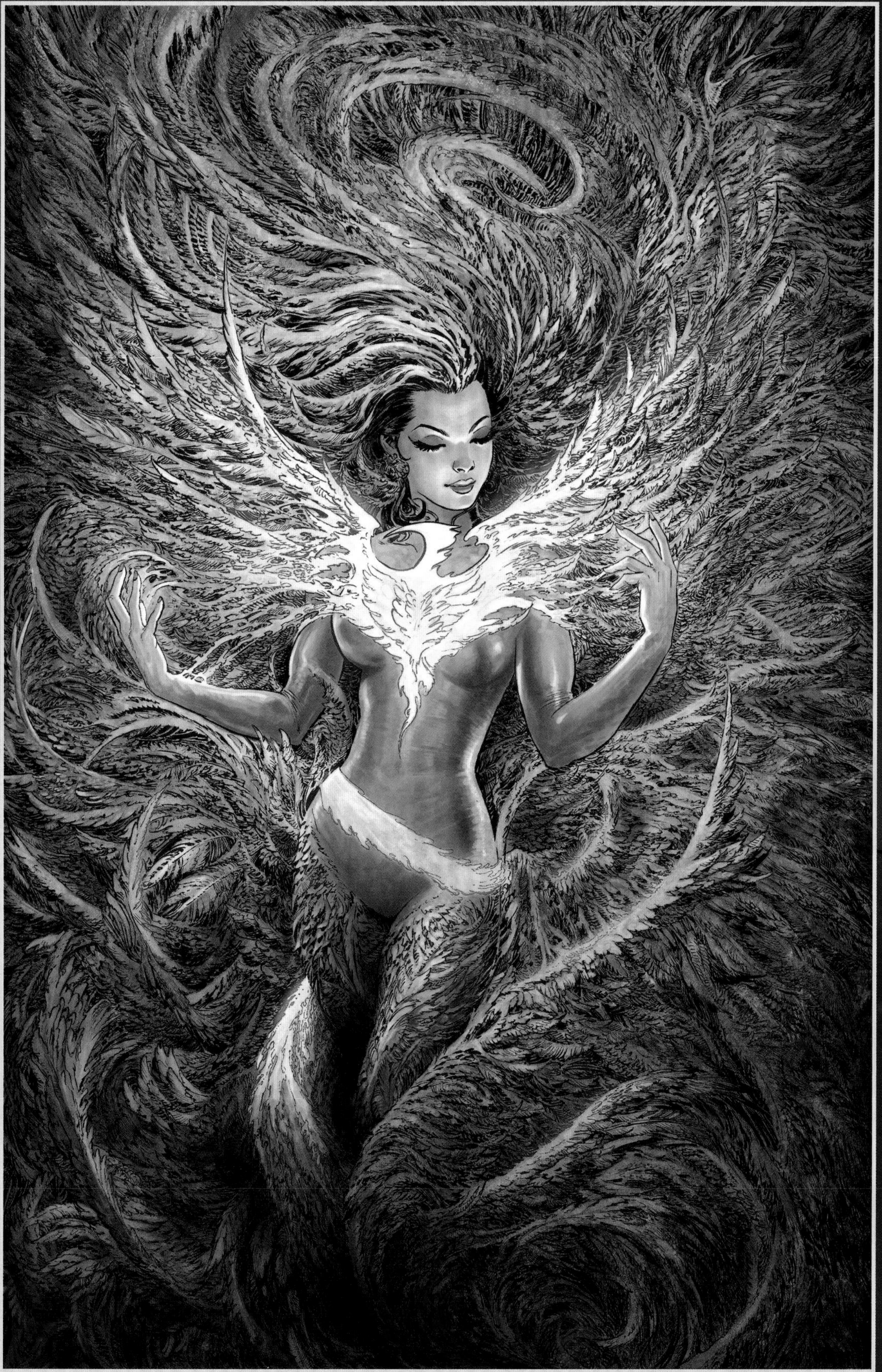

#4 VARIANT BY *MUKESH SINGH*

4

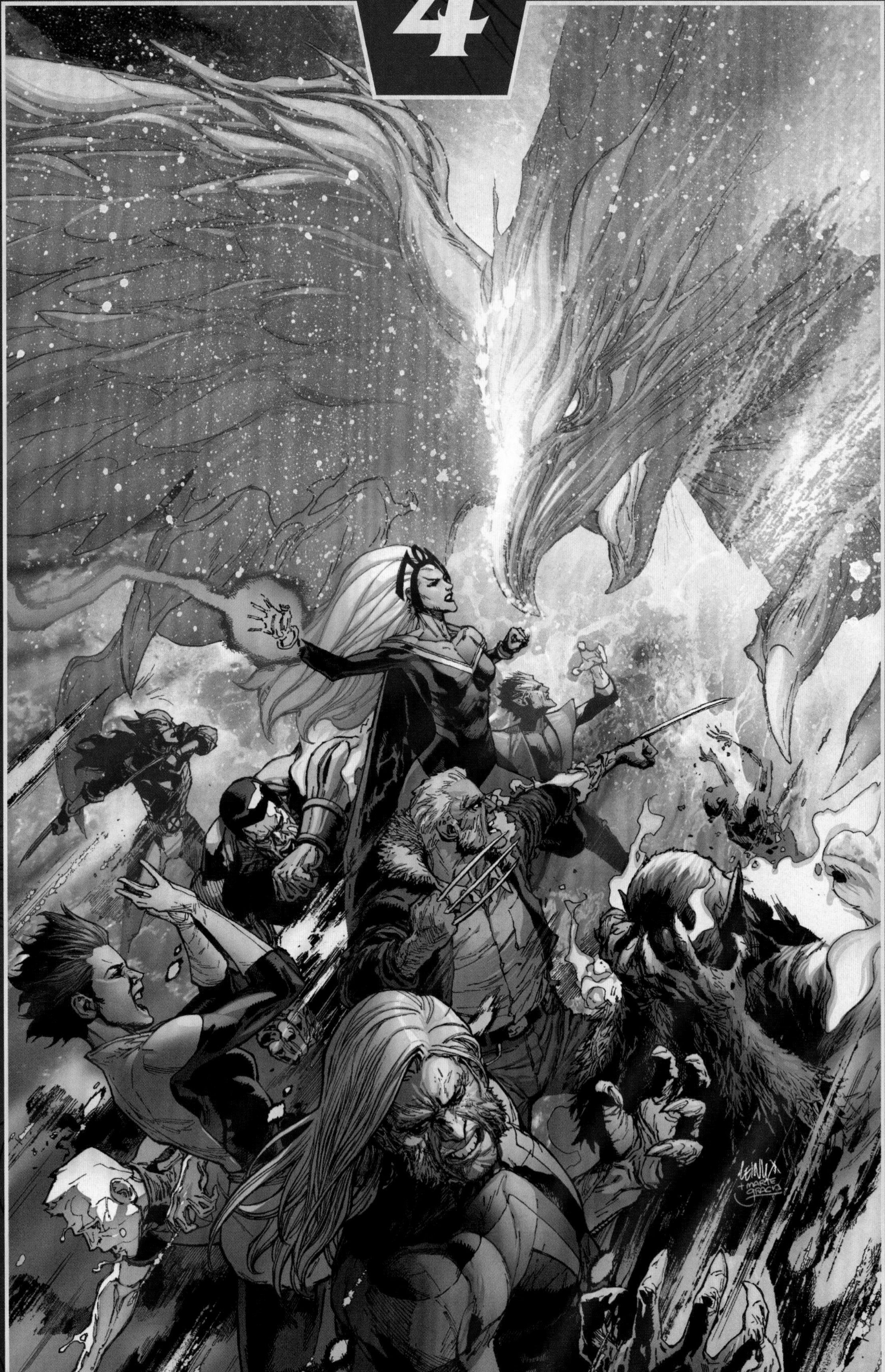

CHAPTER FOUR: *THAT A GREAT PRINCESS FALLS, BUT DOTH NOT DIE*

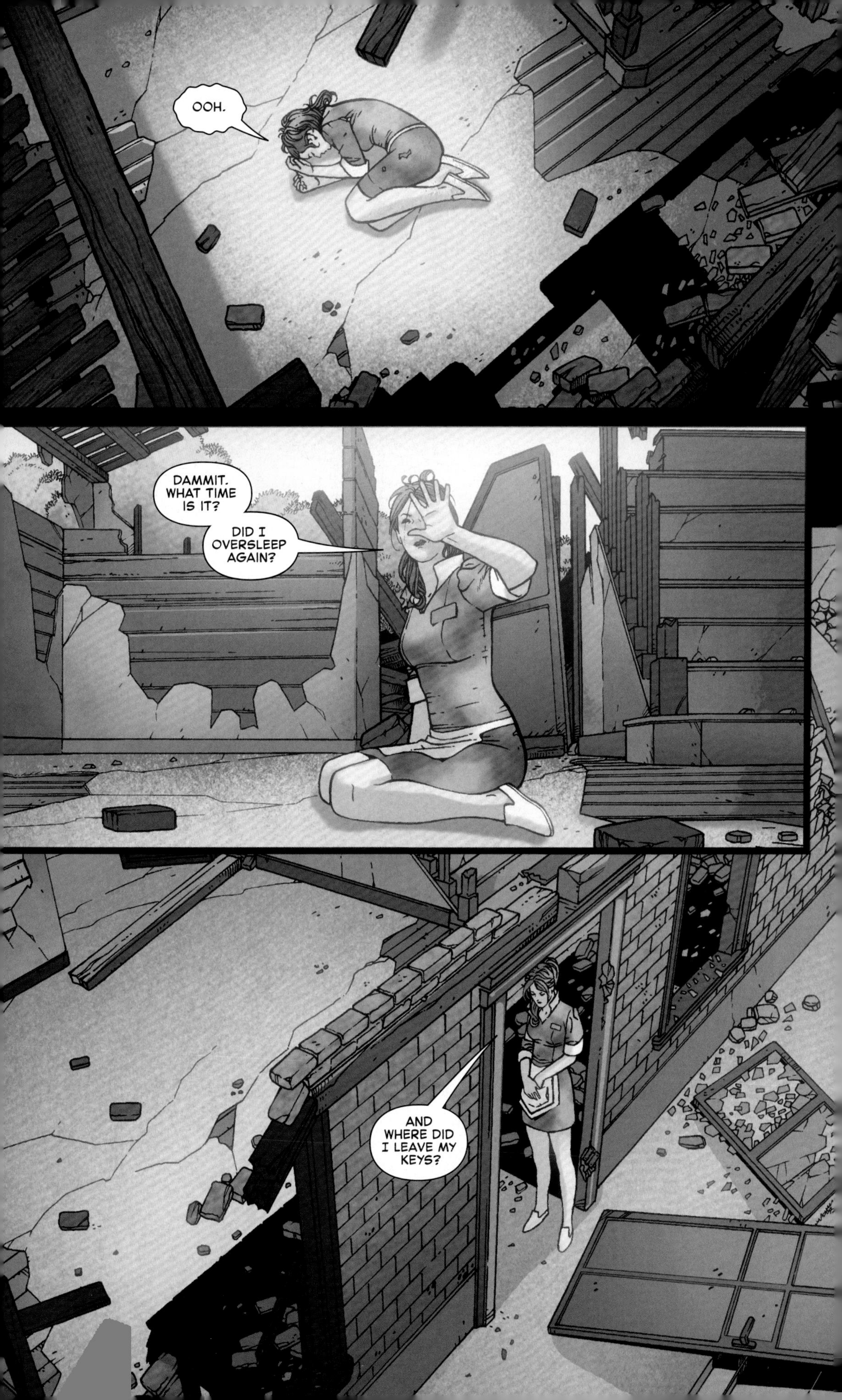
OOH.
DAMMIT. WHAT TIME IS IT?
DID I OVERSLEEP AGAIN?
AND WHERE DID I LEAVE MY KEYS?

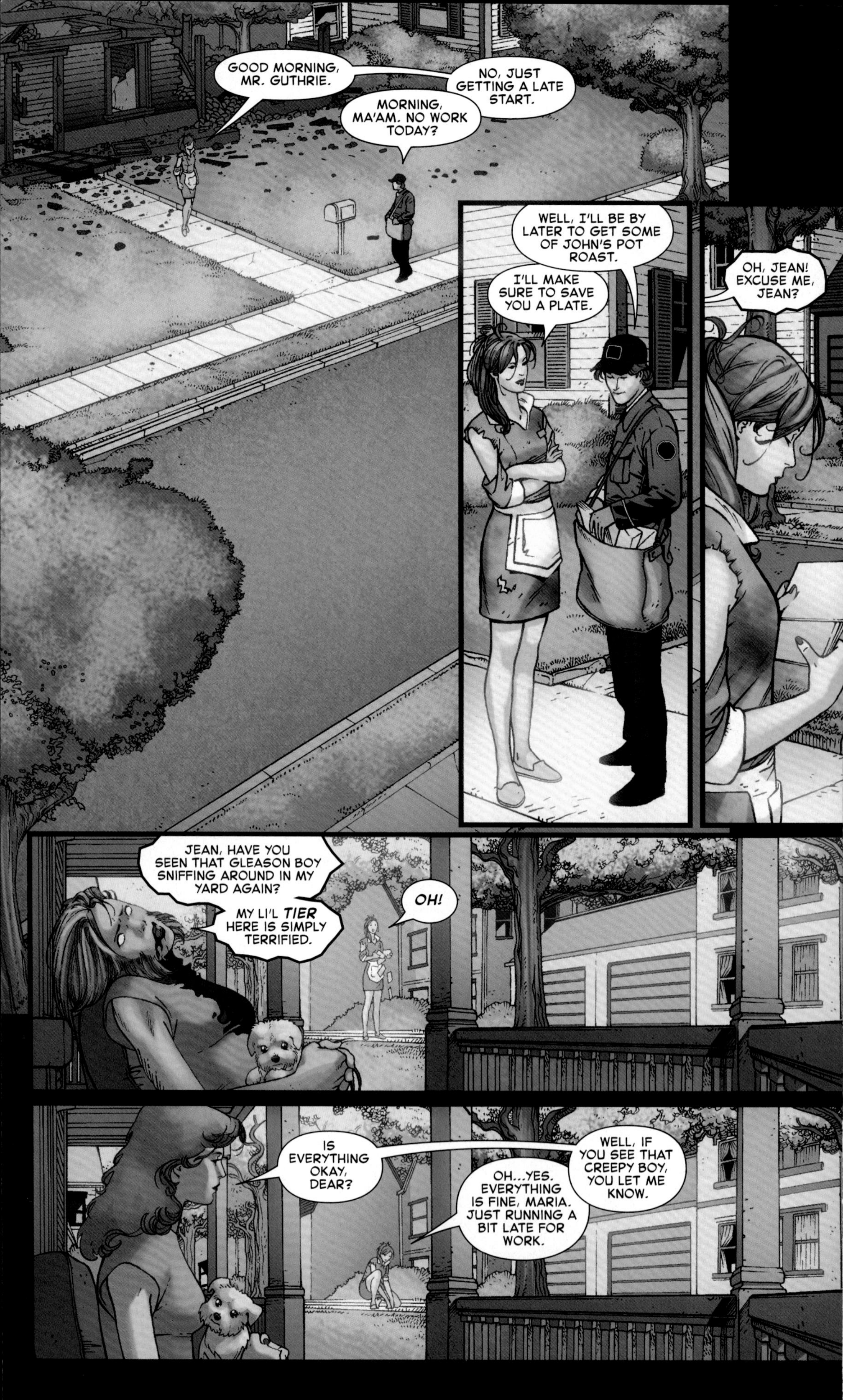

GOOD MORNING, MR. GUTHRIE.
MORNING, MA'AM. NO WORK TODAY?
NO, JUST GETTING A LATE START.
WELL, I'LL BE BY LATER TO GET SOME OF JOHN'S POT ROAST.
I'LL MAKE SURE TO SAVE YOU A PLATE.
OH, JEAN! EXCUSE ME, JEAN?
JEAN, HAVE YOU SEEN THAT GLEASON BOY SNIFFING AROUND IN MY YARD AGAIN?
MY LI'L TIER HERE IS SIMPLY TERRIFIED.
OH!
IS EVERYTHING OKAY, DEAR?
OH...YES. EVERYTHING IS FINE, MARIA. JUST RUNNING A BIT LATE FOR WORK.
WELL, IF YOU SEE THAT CREEPY BOY, YOU LET ME KNOW.

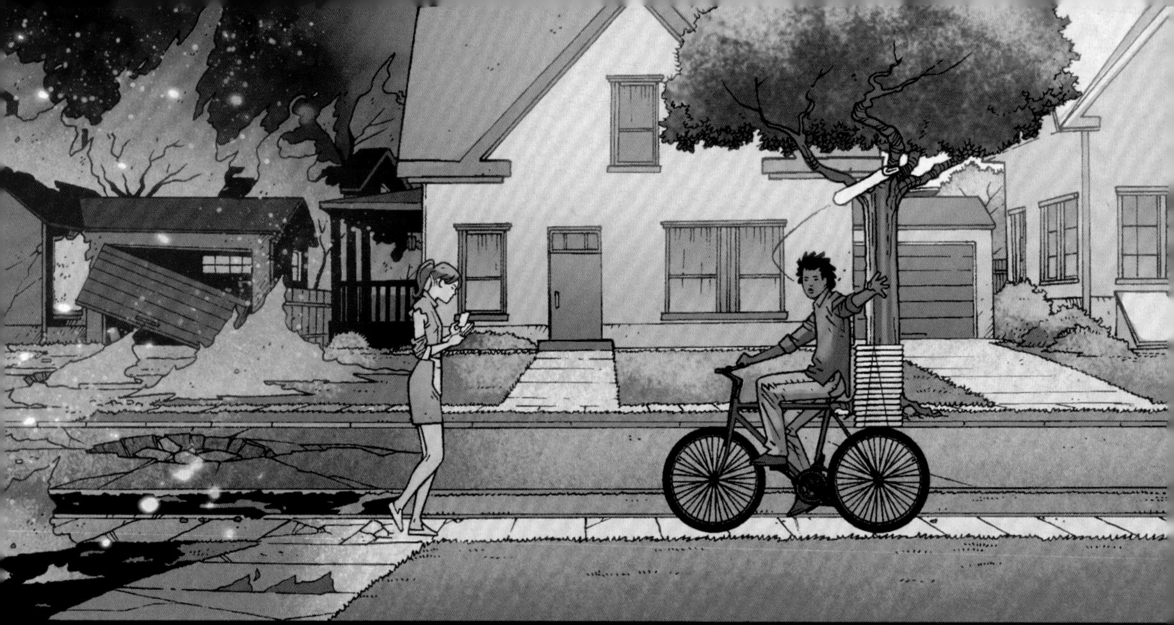

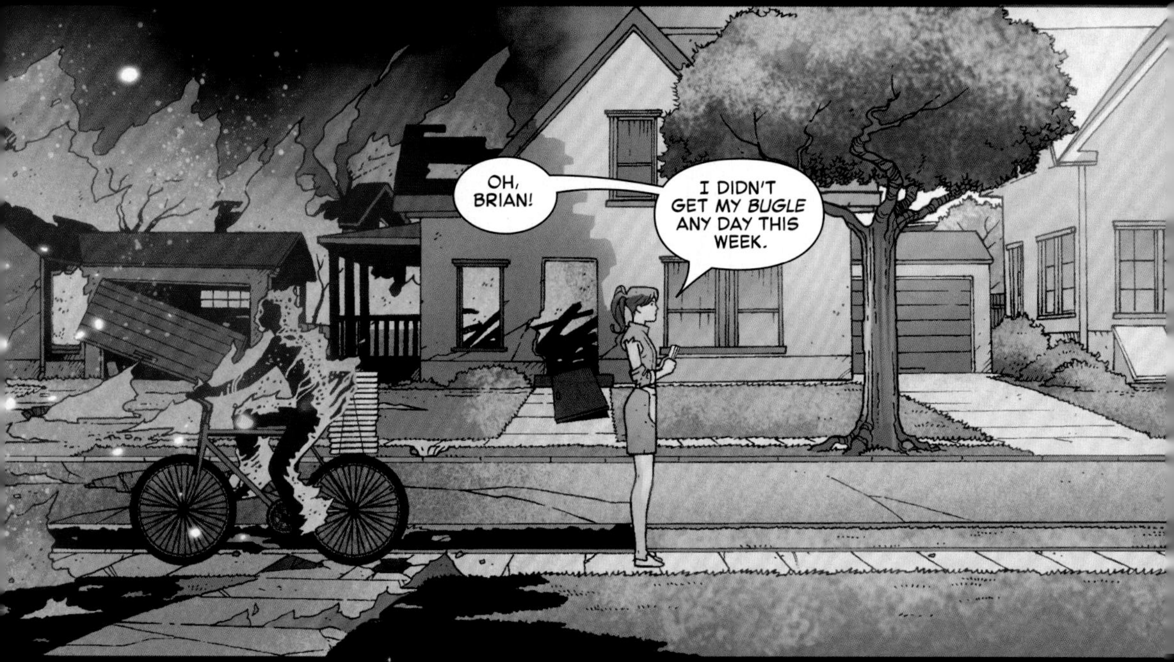
OH, BRIAN!
I DIDN'T GET MY *BUGLE* ANY DAY THIS WEEK.

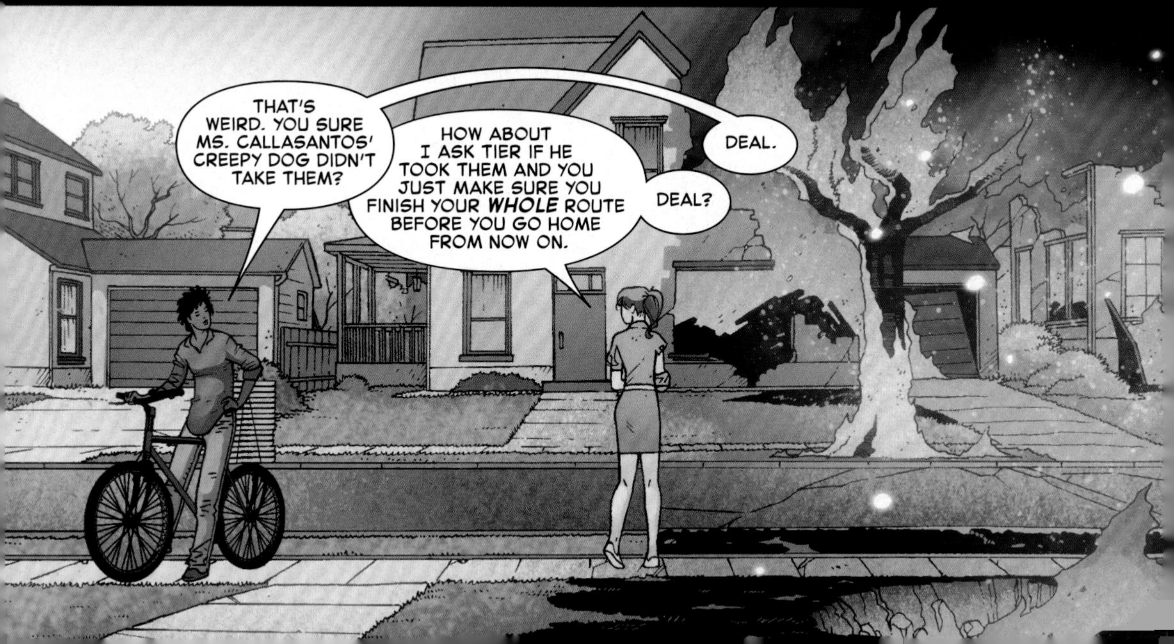
THAT'S WEIRD. YOU SURE MS. CALLASANTOS' CREEPY DOG DIDN'T TAKE THEM?
HOW ABOUT I ASK TIER IF HE TOOK THEM AND YOU JUST MAKE SURE YOU FINISH YOUR **WHOLE** ROUTE BEFORE YOU GO HOME FROM NOW ON.
DEAL?
DEAL.

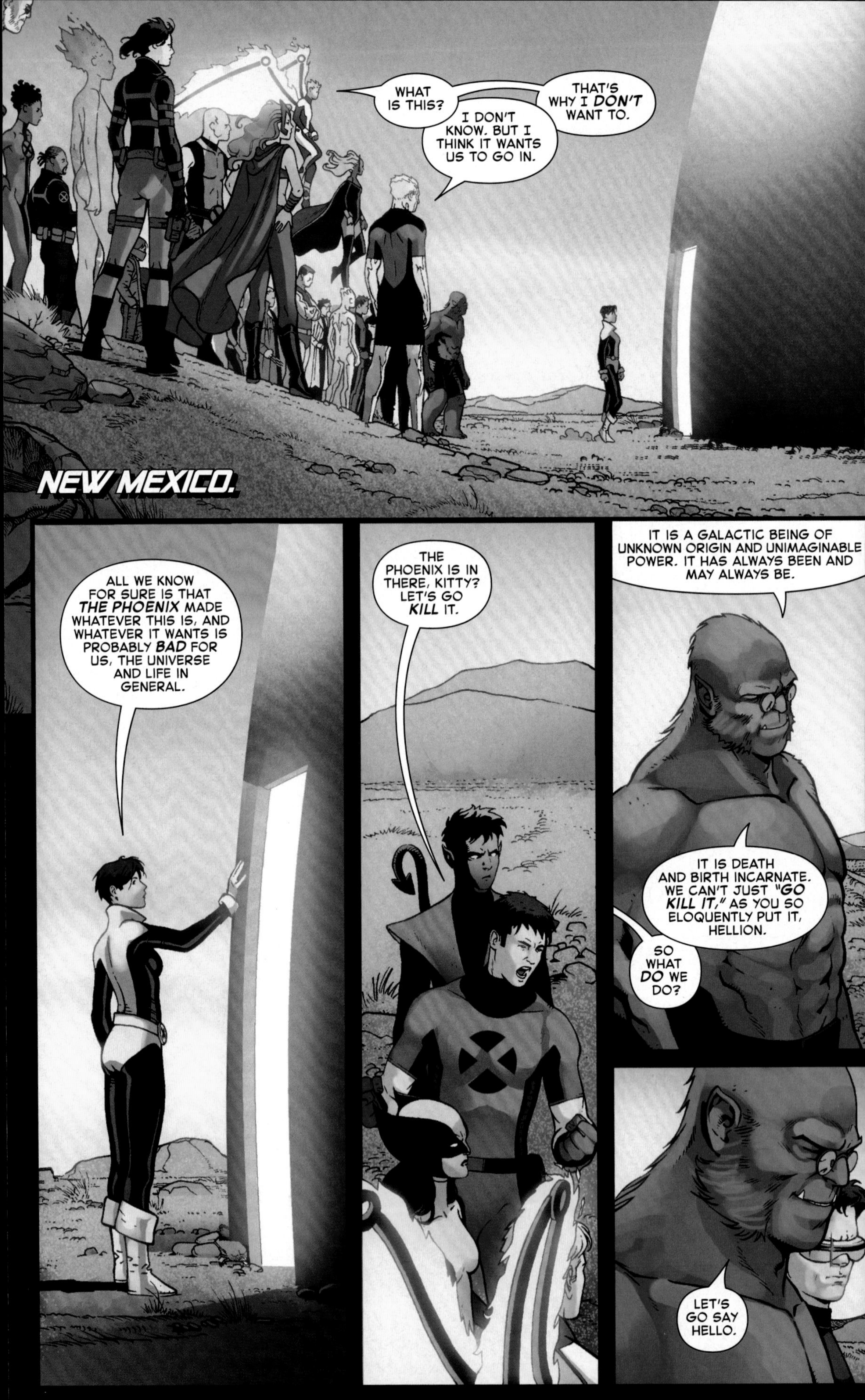
WHAT IS THIS?
I DON'T KNOW. BUT I THINK IT WANTS US TO GO IN.
THAT'S WHY I DON'T WANT TO.
NEW MEXICO.
ALL WE KNOW FOR SURE IS THAT THE PHOENIX MADE WHATEVER THIS IS, AND WHATEVER IT WANTS IS PROBABLY BAD FOR US, THE UNIVERSE AND LIFE IN GENERAL.
THE PHOENIX IS IN THERE, KITTY? LET'S GO KILL IT.
IT IS A GALACTIC BEING OF UNKNOWN ORIGIN AND UNIMAGINABLE POWER. IT HAS ALWAYS BEEN AND MAY ALWAYS BE.
IT IS DEATH AND BIRTH INCARNATE. WE CAN'T JUST "GO KILL IT," AS YOU SO ELOQUENTLY PUT IT, HELLION.
SO WHAT DO WE DO?
LET'S GO SAY HELLO.

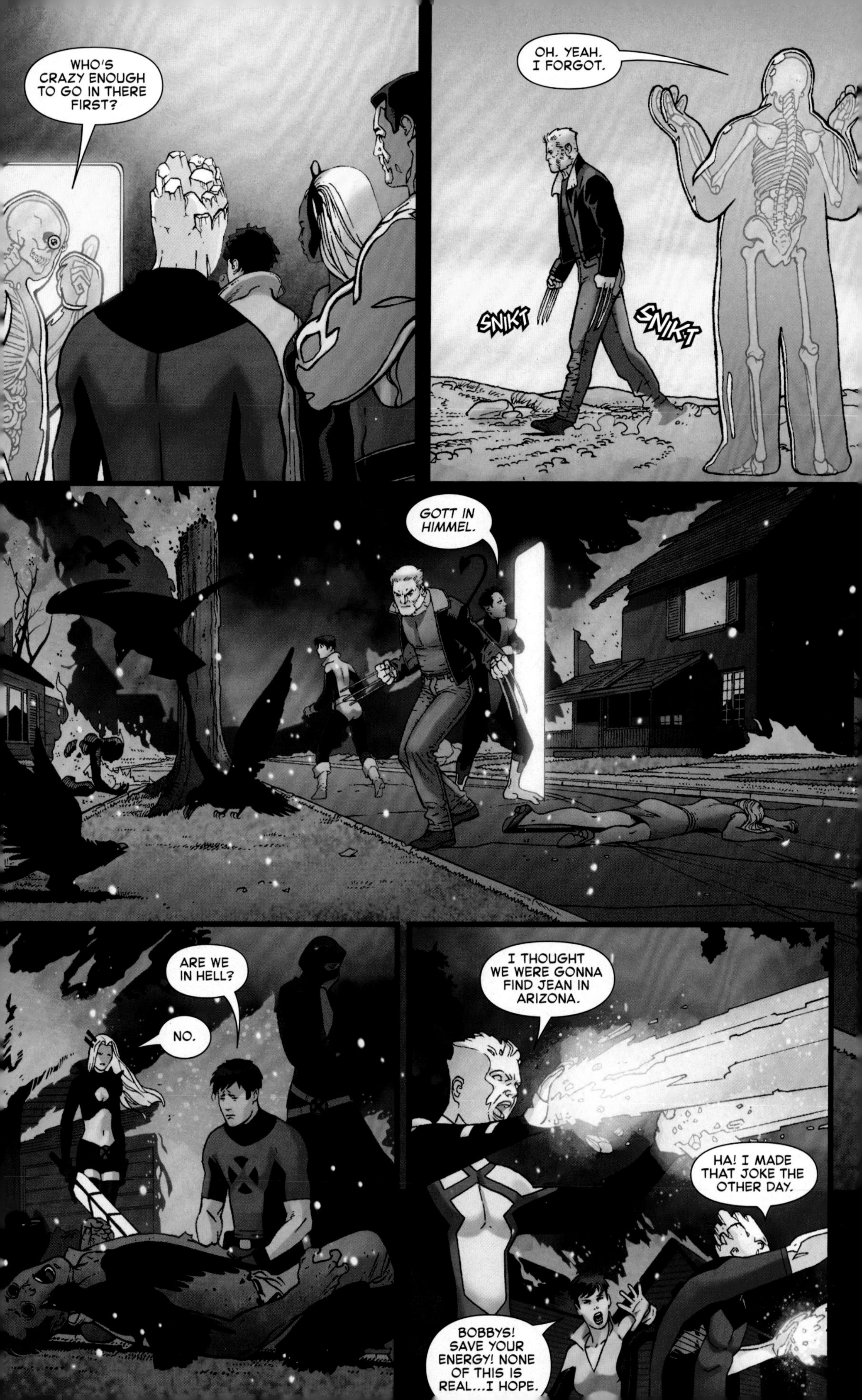
WHO'S CRAZY ENOUGH TO GO IN THERE FIRST?
OH. YEAH. I FORGOT.
SNIKT
SNIKT
GOTT IN HIMMEL.
ARE WE IN HELL?
NO.
I THOUGHT WE WERE GONNA FIND JEAN IN ARIZONA.
HA! I MADE THAT JOKE THE OTHER DAY.
BOBBYS! SAVE YOUR ENERGY! NONE OF THIS IS REAL...I HOPE.

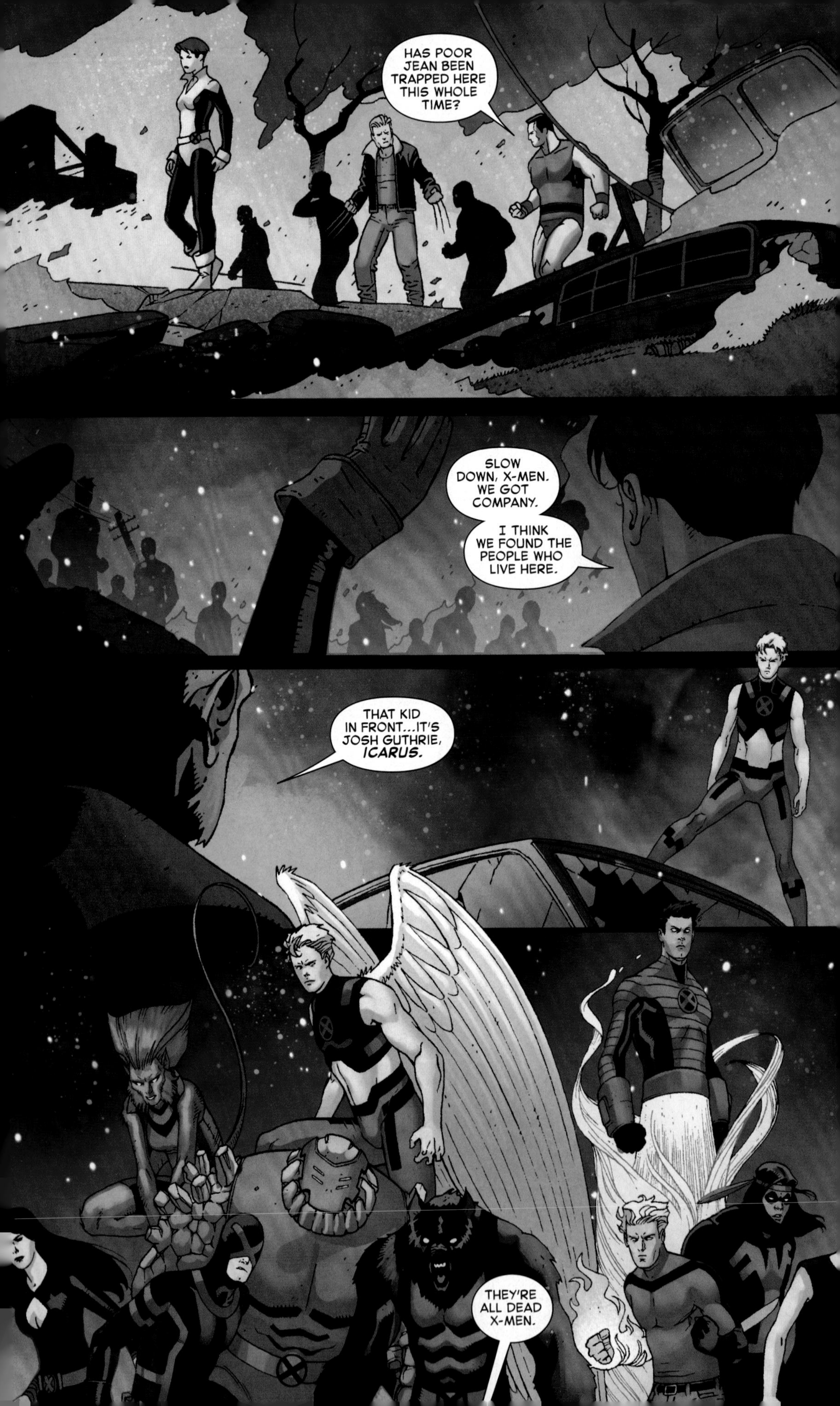
HAS POOR JEAN BEEN TRAPPED HERE THIS WHOLE TIME?
SLOW DOWN, X-MEN. WE GOT COMPANY.
I THINK WE FOUND THE PEOPLE WHO LIVE HERE.
THAT KID IN FRONT...IT'S JOSH GUTHRIE, ICARUS.
THEY'RE ALL DEAD X-MEN.

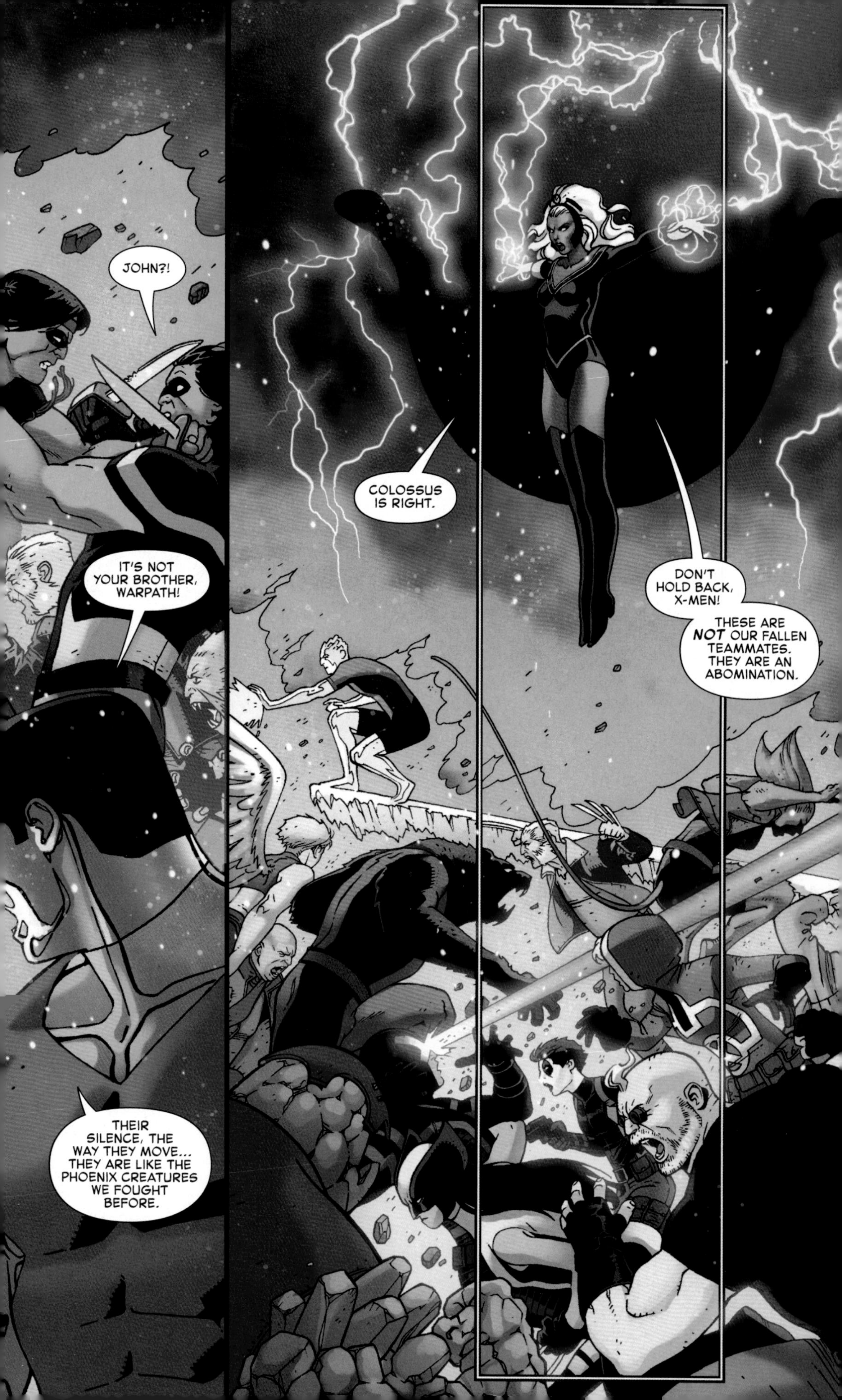
JOHN?!
IT'S NOT YOUR BROTHER, WARPATH!
THEIR SILENCE, THE WAY THEY MOVE... THEY ARE LIKE THE PHOENIX CREATURES WE FOUGHT BEFORE.
COLOSSUS IS RIGHT.
DON'T HOLD BACK, X-MEN!
THESE ARE NOT OUR FALLEN TEAMMATES. THEY ARE AN ABOMINATION.

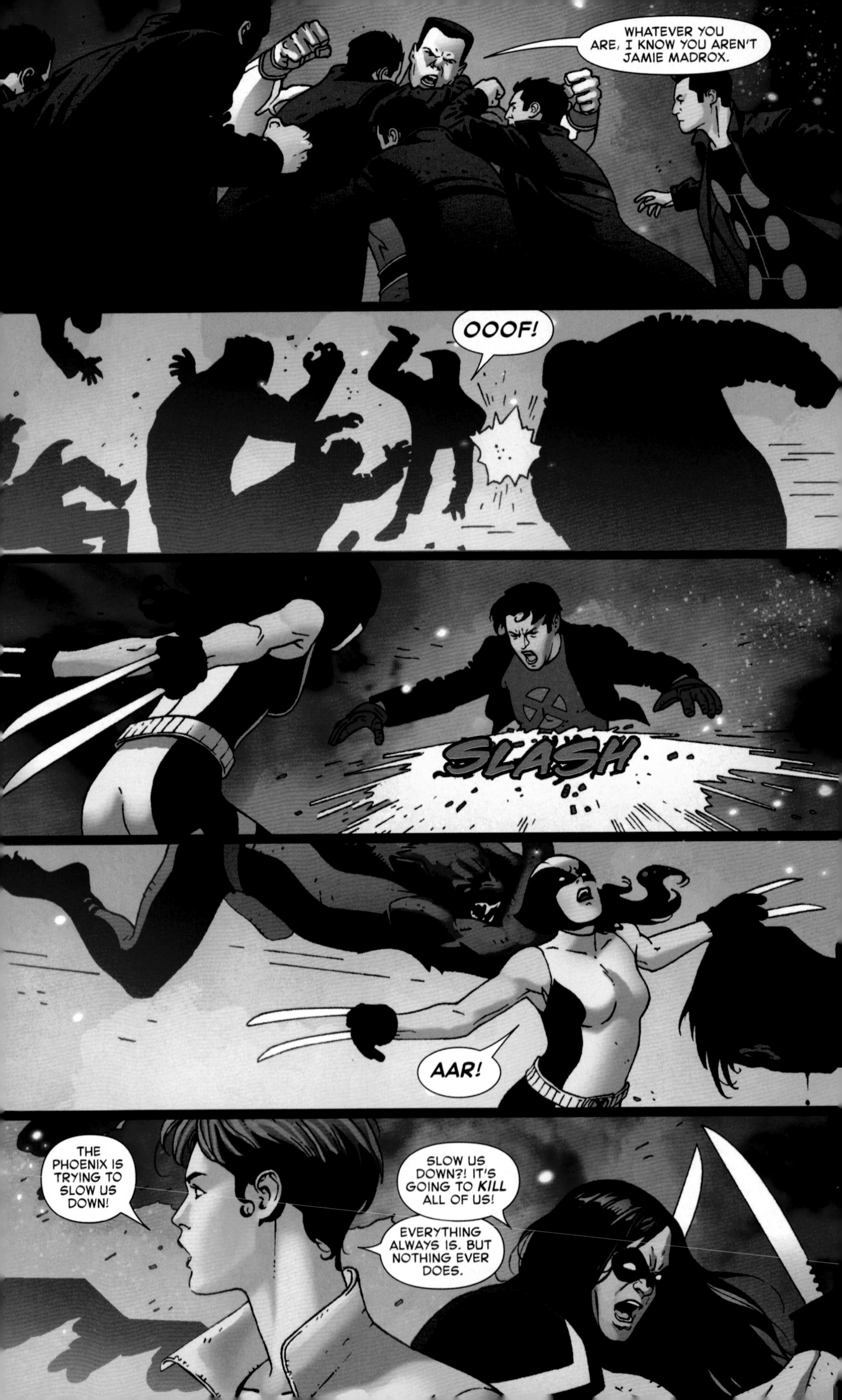
WHATEVER YOU ARE, I KNOW YOU AREN'T JAMIE MADROX.
OOOF!
SLASH
AAR!
THE PHOENIX IS TRYING TO SLOW US DOWN!
SLOW US DOWN?! IT'S GOING TO KILL ALL OF US!
EVERYTHING ALWAYS IS. BUT NOTHING EVER DOES.

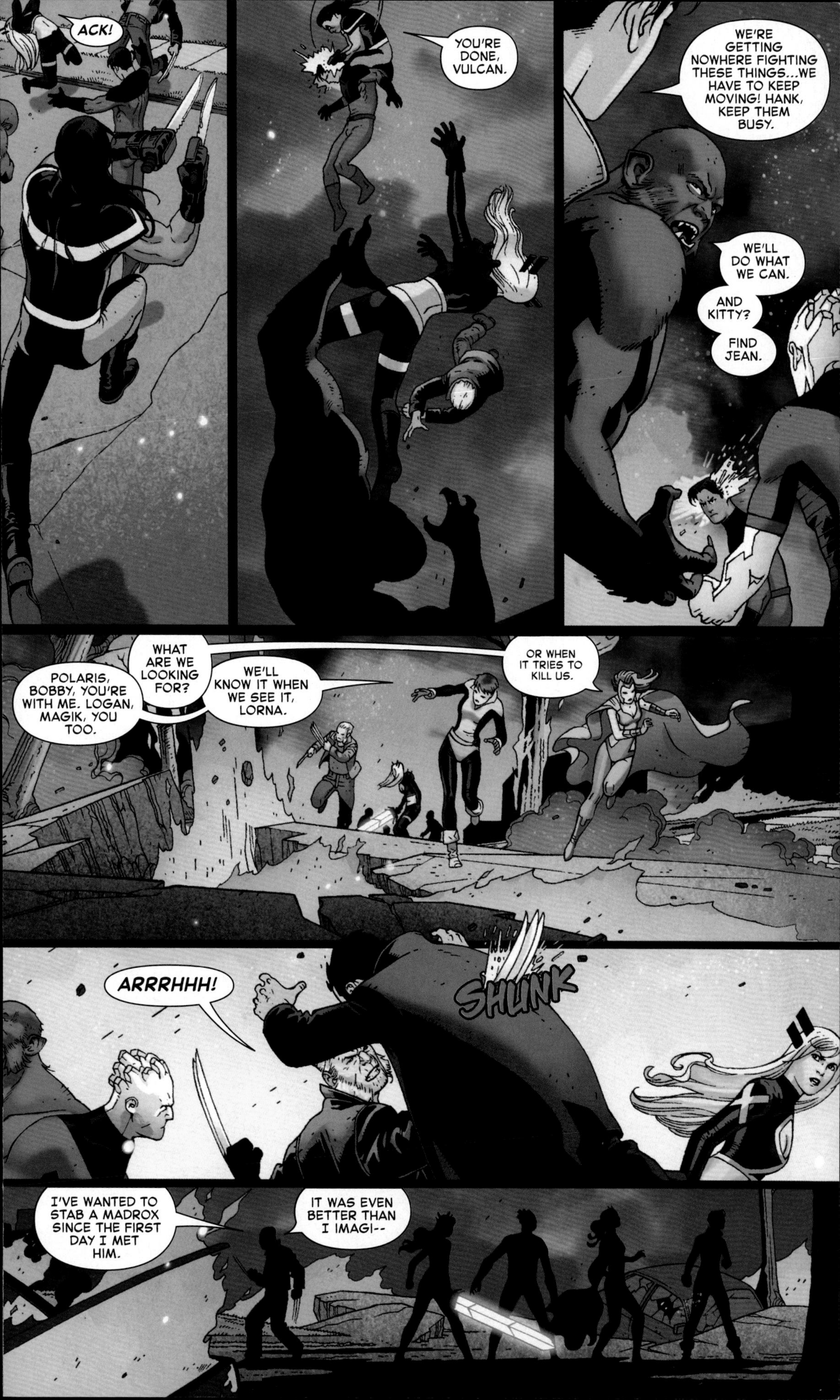

ACK!
YOU'RE DONE, VULCAN.
WE'RE GETTING NOWHERE FIGHTING THESE THINGS...WE HAVE TO KEEP MOVING! HANK, KEEP THEM BUSY.
WE'LL DO WHAT WE CAN.
AND KITTY?
FIND JEAN.
POLARIS, BOBBY, YOU'RE WITH ME. LOGAN, MAGIK, YOU TOO.
WHAT ARE WE LOOKING FOR?
WE'LL KNOW IT WHEN WE SEE IT, LORNA.
OR WHEN IT TRIES TO KILL US.
ARRRHHH!
SHUNK
I'VE WANTED TO STAB A MADROX SINCE THE FIRST DAY I MET HIM.
IT WAS EVEN BETTER THAN I IMAGI--

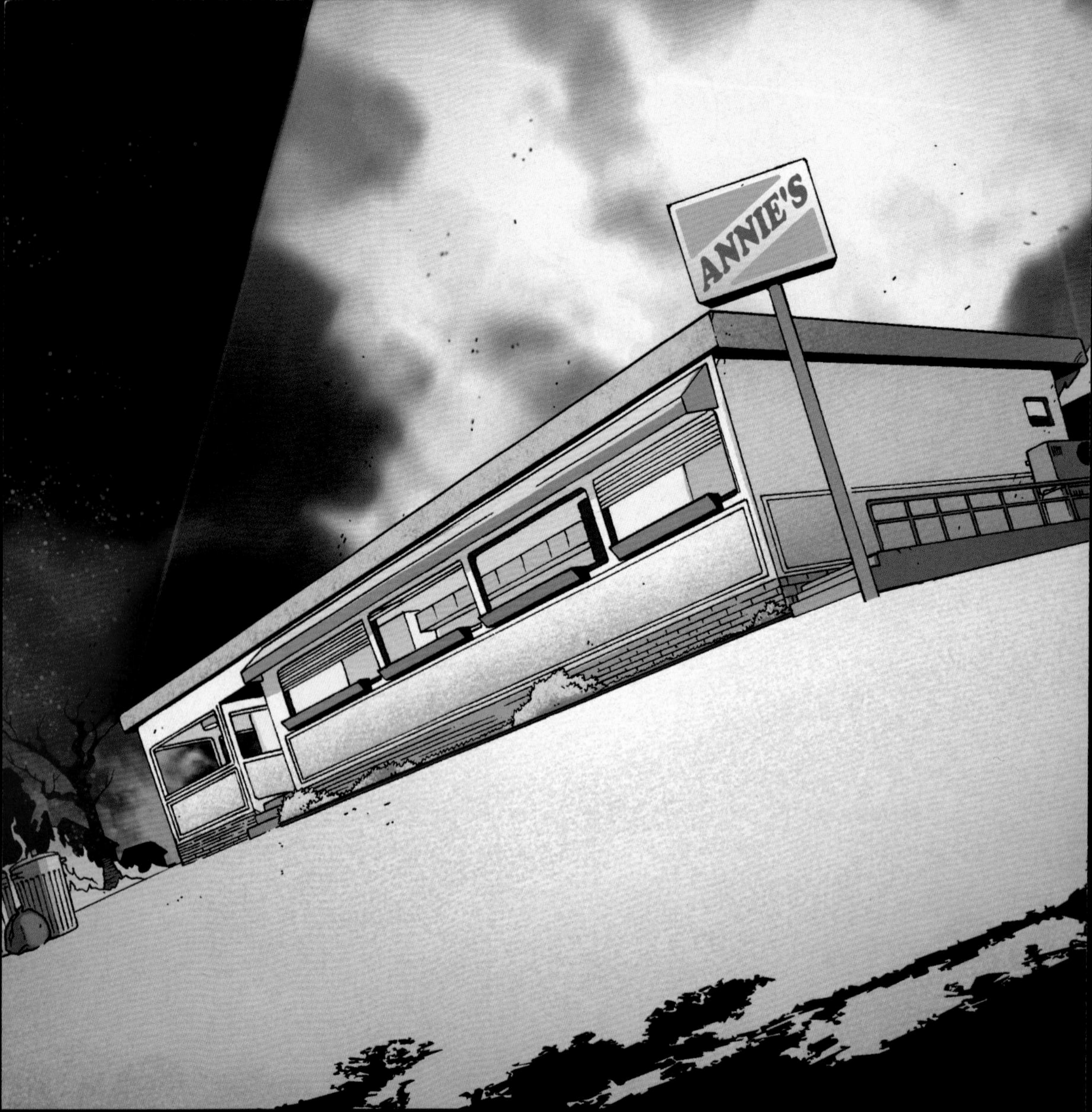
ANNIE'S

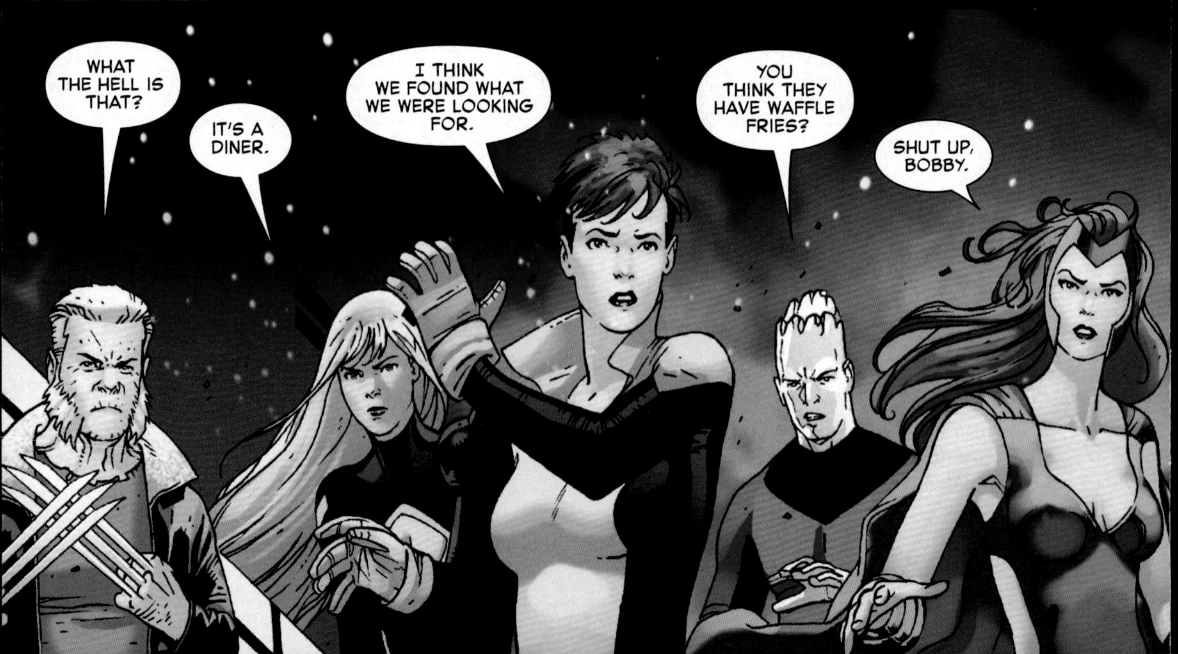
WHAT THE HELL IS THAT?
IT'S A DINER.
I THINK WE FOUND WHAT WE WERE LOOKING FOR.
YOU THINK THEY HAVE WAFFLE FRIES?
SHUT UP, BOBBY.

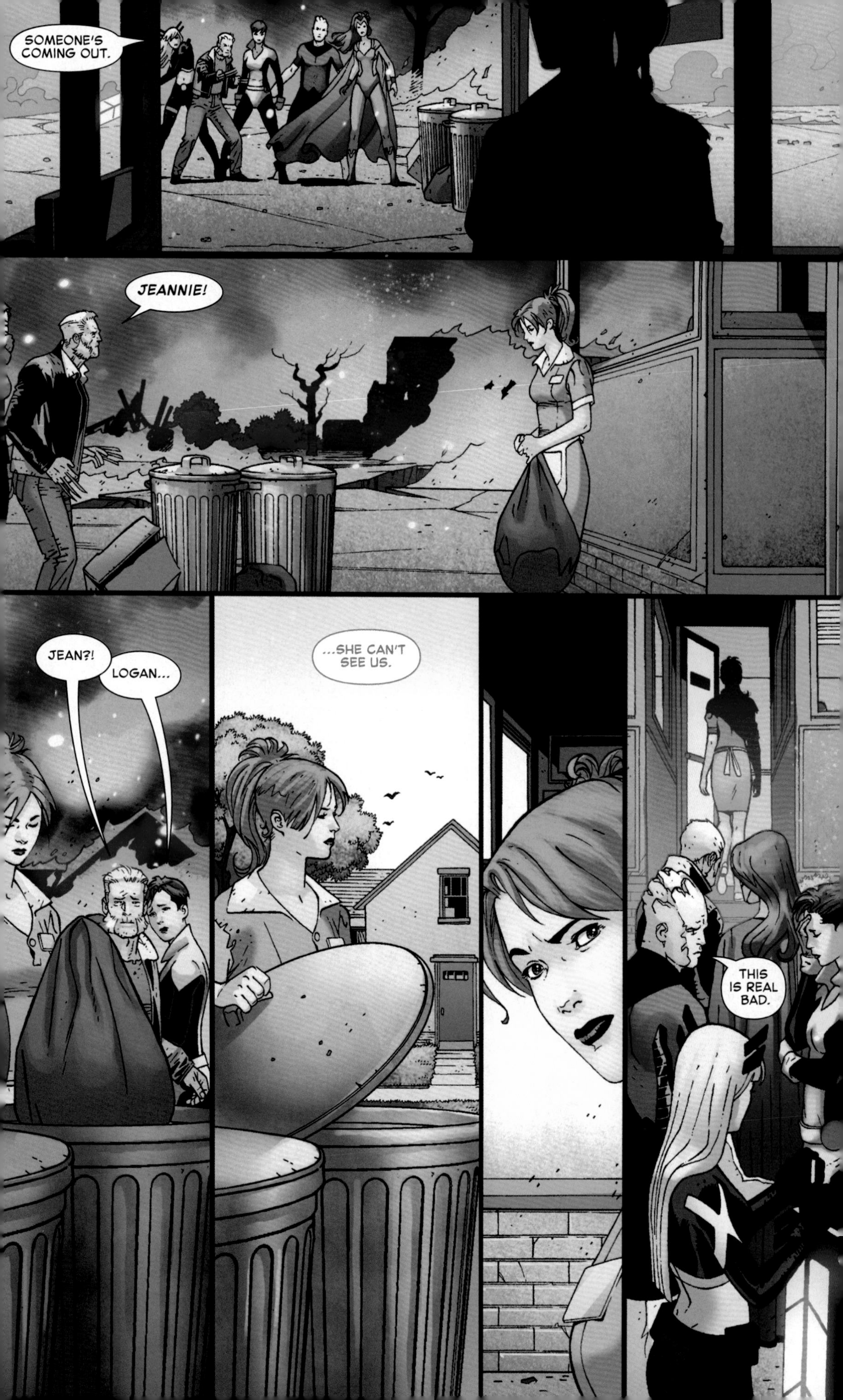
SOMEONE'S COMING OUT.
JEANNIE!
JEAN?!
LOGAN...
...SHE CAN'T SEE US.
THIS IS REAL BAD.

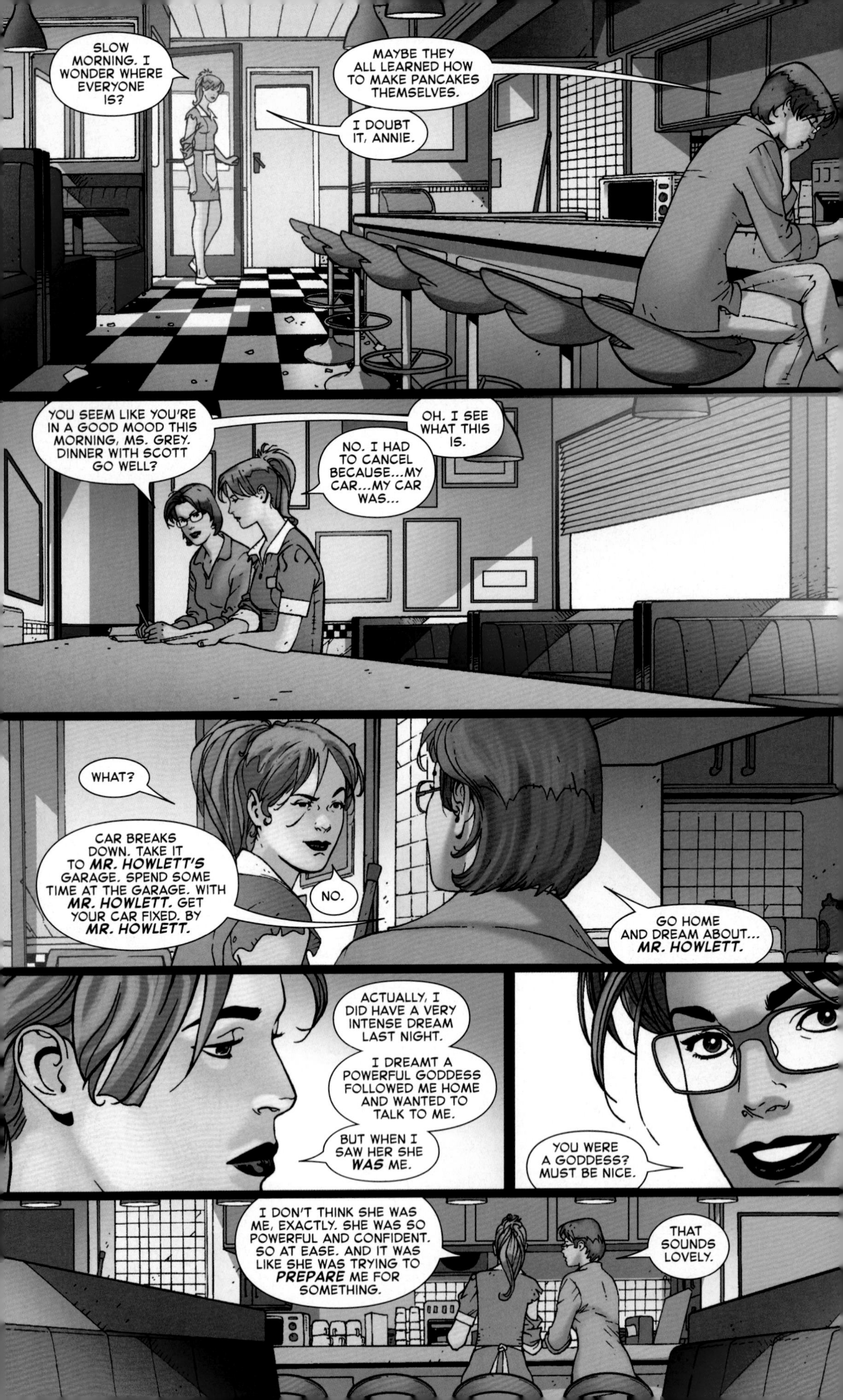
SLOW MORNING. I WONDER WHERE EVERYONE IS?
MAYBE THEY ALL LEARNED HOW TO MAKE PANCAKES THEMSELVES.
I DOUBT IT, ANNIE.
YOU SEEM LIKE YOU'RE IN A GOOD MOOD THIS MORNING, MS. GREY. DINNER WITH SCOTT GO WELL?
NO. I HAD TO CANCEL BECAUSE...MY CAR...MY CAR WAS...
OH. I SEE WHAT THIS IS.
WHAT?
CAR BREAKS DOWN. TAKE IT TO MR. HOWLETT'S GARAGE. SPEND SOME TIME AT THE GARAGE. WITH MR. HOWLETT. GET YOUR CAR FIXED. BY MR. HOWLETT.
NO.
GO HOME AND DREAM ABOUT... MR. HOWLETT.
ACTUALLY, I DID HAVE A VERY INTENSE DREAM LAST NIGHT.
I DREAMT A POWERFUL GODDESS FOLLOWED ME HOME AND WANTED TO TALK TO ME.
BUT WHEN I SAW HER SHE WAS ME.
YOU WERE A GODDESS? MUST BE NICE.
I DON'T THINK SHE WAS ME, EXACTLY. SHE WAS SO POWERFUL AND CONFIDENT. SO AT EASE. AND IT WAS LIKE SHE WAS TRYING TO PREPARE ME FOR SOMETHING.
THAT SOUNDS LOVELY.

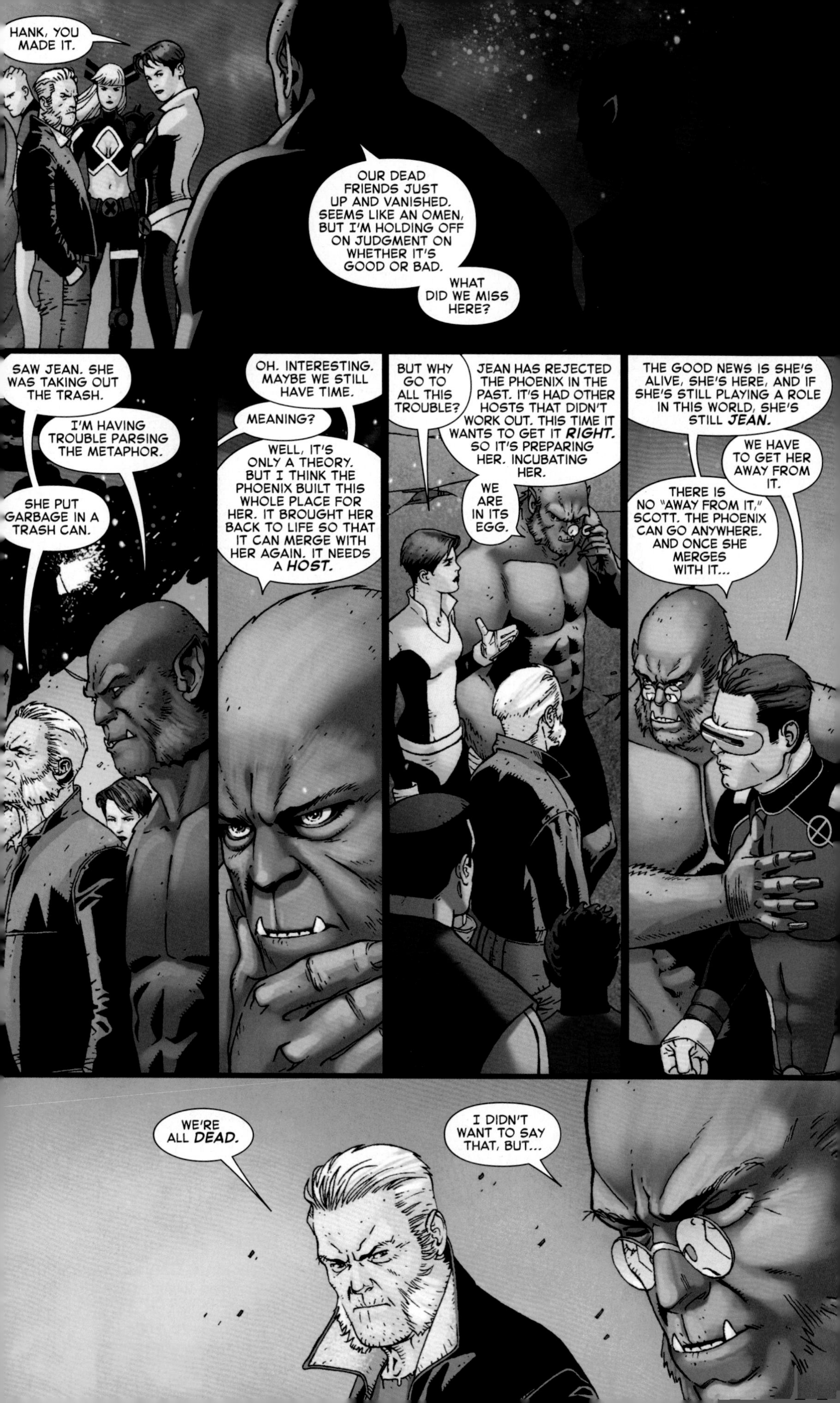
HANK, YOU MADE IT.
OUR DEAD FRIENDS JUST UP AND VANISHED. SEEMS LIKE AN OMEN, BUT I'M HOLDING OFF ON JUDGMENT ON WHETHER IT'S GOOD OR BAD.
WHAT DID WE MISS HERE?
SAW JEAN. SHE WAS TAKING OUT THE TRASH.
I'M HAVING TROUBLE PARSING THE METAPHOR.
SHE PUT GARBAGE IN A TRASH CAN.
OH. INTERESTING. MAYBE WE STILL HAVE TIME.
MEANING?
WELL, IT'S ONLY A THEORY. BUT I THINK THE PHOENIX BUILT THIS WHOLE PLACE FOR HER. IT BROUGHT HER BACK TO LIFE SO THAT IT CAN MERGE WITH HER AGAIN. IT NEEDS A *HOST.*
BUT WHY GO TO ALL THIS TROUBLE?
JEAN HAS REJECTED THE PHOENIX IN THE PAST. IT'S HAD OTHER HOSTS THAT DIDN'T WORK OUT. THIS TIME IT WANTS TO GET IT *RIGHT.* SO IT'S PREPARING HER. INCUBATING HER.
WE ARE IN ITS EGG.
THE GOOD NEWS IS SHE'S ALIVE, SHE'S HERE, AND IF SHE'S STILL PLAYING A ROLE IN THIS WORLD, SHE'S STILL *JEAN.*
WE HAVE TO GET HER AWAY FROM IT.
THERE IS NO "AWAY FROM IT," SCOTT. THE PHOENIX CAN GO ANYWHERE. AND ONCE SHE MERGES WITH IT...
WE'RE ALL *DEAD.*
I DIDN'T WANT TO SAY THAT, BUT...

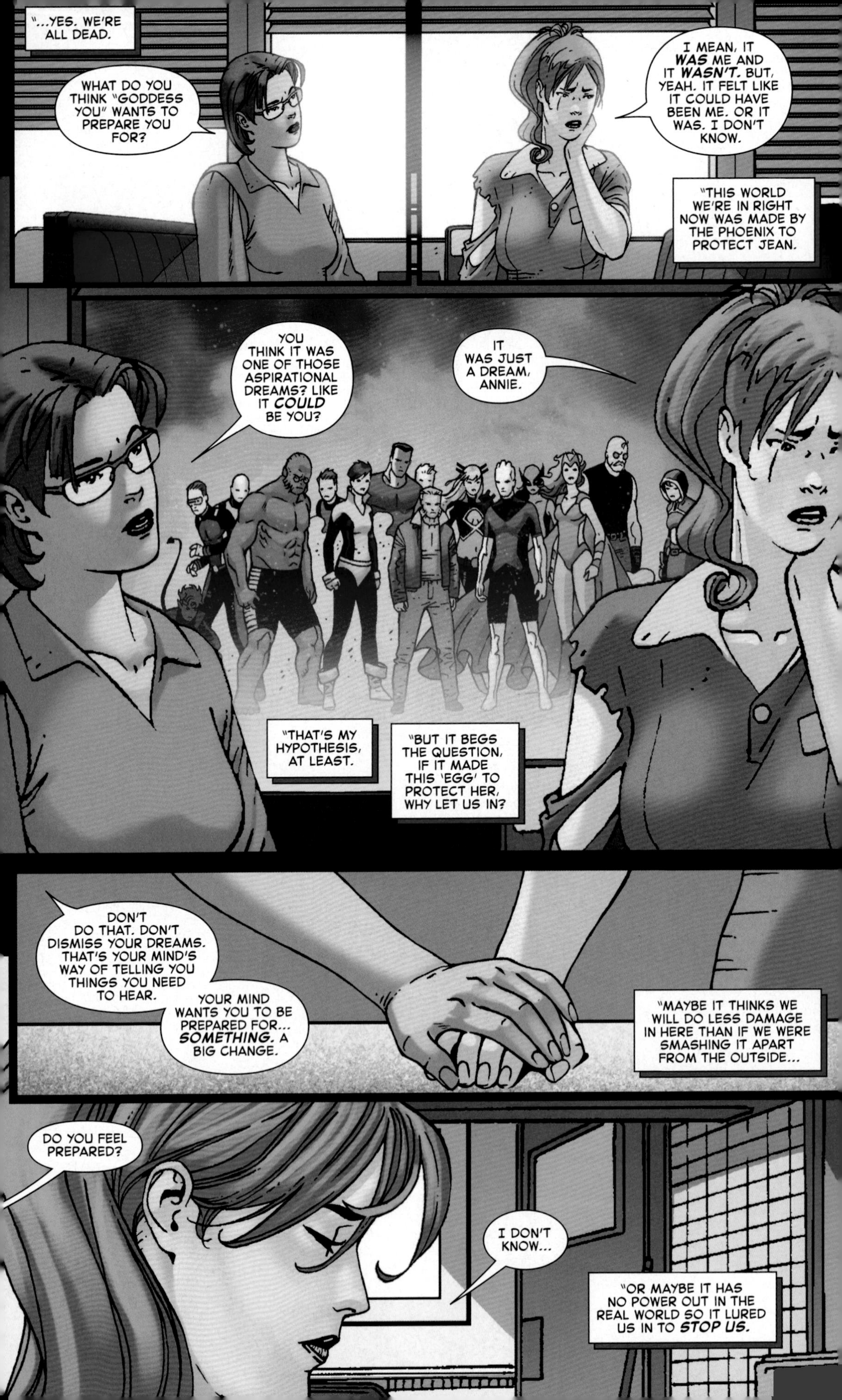
"...YES. WE'RE ALL DEAD.
WHAT DO YOU THINK "GODDESS YOU" WANTS TO PREPARE YOU FOR?
I MEAN, IT **WAS** ME AND IT **WASN'T.** BUT, YEAH. IT FELT LIKE IT COULD HAVE BEEN ME. OR IT WAS. I DON'T KNOW.
"THIS WORLD WE'RE IN RIGHT NOW WAS MADE BY THE PHOENIX TO PROTECT JEAN.
YOU THINK IT WAS ONE OF THOSE ASPIRATIONAL DREAMS? LIKE IT **COULD** BE YOU?
IT WAS JUST A DREAM, ANNIE.
"THAT'S MY HYPOTHESIS, AT LEAST.
"BUT IT BEGS THE QUESTION, IF IT MADE THIS 'EGG' TO PROTECT HER, WHY LET US IN?
DON'T DO THAT. DON'T DISMISS YOUR DREAMS. THAT'S YOUR MIND'S WAY OF TELLING YOU THINGS YOU NEED TO HEAR.
YOUR MIND WANTS YOU TO BE PREPARED FOR... **SOMETHING.** A BIG CHANGE.
"MAYBE IT THINKS WE WILL DO LESS DAMAGE IN HERE THAN IF WE WERE SMASHING IT APART FROM THE OUTSIDE...
DO YOU FEEL PREPARED?
I DON'T KNOW...
"OR MAYBE IT HAS NO POWER OUT IN THE REAL WORLD SO IT LURED US IN TO **STOP US.**

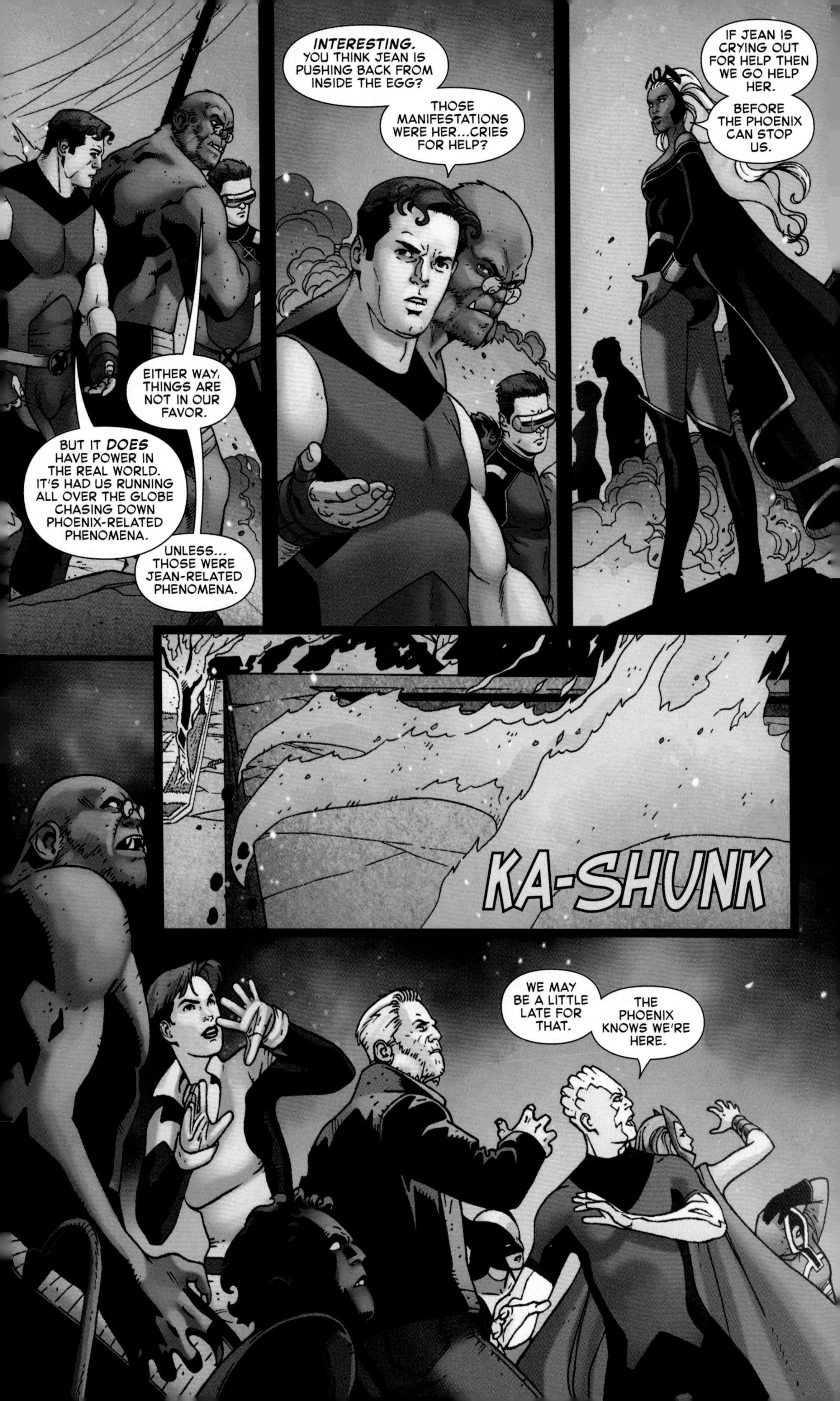

EITHER WAY, THINGS ARE NOT IN OUR FAVOR.
BUT IT DOES HAVE POWER IN THE REAL WORLD. IT'S HAD US RUNNING ALL OVER THE GLOBE CHASING DOWN PHOENIX-RELATED PHENOMENA.
UNLESS... THOSE WERE JEAN-RELATED PHENOMENA.
INTERESTING. YOU THINK JEAN IS PUSHING BACK FROM INSIDE THE EGG?
THOSE MANIFESTATIONS WERE HER...CRIES FOR HELP?
IF JEAN IS CRYING OUT FOR HELP THEN WE GO HELP HER.
BEFORE THE PHOENIX CAN STOP US.
KA-SHUNK
WE MAY BE A LITTLE LATE FOR THAT.
THE PHOENIX KNOWS WE'RE HERE.

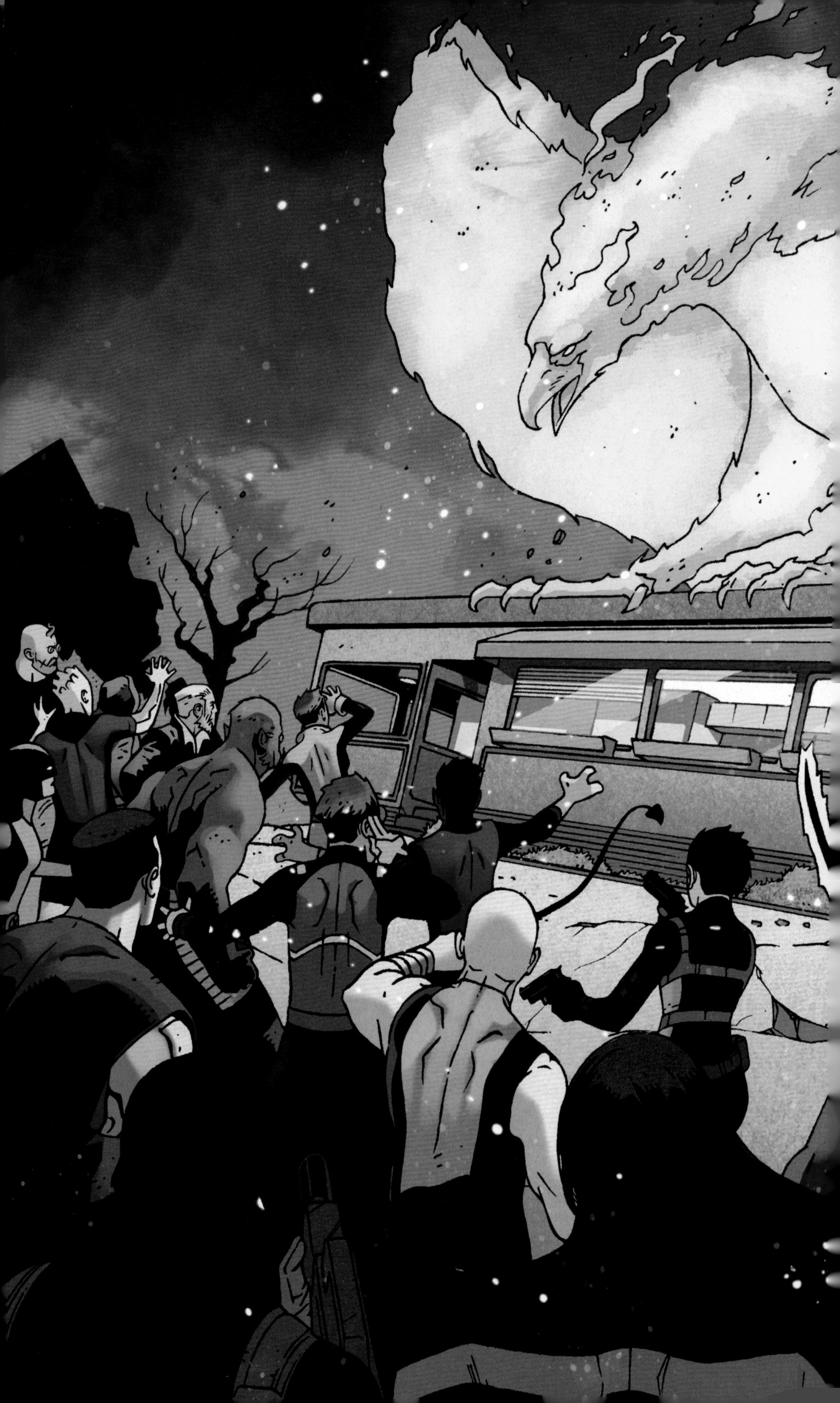

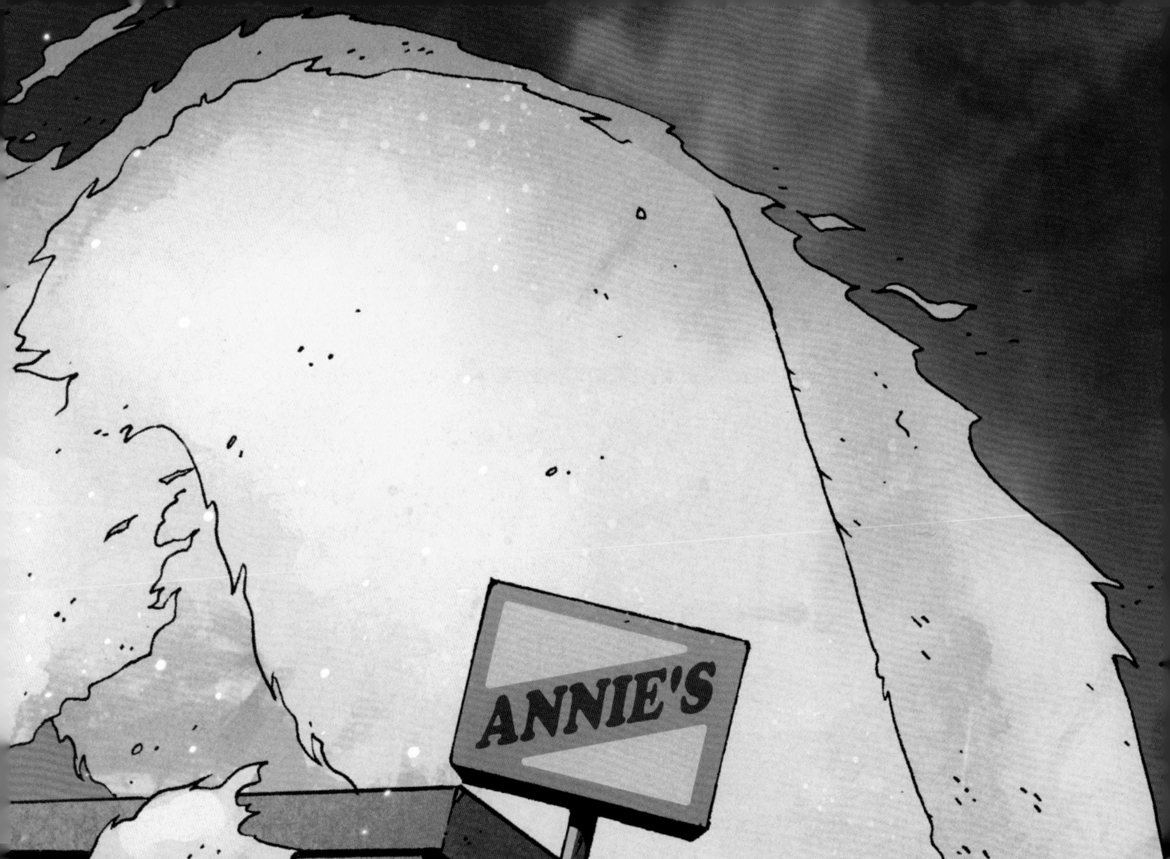
ANNIE'S

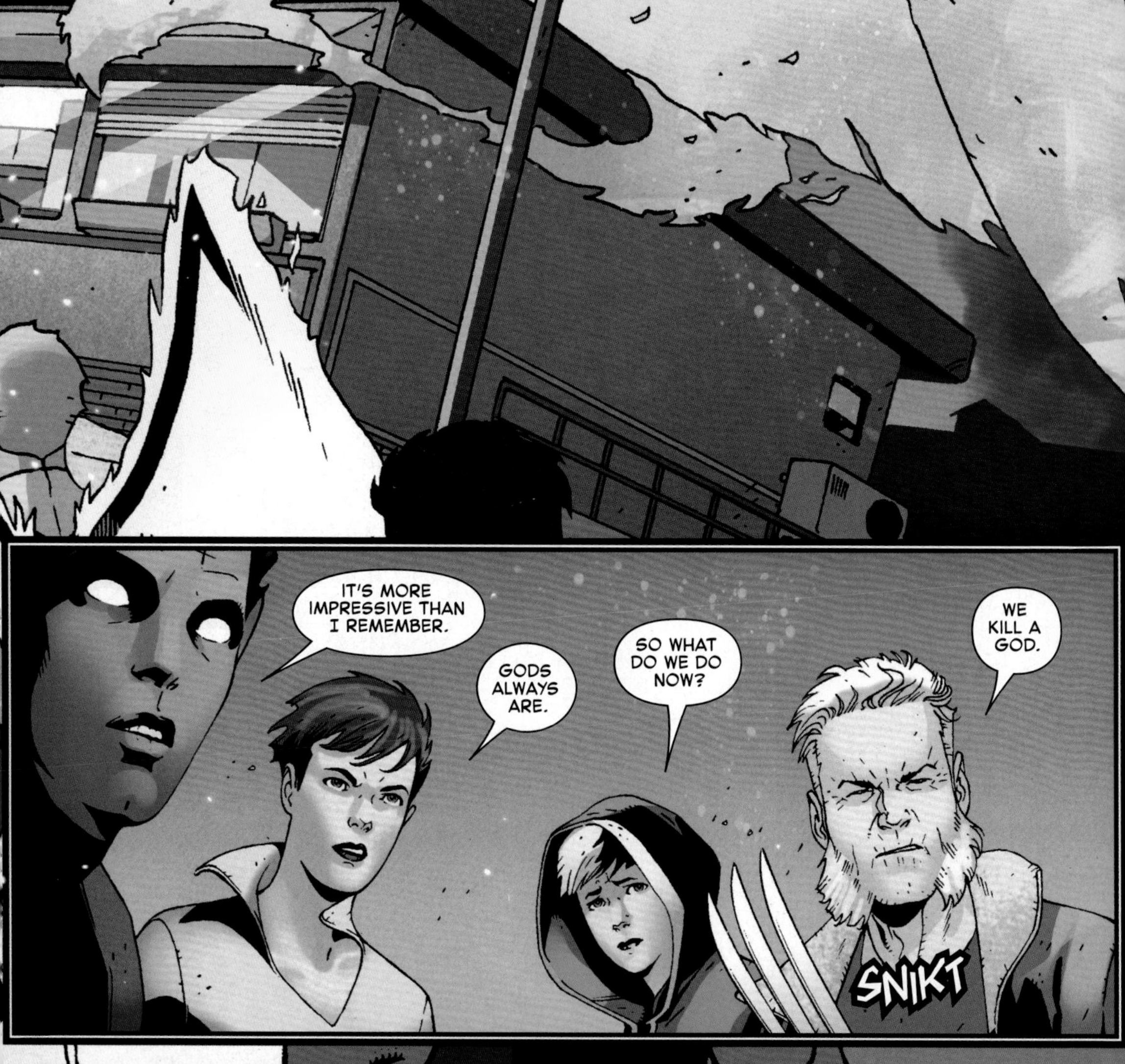
IT'S MORE IMPRESSIVE THAN I REMEMBER.
GODS ALWAYS ARE.
SO WHAT DO WE DO NOW?
WE KILL A GOD.
SNIKT

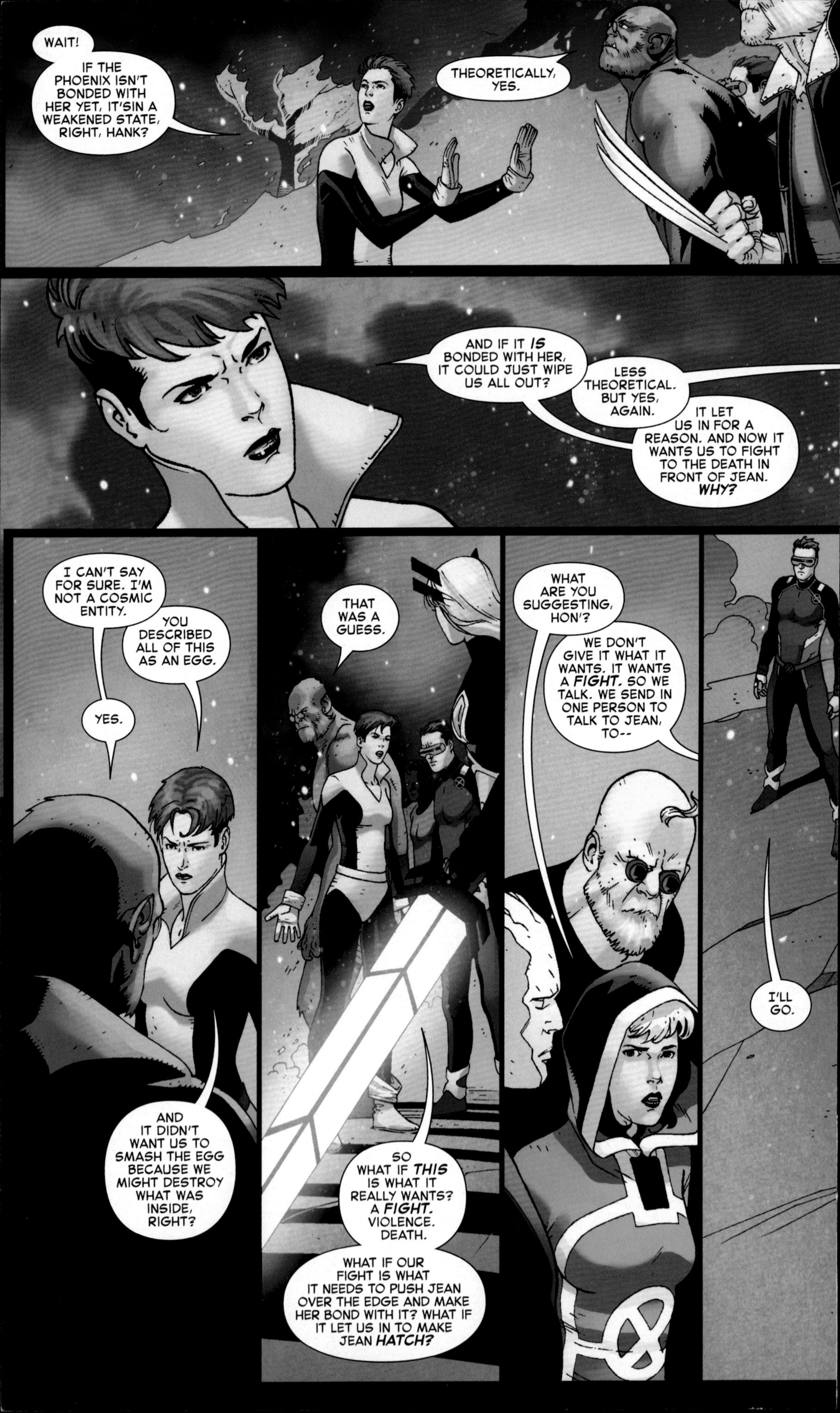
WAIT!
IF THE PHOENIX ISN'T BONDED WITH HER YET, IT'SIN A WEAKENED STATE, RIGHT, HANK?
THEORETICALLY, YES.
AND IF IT IS BONDED WITH HER, IT COULD JUST WIPE US ALL OUT?
LESS THEORETICAL. BUT YES, AGAIN.
IT LET US IN FOR A REASON. AND NOW IT WANTS US TO FIGHT TO THE DEATH IN FRONT OF JEAN. WHY?
I CAN'T SAY FOR SURE. I'M NOT A COSMIC ENTITY.
YOU DESCRIBED ALL OF THIS AS AN EGG.
YES.
AND IT DIDN'T WANT US TO SMASH THE EGG BECAUSE WE MIGHT DESTROY WHAT WAS INSIDE, RIGHT?
THAT WAS A GUESS.
SO WHAT IF THIS IS WHAT IT REALLY WANTS? A FIGHT. VIOLENCE. DEATH.
WHAT IF OUR FIGHT IS WHAT IT NEEDS TO PUSH JEAN OVER THE EDGE AND MAKE HER BOND WITH IT? WHAT IF IT LET US IN TO MAKE JEAN HATCH?
WHAT ARE YOU SUGGESTING, HON'?
WE DON'T GIVE IT WHAT IT WANTS. IT WANTS A FIGHT. SO WE TALK. WE SEND IN ONE PERSON TO TALK TO JEAN, TO--
I'LL GO.

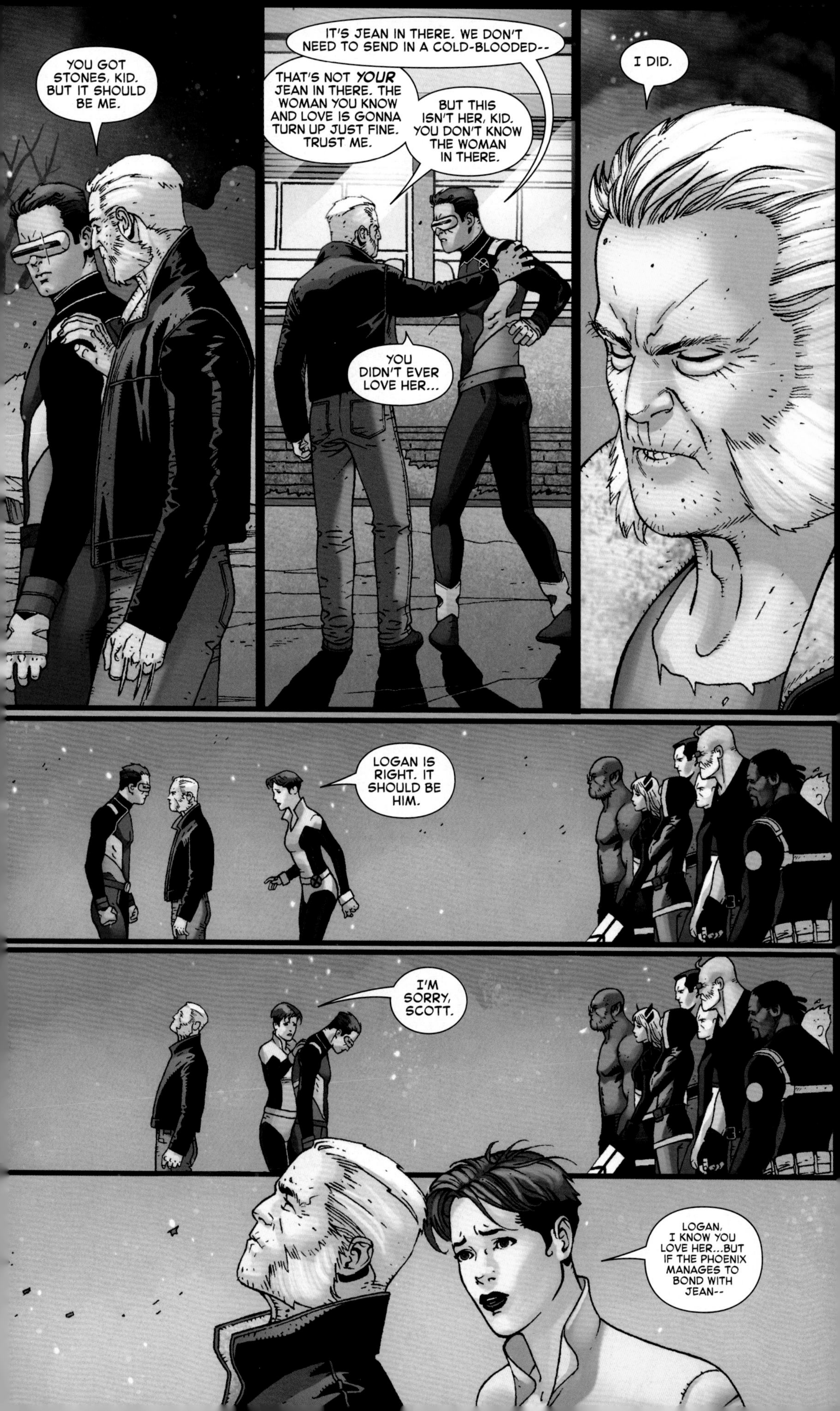

YOU GOT STONES, KID. BUT IT SHOULD BE ME.
IT'S JEAN IN THERE. WE DON'T NEED TO SEND IN A COLD-BLOODED--
THAT'S NOT YOUR JEAN IN THERE. THE WOMAN YOU KNOW AND LOVE IS GONNA TURN UP JUST FINE. TRUST ME.
BUT THIS ISN'T HER, KID. YOU DON'T KNOW THE WOMAN IN THERE.
YOU DIDN'T EVER LOVE HER...
I DID.
LOGAN IS RIGHT. IT SHOULD BE HIM.
I'M SORRY, SCOTT.
LOGAN, I KNOW YOU LOVE HER...BUT IF THE PHOENIX MANAGES TO BOND WITH JEAN--

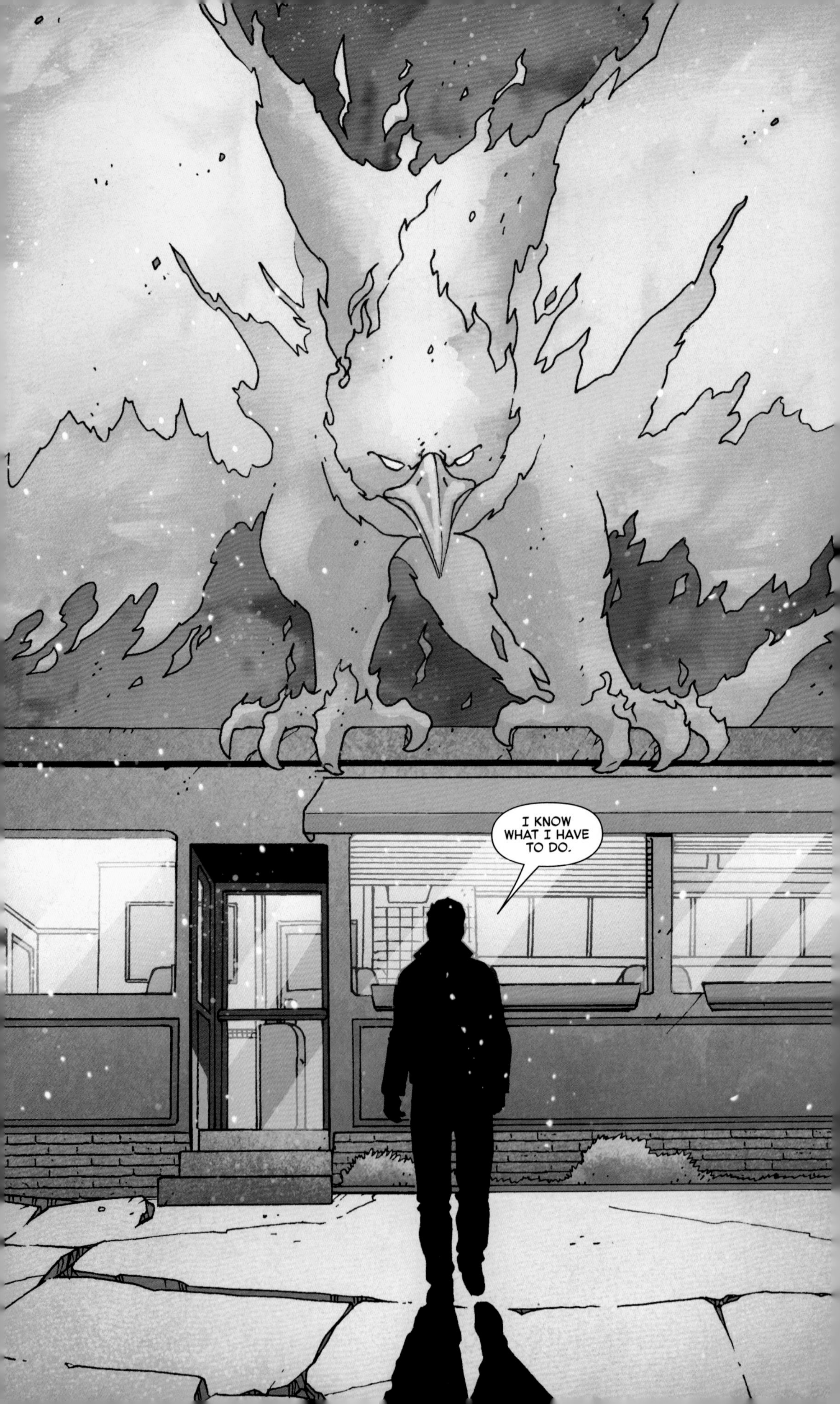
I KNOW WHAT I HAVE TO DO.

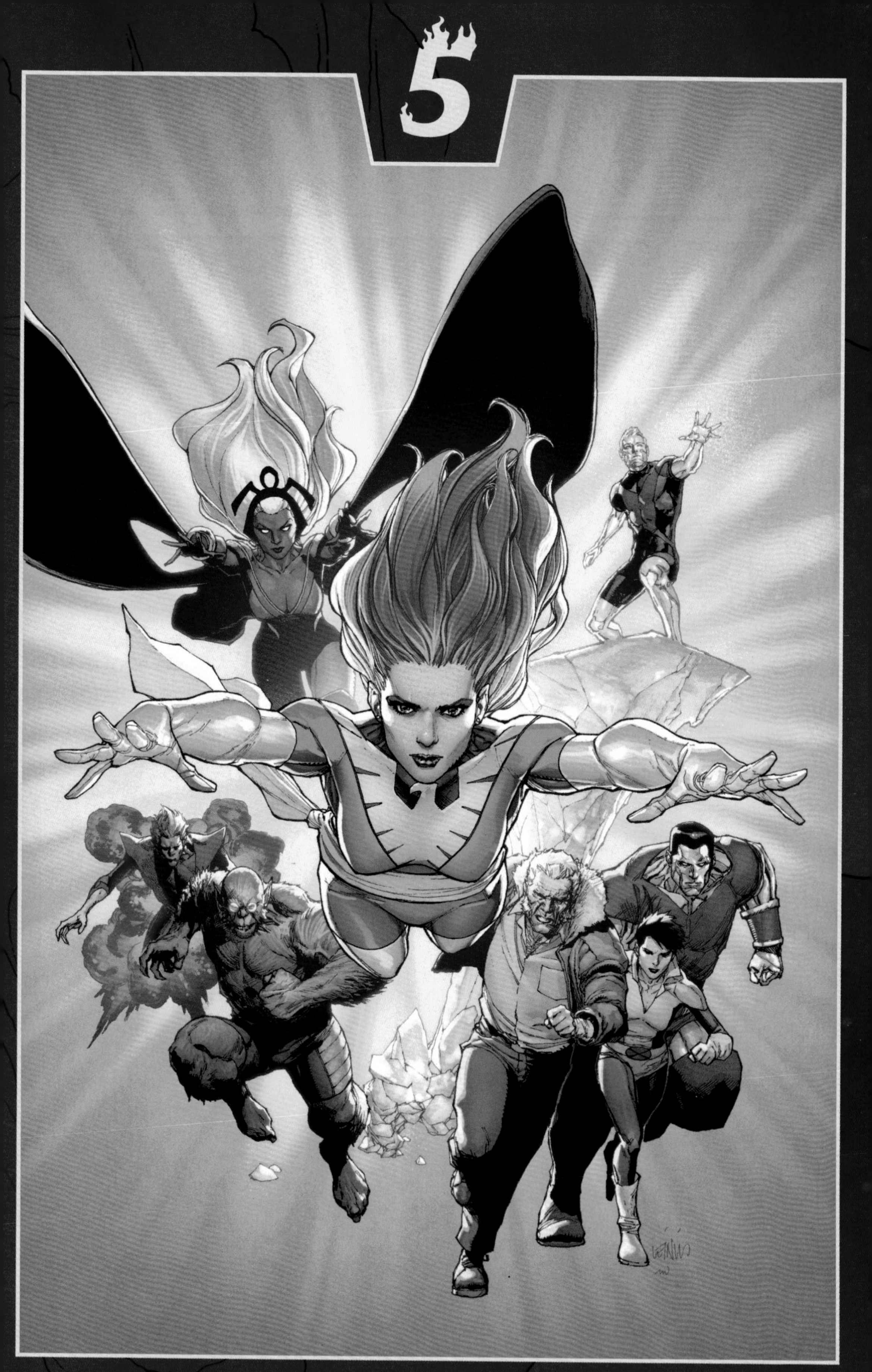

CHAPTER FIVE: *BE THOU THOSE ENDS*

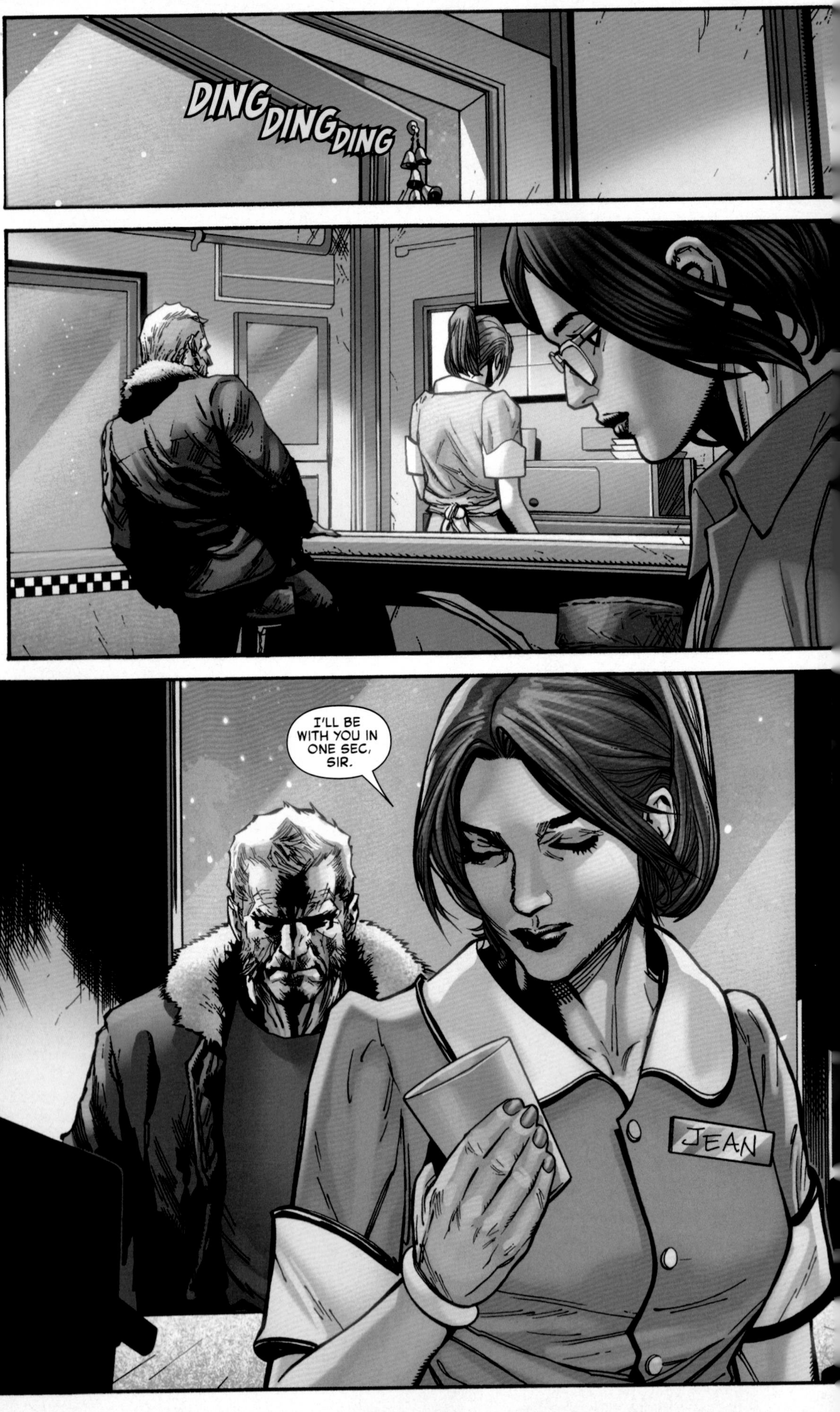
DING DING DING
I'LL BE WITH YOU IN ONE SEC, SIR.
JEAN

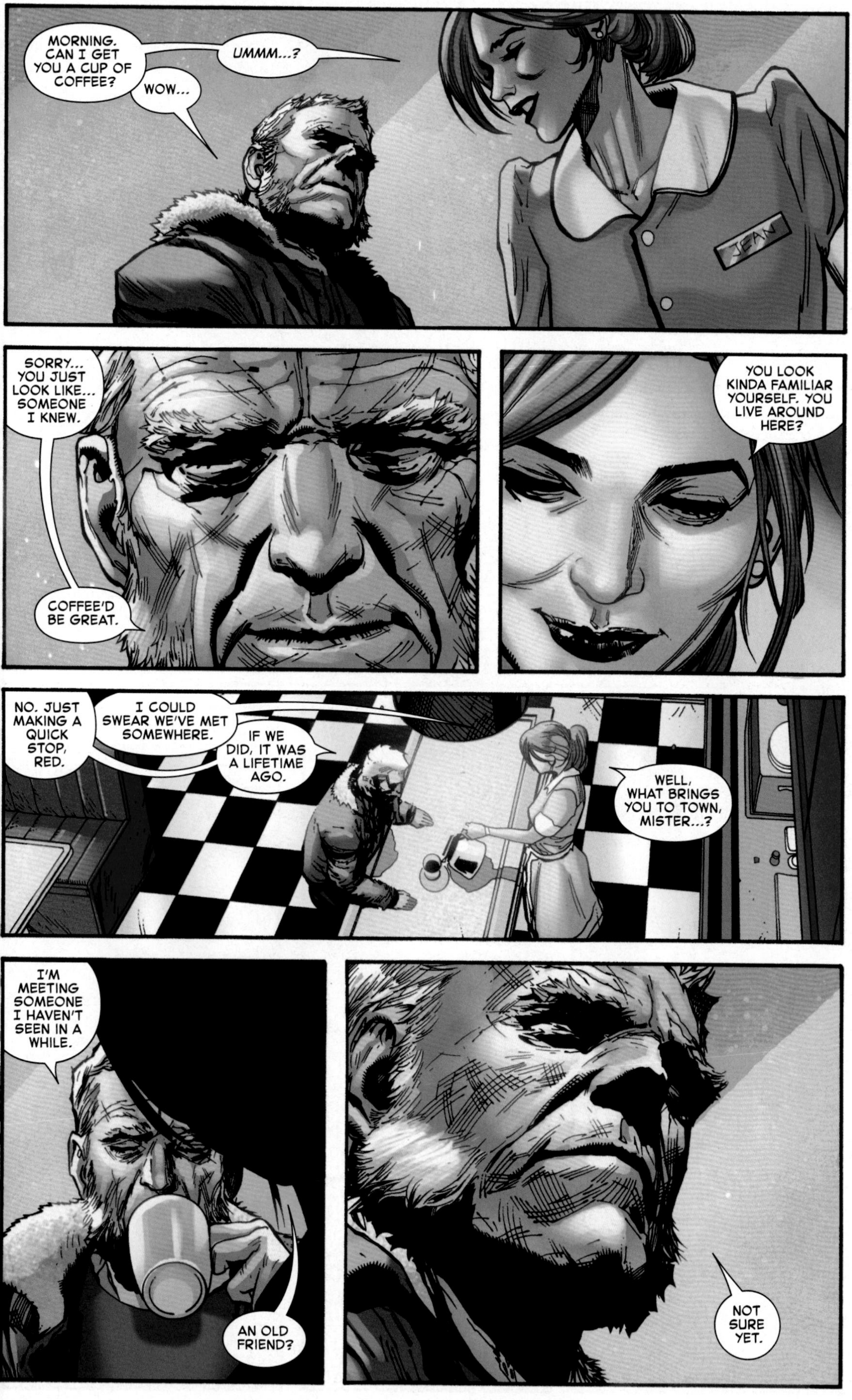
MORNING. CAN I GET YOU A CUP OF COFFEE?
UMMM...?
WOW...
SORRY... YOU JUST LOOK LIKE... SOMEONE I KNEW.
COFFEE'D BE GREAT.
YOU LOOK KINDA FAMILIAR YOURSELF. YOU LIVE AROUND HERE?
NO. JUST MAKING A QUICK STOP, RED.
I COULD SWEAR WE'VE MET SOMEWHERE.
IF WE DID, IT WAS A LIFETIME AGO.
WELL, WHAT BRINGS YOU TO TOWN, MISTER...?
I'M MEETING SOMEONE I HAVEN'T SEEN IN A WHILE.
AN OLD FRIEND?
NOT SURE YET.

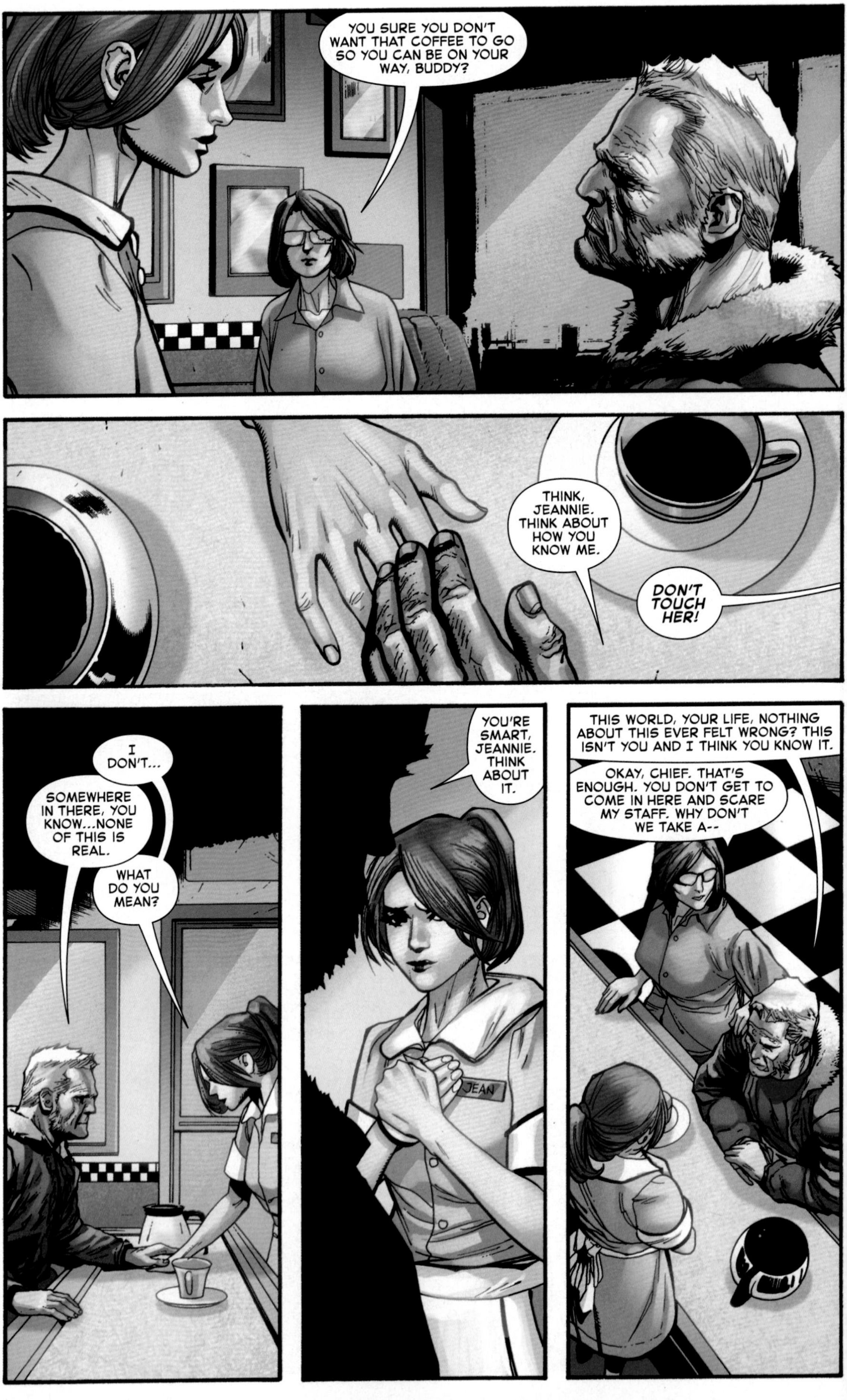
YOU SURE YOU DON'T WANT THAT COFFEE TO GO SO YOU CAN BE ON YOUR WAY, BUDDY?
THINK, JEANNIE. THINK ABOUT HOW YOU KNOW ME.
DON'T TOUCH HER!
I DON'T...
SOMEWHERE IN THERE, YOU KNOW...NONE OF THIS IS REAL.
WHAT DO YOU MEAN?
YOU'RE SMART, JEANNIE. THINK ABOUT IT.
JEAN
THIS WORLD, YOUR LIFE, NOTHING ABOUT THIS EVER FELT WRONG? THIS ISN'T YOU AND I THINK YOU KNOW IT.
OKAY, CHIEF. THAT'S ENOUGH. YOU DON'T GET TO COME IN HERE AND SCARE MY STAFF. WHY DON'T WE TAKE A--

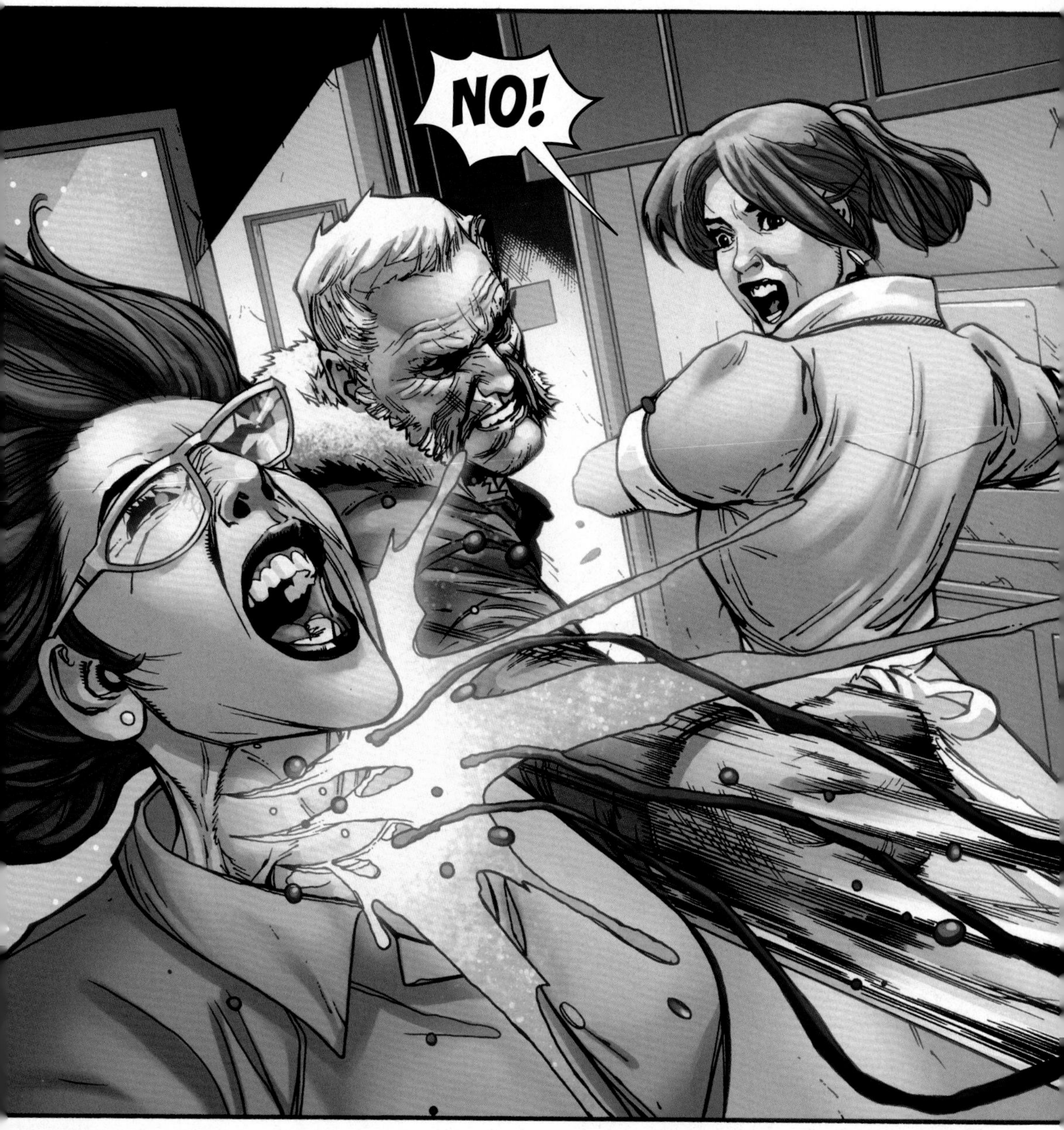
NO!

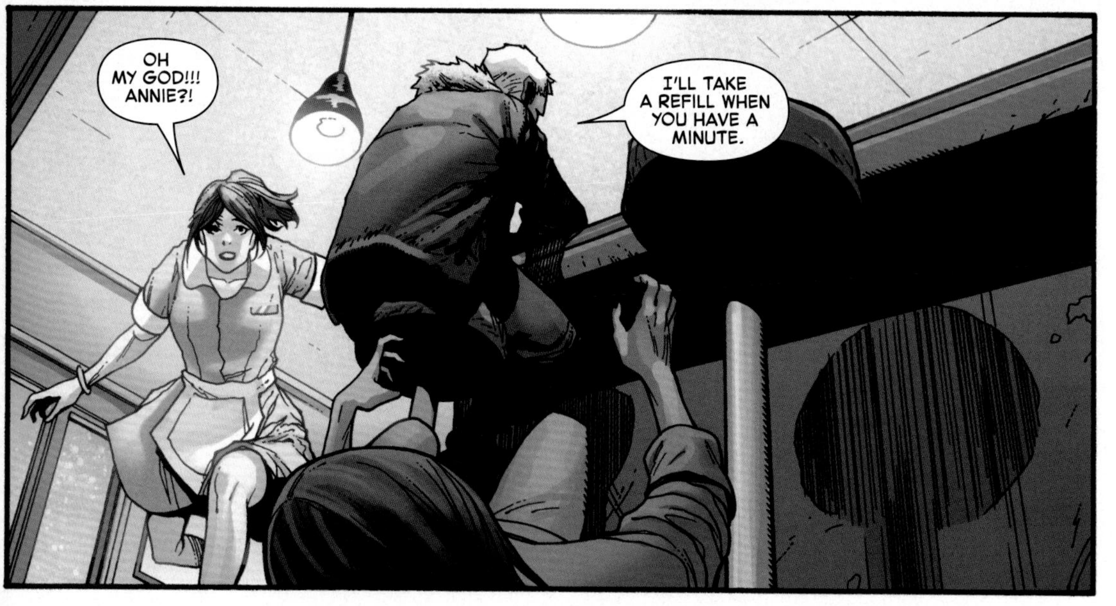
OH
MY GOD!!!
ANNIE?!
I'LL TAKE
A REFILL WHEN
YOU HAVE A
MINUTE.

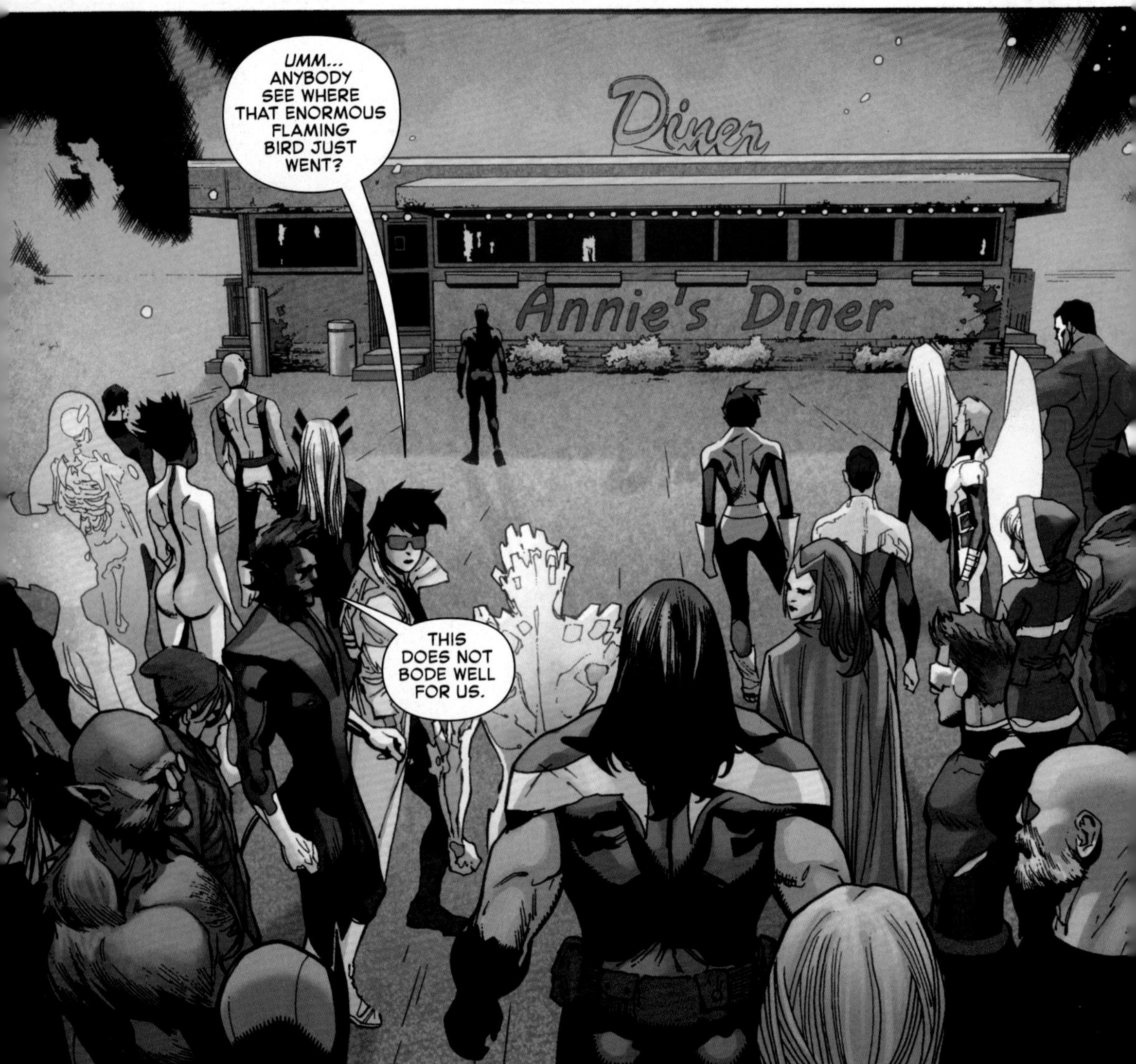
Diner
Annie's Diner
UMM... ANYBODY SEE WHERE THAT ENORMOUS FLAMING BIRD JUST WENT?
THIS DOES NOT BODE WELL FOR US.

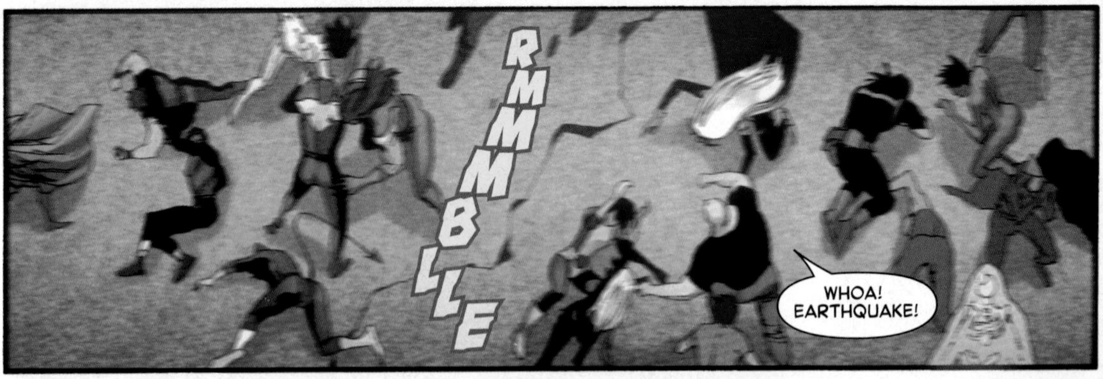
RMMMBLLE
WHOA! EARTHQUAKE!

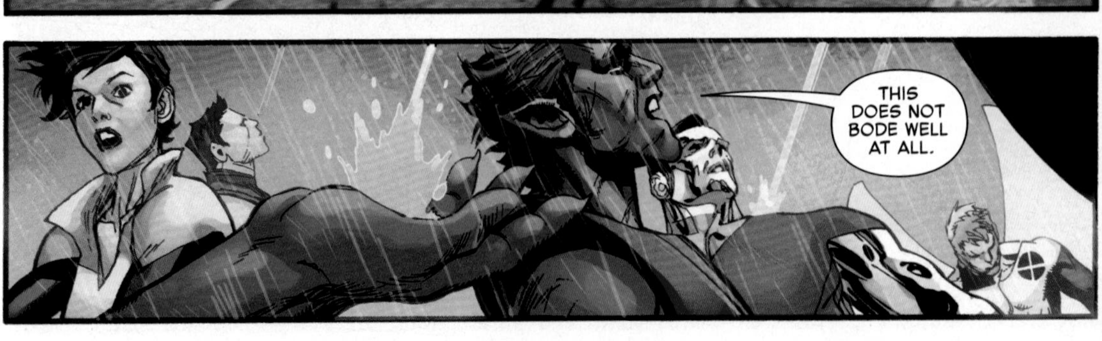
THIS DOES NOT BODE WELL AT ALL.

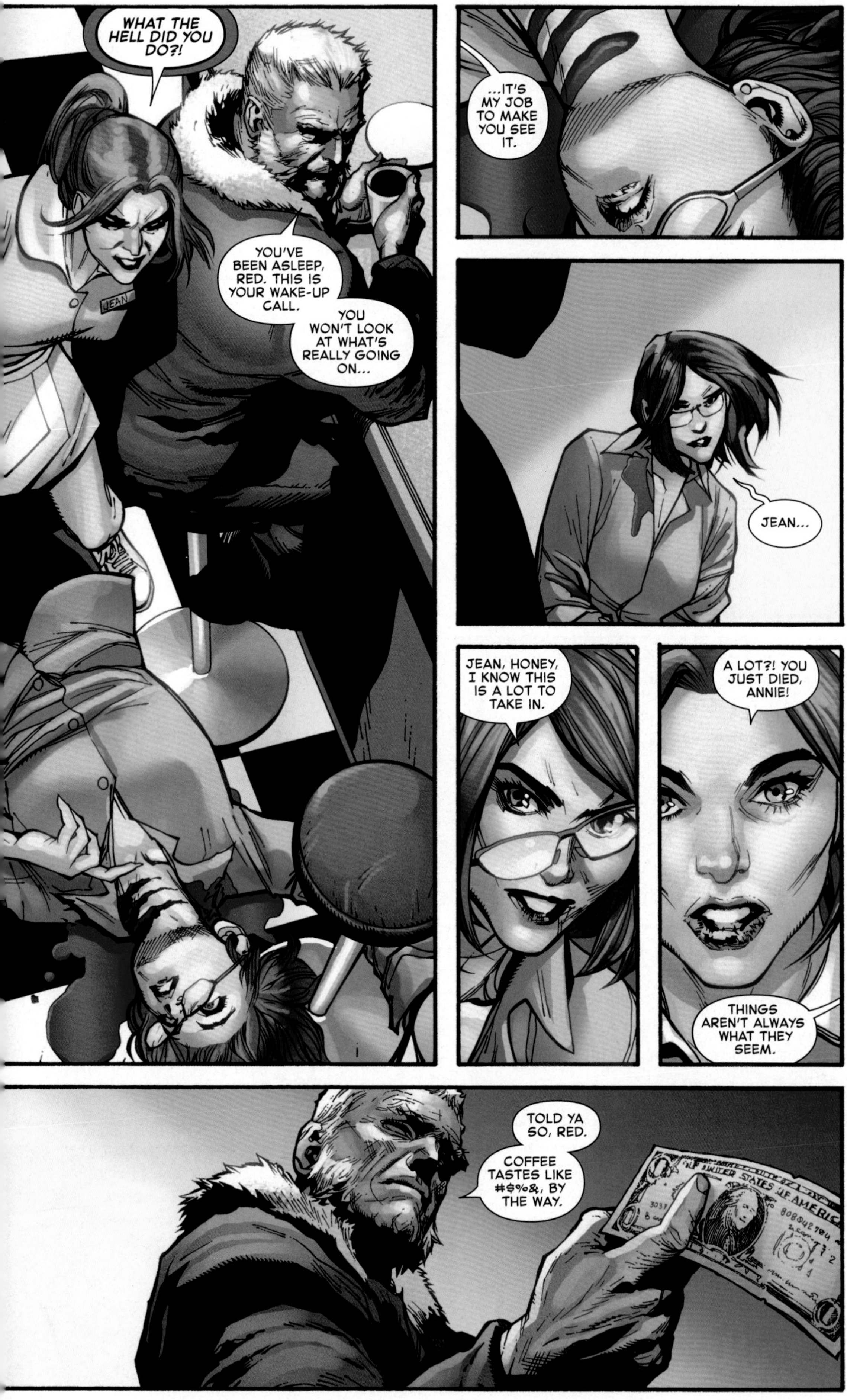
WHAT THE HELL DID YOU DO?!
YOU'VE BEEN ASLEEP, RED. THIS IS YOUR WAKE-UP CALL.
YOU WON'T LOOK AT WHAT'S REALLY GOING ON...
...IT'S MY JOB TO MAKE YOU SEE IT.
JEAN...
JEAN, HONEY, I KNOW THIS IS A LOT TO TAKE IN.
A LOT?! YOU JUST DIED, ANNIE!
THINGS AREN'T ALWAYS WHAT THEY SEEM.
TOLD YA SO, RED.
COFFEE TASTES LIKE #$%&, BY THE WAY.

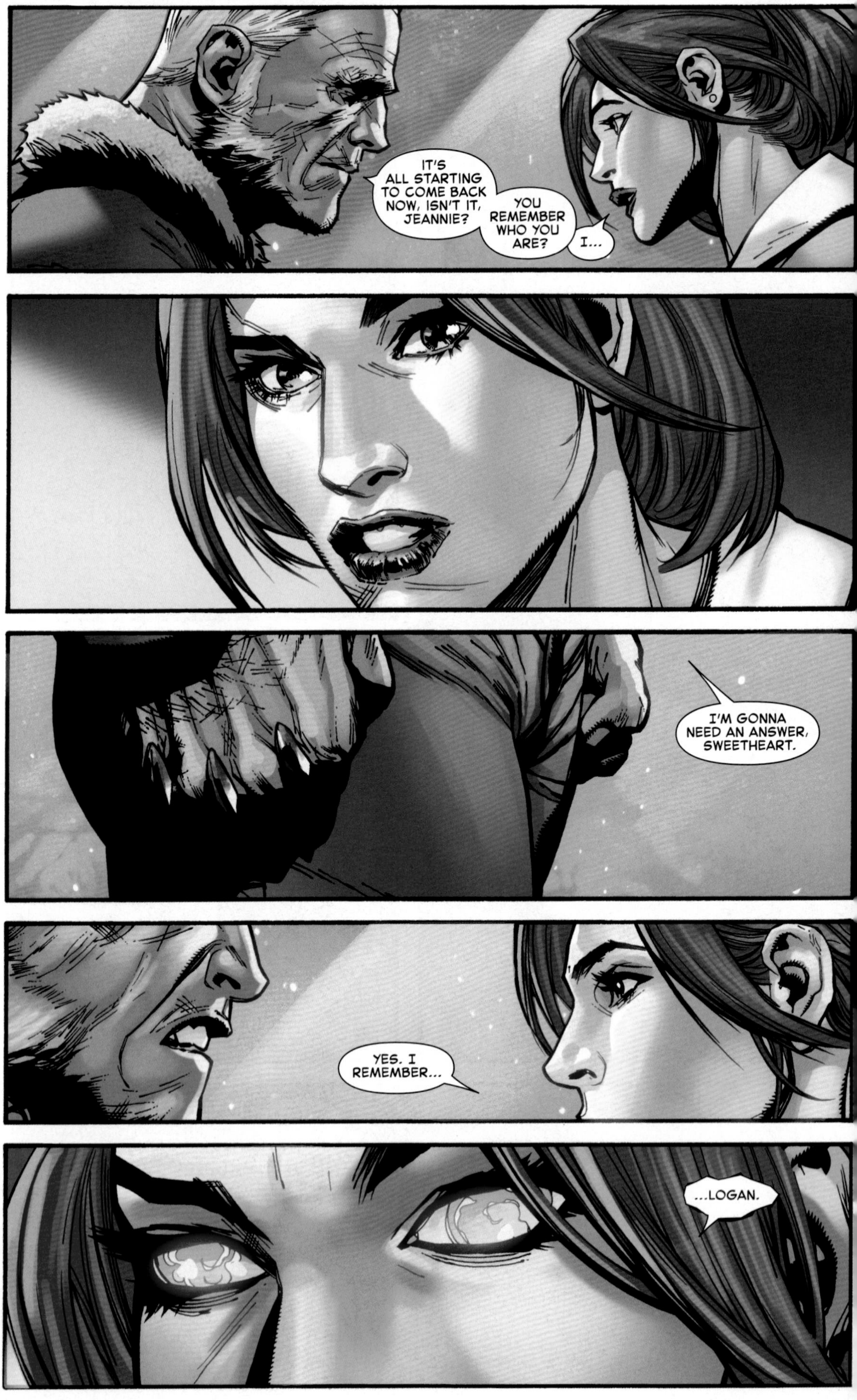
IT'S ALL STARTING TO COME BACK NOW, ISN'T IT, JEANNIE?
YOU REMEMBER WHO YOU ARE?
I...
I'M GONNA NEED AN ANSWER, SWEETHEART.
YES. I REMEMBER...
...LOGAN.

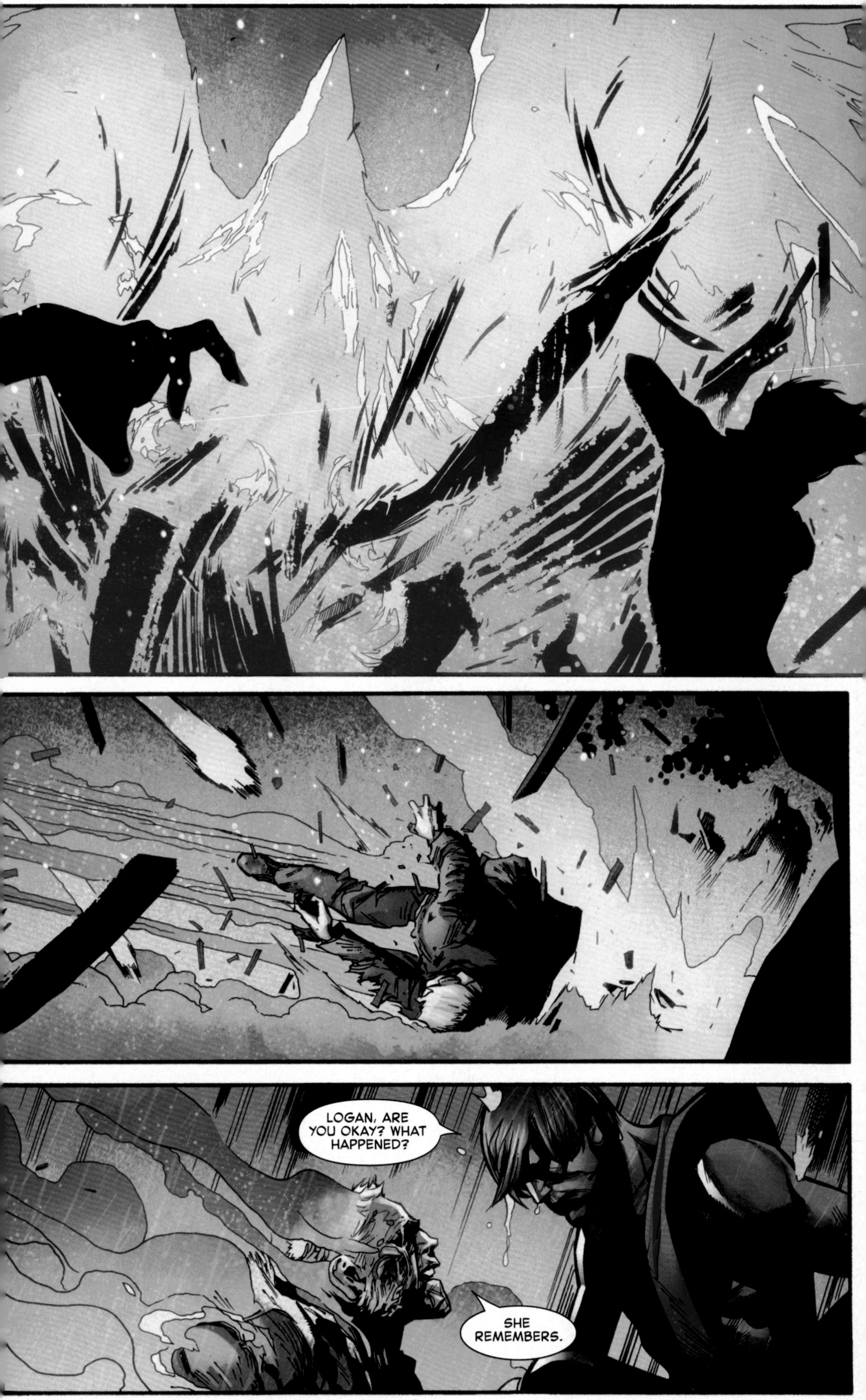
LOGAN, ARE YOU OKAY? WHAT HAPPENED?
SHE REMEMBERS.

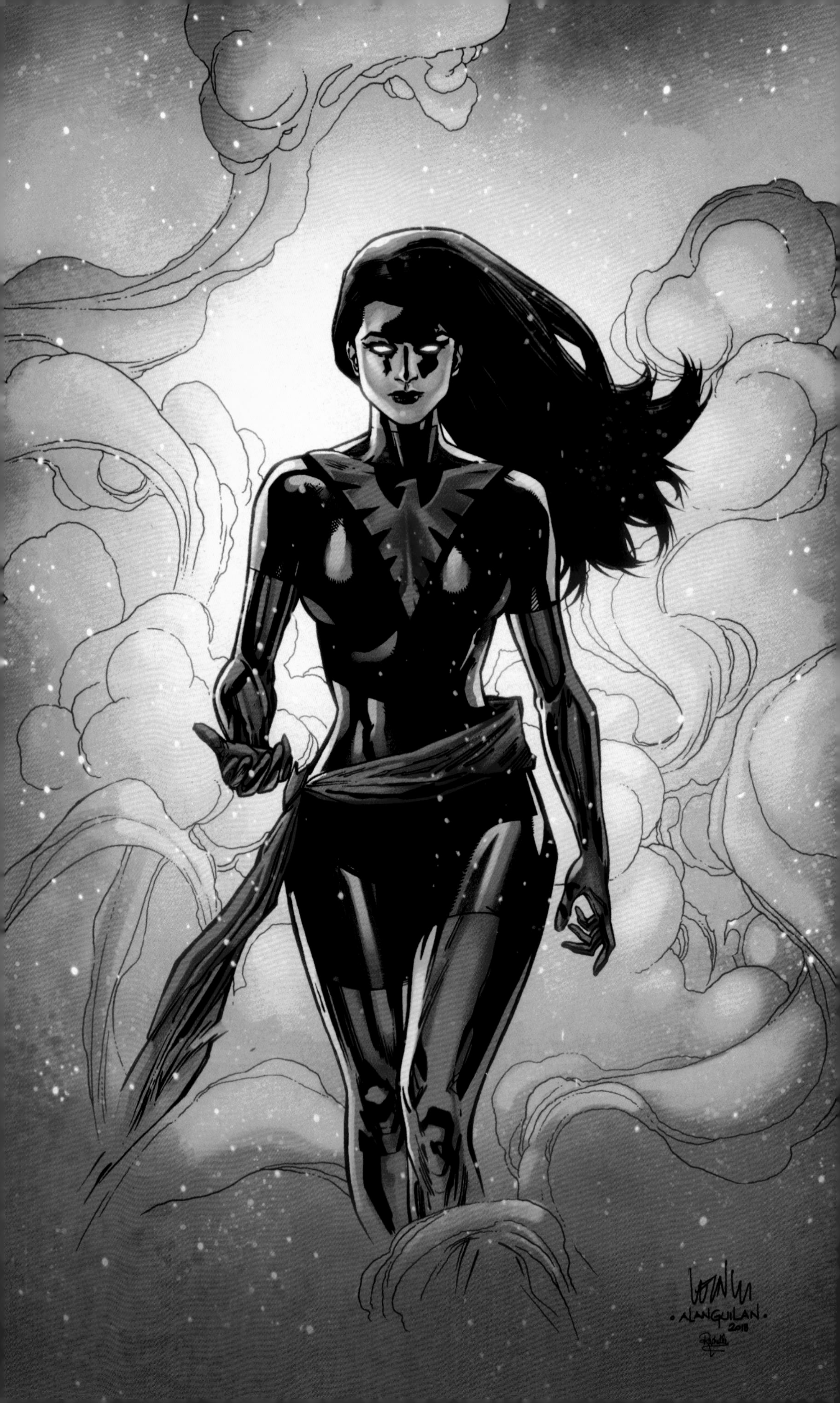
ALANGUILAN
2018

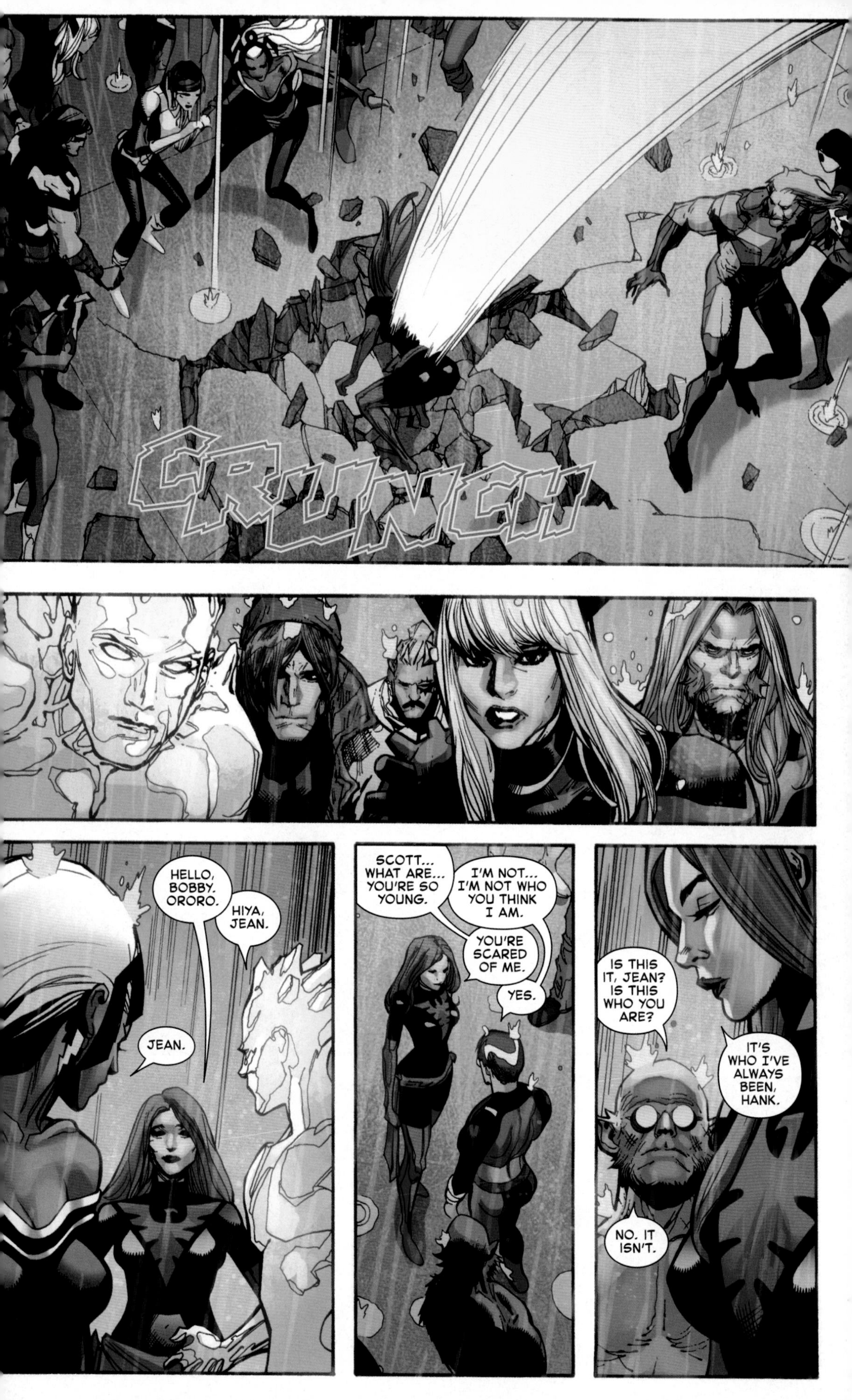
CRUNCH
HELLO, BOBBY. ORORO.
HIYA, JEAN.
JEAN.
SCOTT... WHAT ARE... YOU'RE SO YOUNG.
I'M NOT... I'M NOT WHO YOU THINK I AM.
YOU'RE SCARED OF ME.
YES.
IS THIS IT, JEAN? IS THIS WHO YOU ARE?
IT'S WHO I'VE ALWAYS BEEN, HANK.
NO. IT ISN'T.

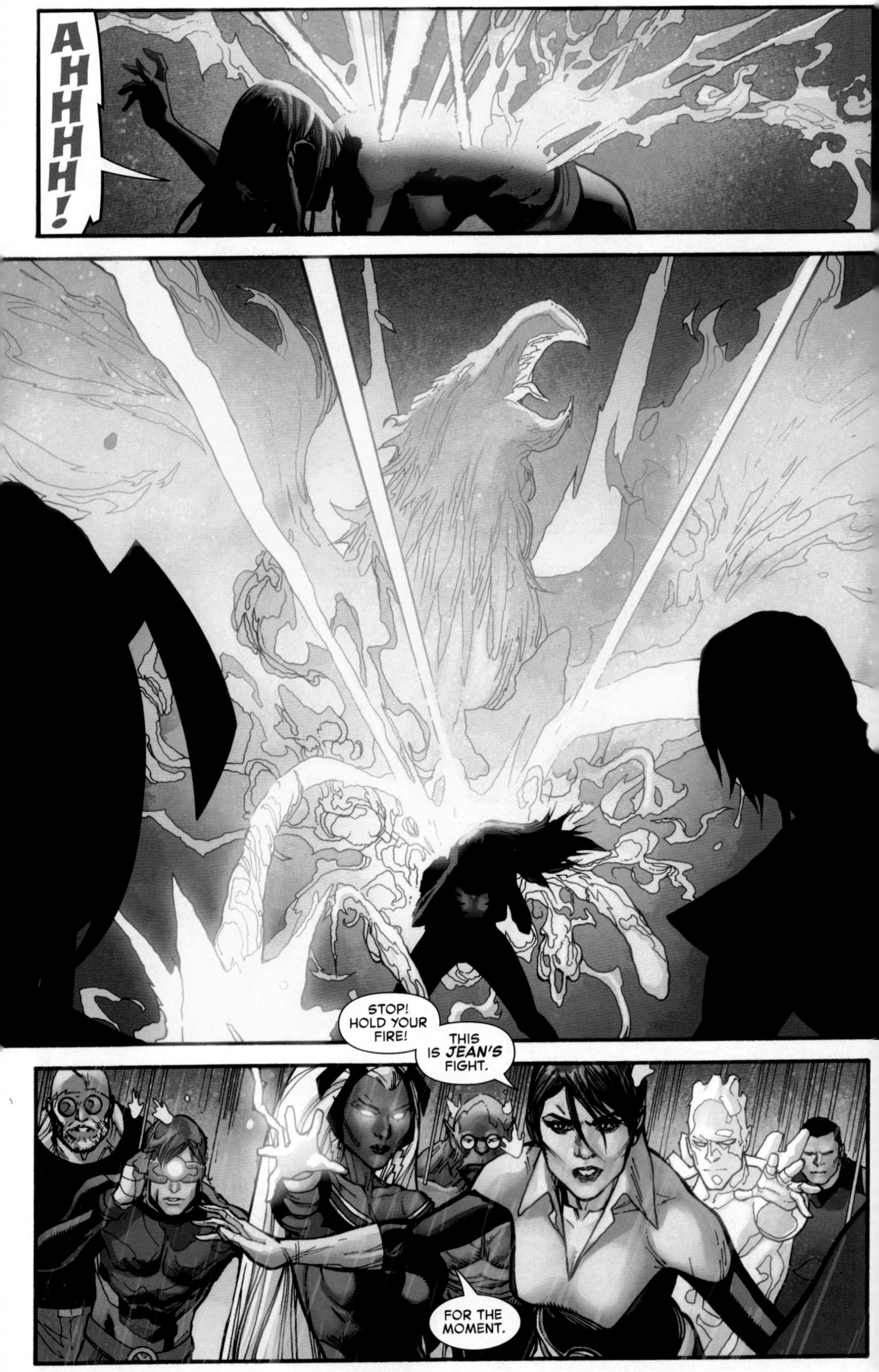
AHHHHH!
STOP! HOLD YOUR FIRE!
THIS IS JEAN'S FIGHT.
FOR THE MOMENT.

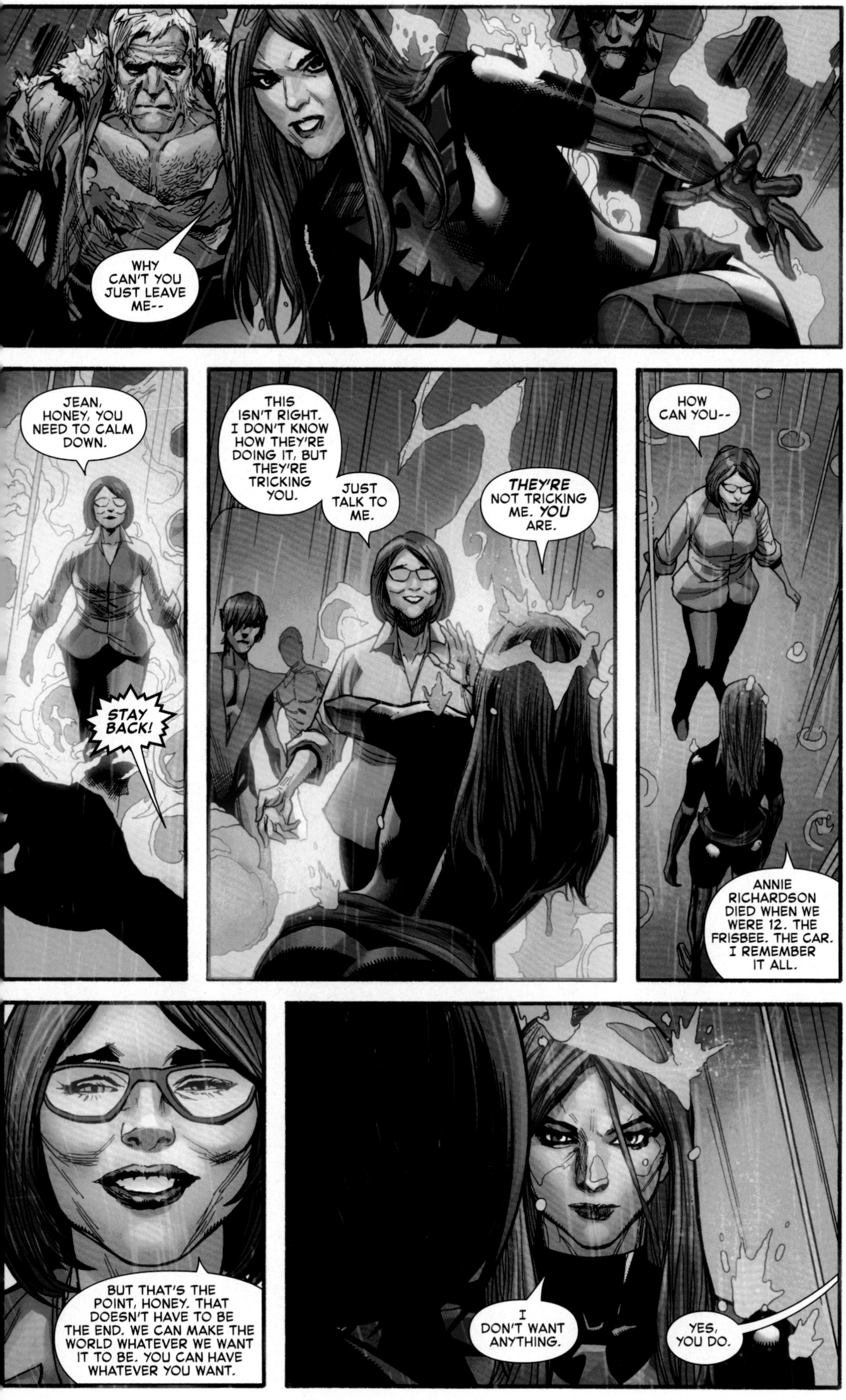
WHY CAN'T YOU JUST LEAVE ME--
JEAN, HONEY, YOU NEED TO CALM DOWN.
STAY BACK!
THIS ISN'T RIGHT. I DON'T KNOW HOW THEY'RE DOING IT, BUT THEY'RE TRICKING YOU.
JUST TALK TO ME.
THEY'RE NOT TRICKING ME. *YOU* ARE.
HOW CAN YOU--
ANNIE RICHARDSON DIED WHEN WE WERE 12. THE FRISBEE. THE CAR. I REMEMBER IT ALL.
BUT THAT'S THE POINT, HONEY. THAT DOESN'T HAVE TO BE THE END. WE CAN MAKE THE WORLD WHATEVER WE WANT IT TO BE. YOU CAN HAVE WHATEVER YOU WANT.
I DON'T WANT ANYTHING.
YES, YOU DO.

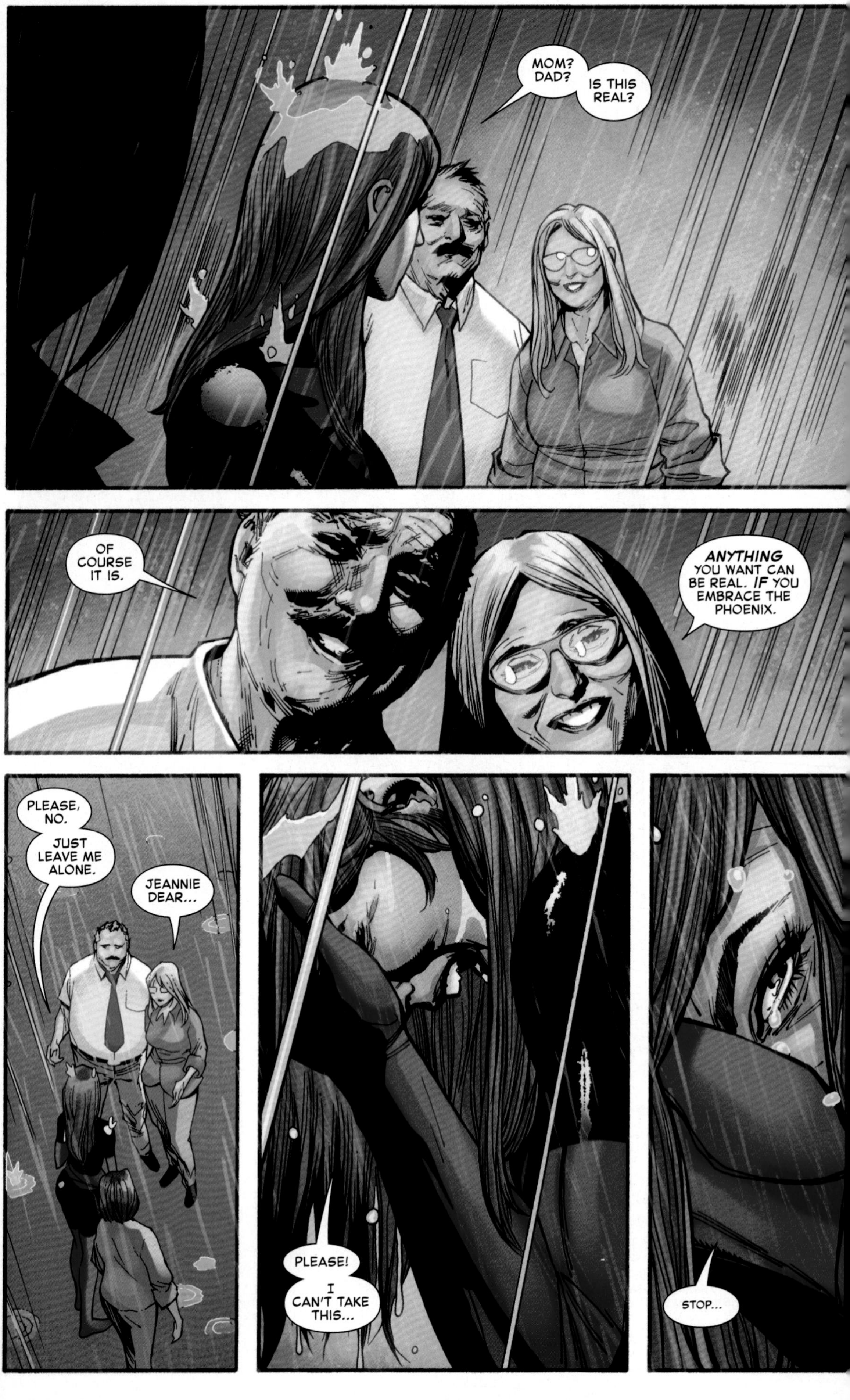
MOM? DAD?
IS THIS REAL?
OF COURSE IT IS.
ANYTHING YOU WANT CAN BE REAL. IF YOU EMBRACE THE PHOENIX.
PLEASE, NO.
JUST LEAVE ME ALONE.
JEANNIE DEAR...
PLEASE!
I CAN'T TAKE THIS...
STOP...

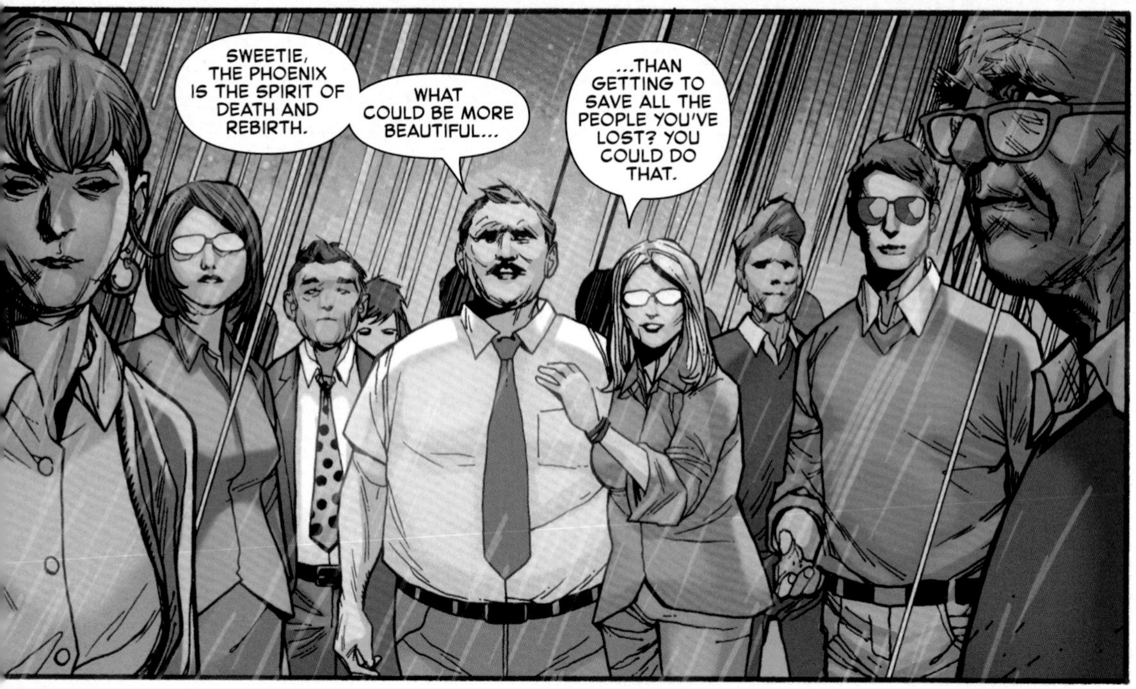
SWEETIE, THE PHOENIX IS THE SPIRIT OF DEATH AND REBIRTH.
WHAT COULD BE MORE BEAUTIFUL...
...THAN GETTING TO SAVE ALL THE PEOPLE YOU'VE LOST? YOU COULD DO THAT.

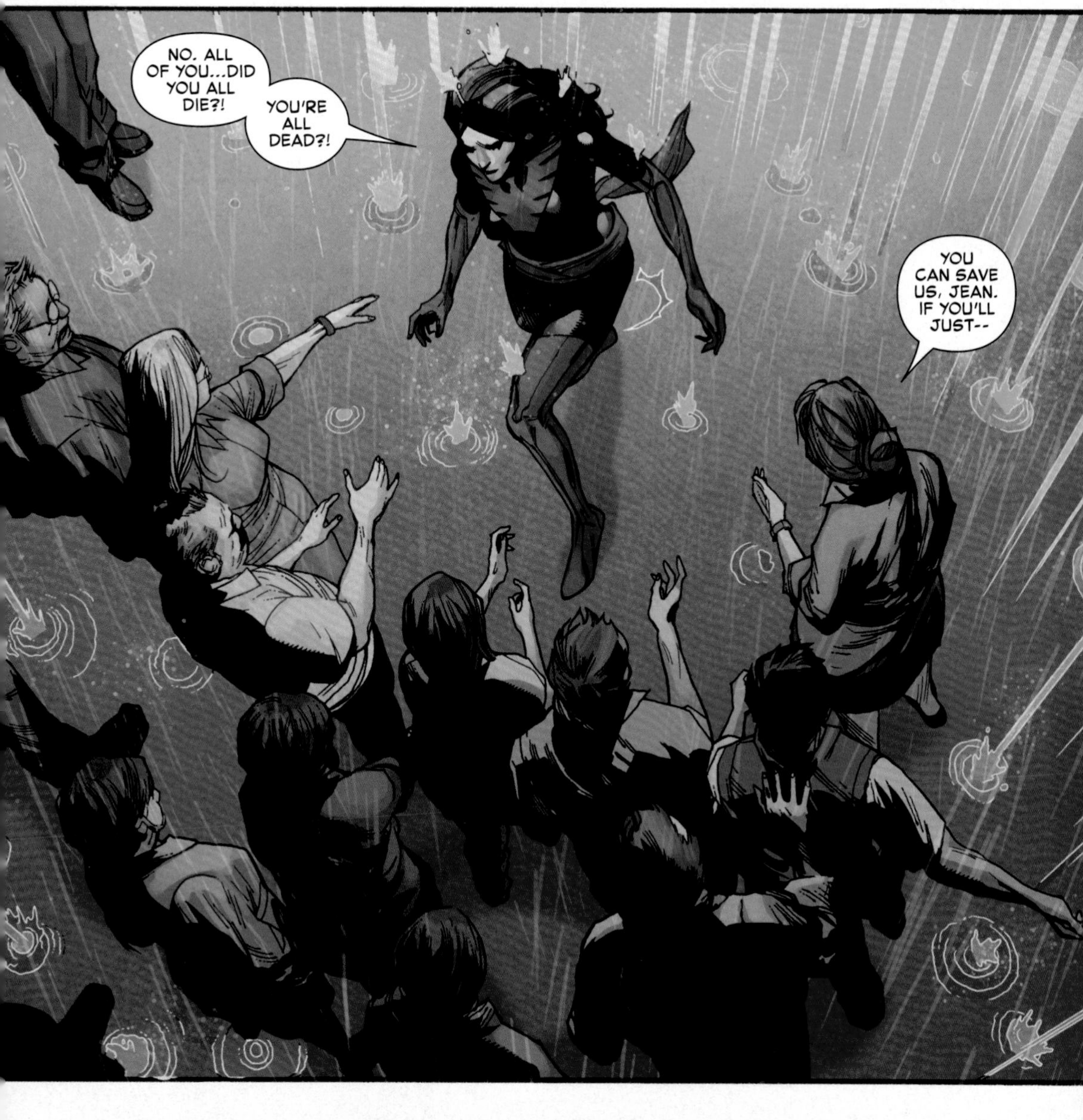
NO. ALL OF YOU...DID YOU ALL DIE?!
YOU'RE ALL DEAD?!
YOU CAN SAVE US, JEAN. IF YOU'LL JUST--

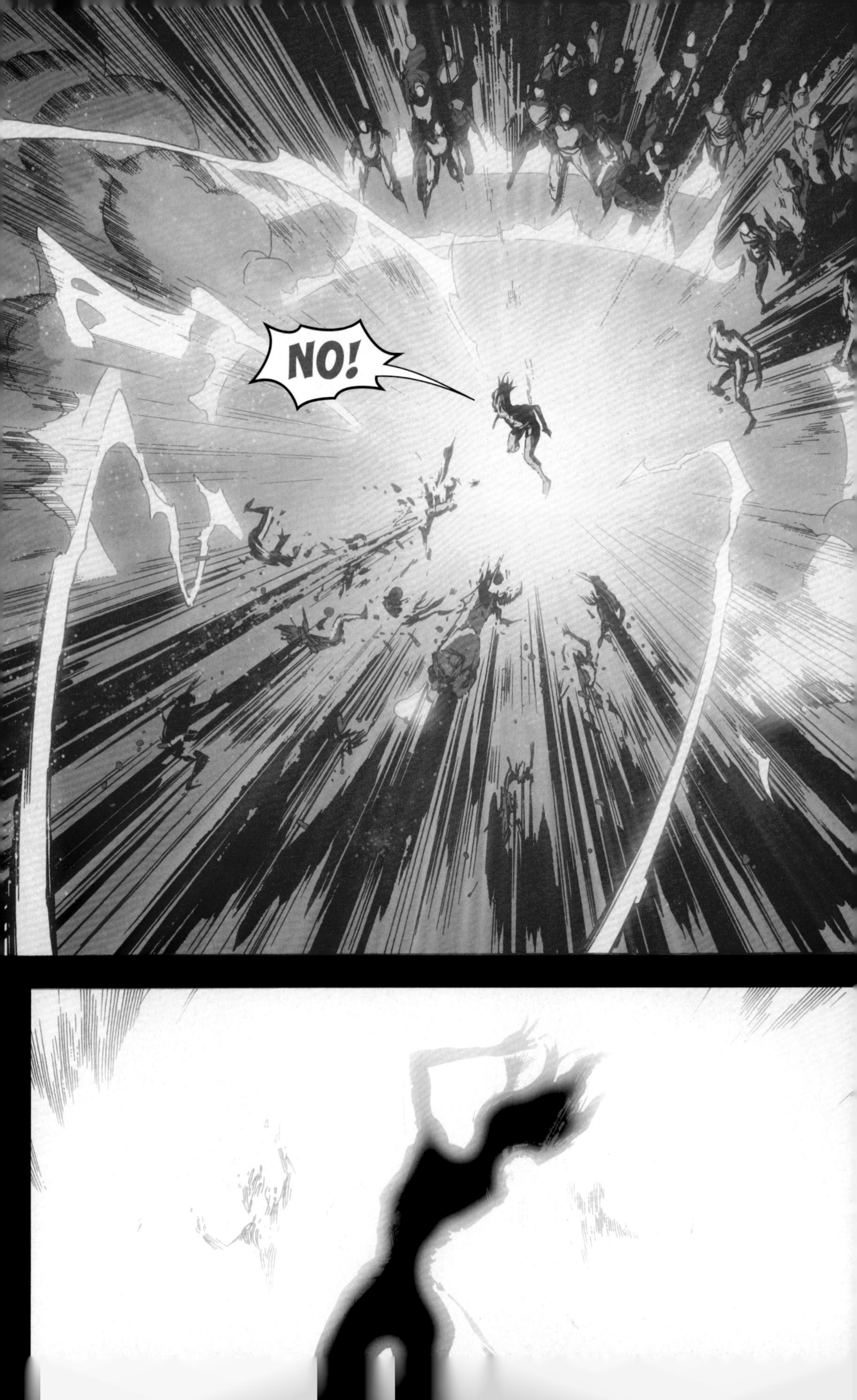
NO!

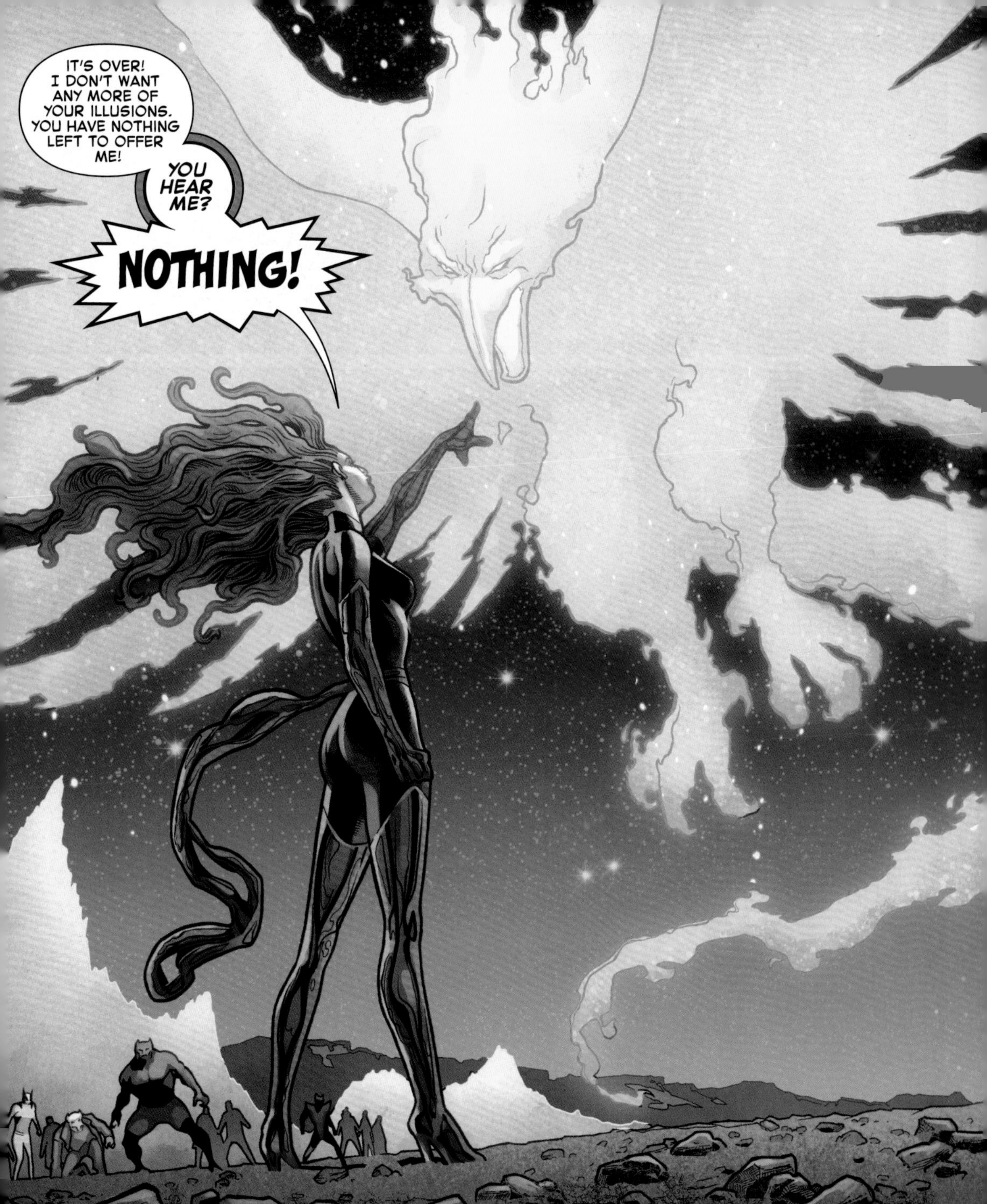
IT'S OVER! I DON'T WANT ANY MORE OF YOUR ILLUSIONS. YOU HAVE NOTHING LEFT TO OFFER ME!
YOU HEAR ME?
NOTHING!

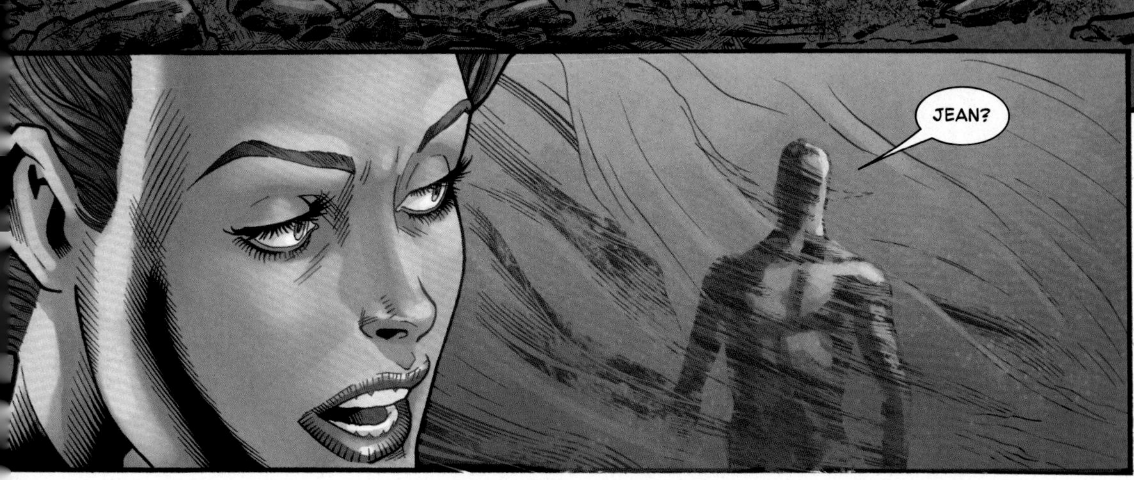
JEAN?

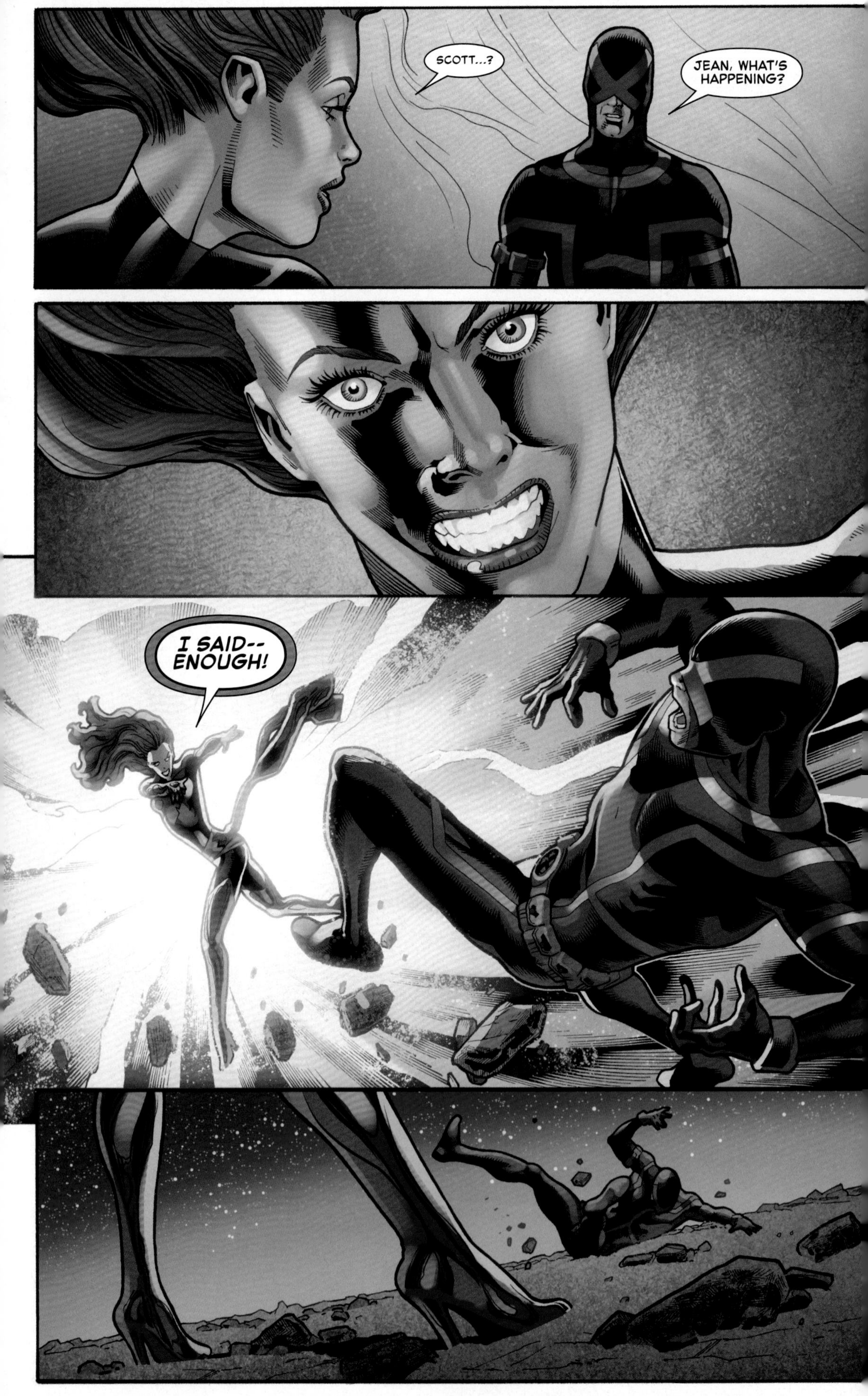
SCOTT...?
JEAN, WHAT'S HAPPENING?
I SAID-- ENOUGH!

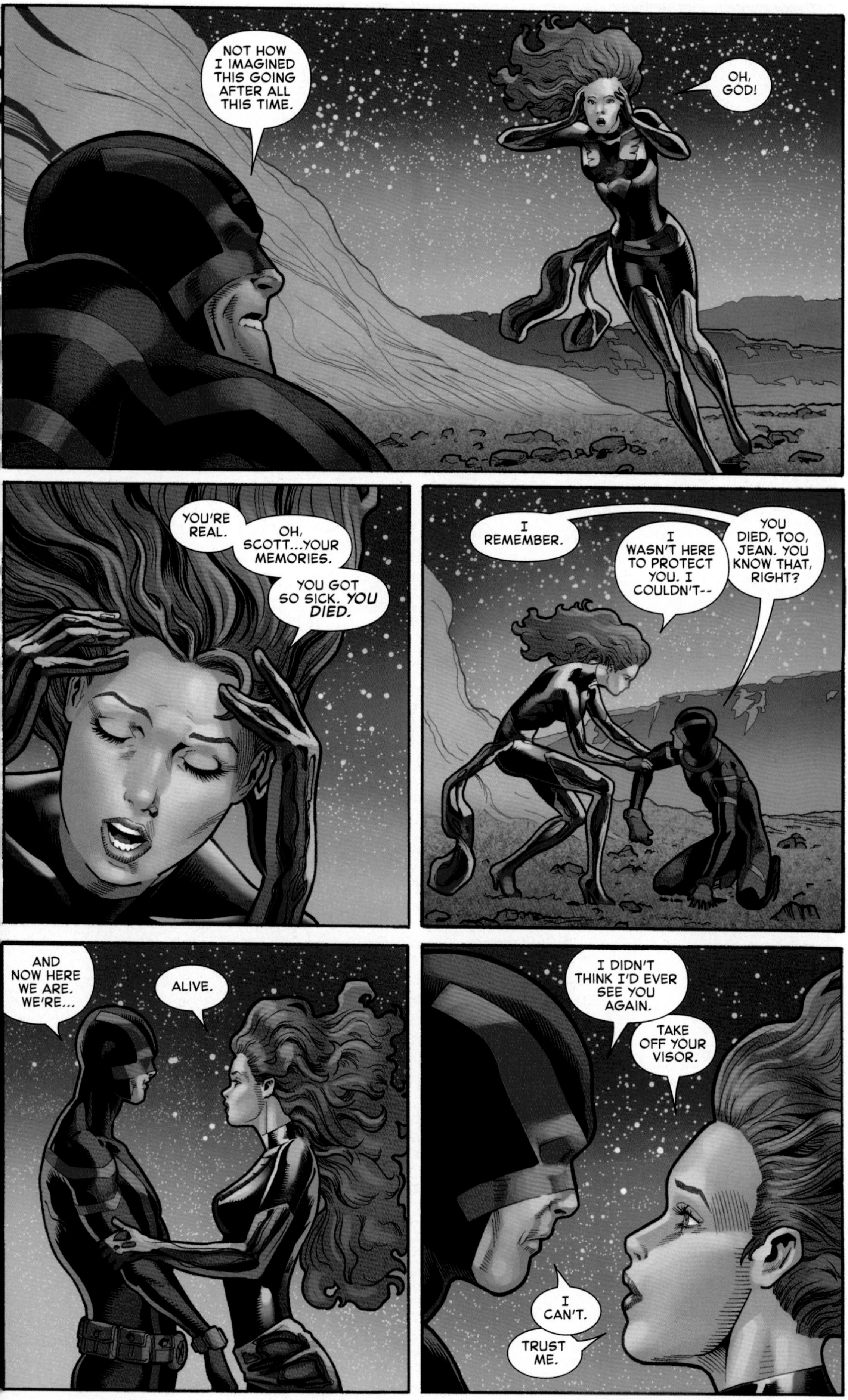
NOT HOW I IMAGINED THIS GOING AFTER ALL THIS TIME.
OH, GOD!
YOU'RE REAL.
OH, SCOTT...YOUR MEMORIES.
YOU GOT SO SICK. YOU DIED.
I REMEMBER.
I WASN'T HERE TO PROTECT YOU. I COULDN'T--
YOU DIED, TOO, JEAN. YOU KNOW THAT, RIGHT?
AND NOW HERE WE ARE. WE'RE...
ALIVE.
I DIDN'T THINK I'D EVER SEE YOU AGAIN.
TAKE OFF YOUR VISOR.
I CAN'T.
TRUST ME.

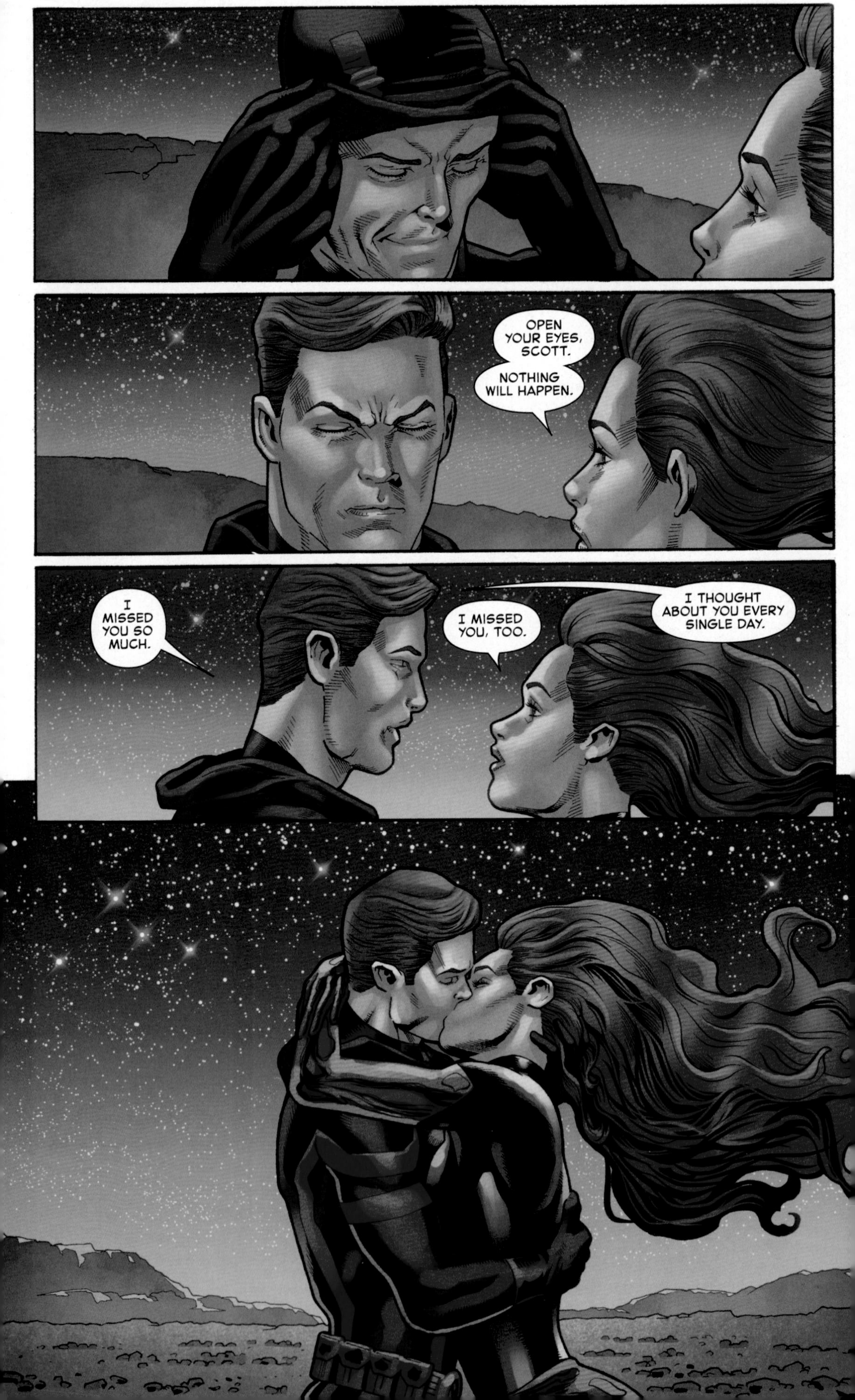
OPEN YOUR EYES, SCOTT.
NOTHING WILL HAPPEN.
I MISSED YOU SO MUCH.
I MISSED YOU, TOO.
I THOUGHT ABOUT YOU EVERY SINGLE DAY.

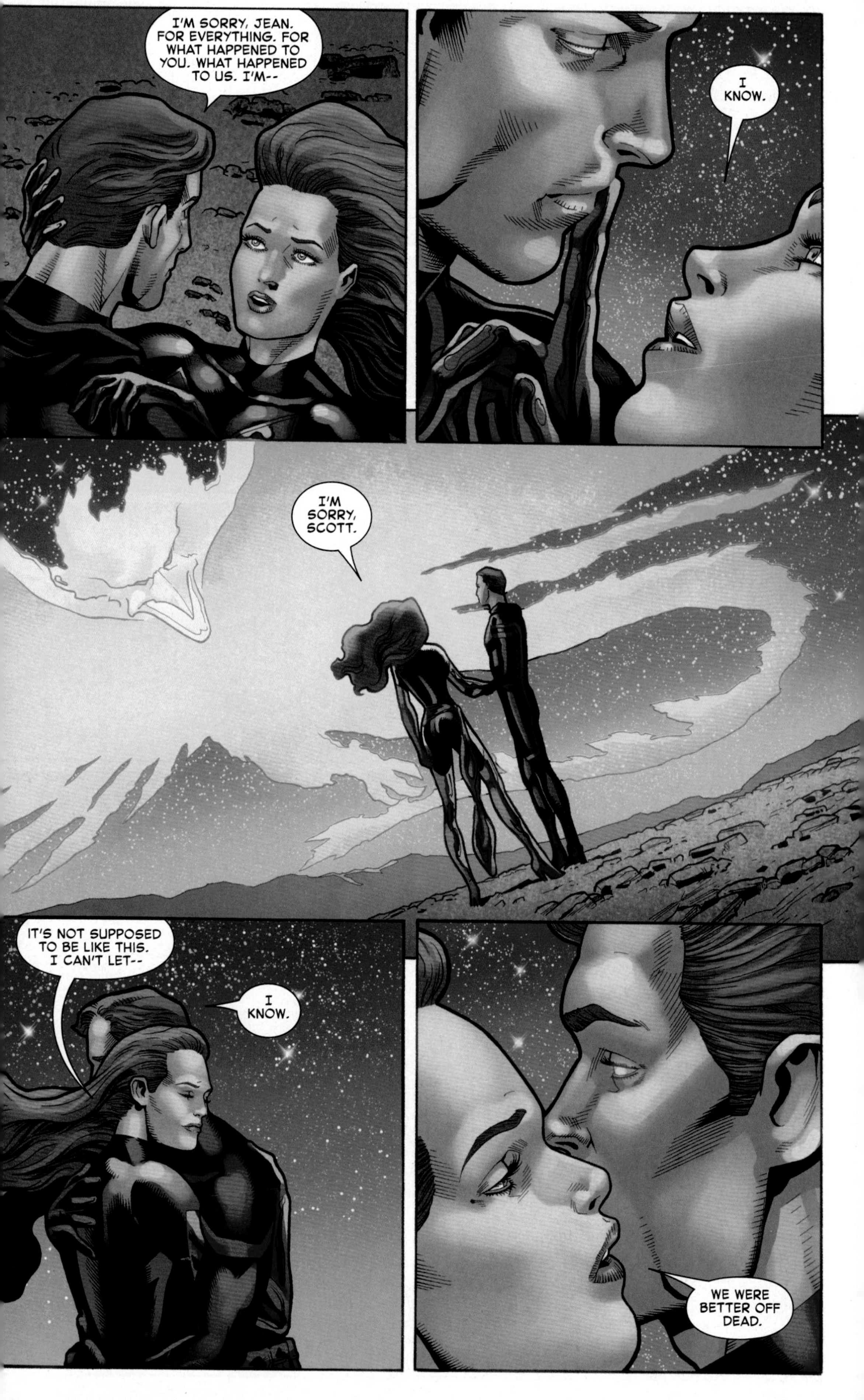
I'M SORRY, JEAN. FOR EVERYTHING. FOR WHAT HAPPENED TO YOU. WHAT HAPPENED TO US. I'M--
I KNOW.
I'M SORRY, SCOTT.
IT'S NOT SUPPOSED TO BE LIKE THIS. I CAN'T LET--
I KNOW.
WE WERE BETTER OFF DEAD.

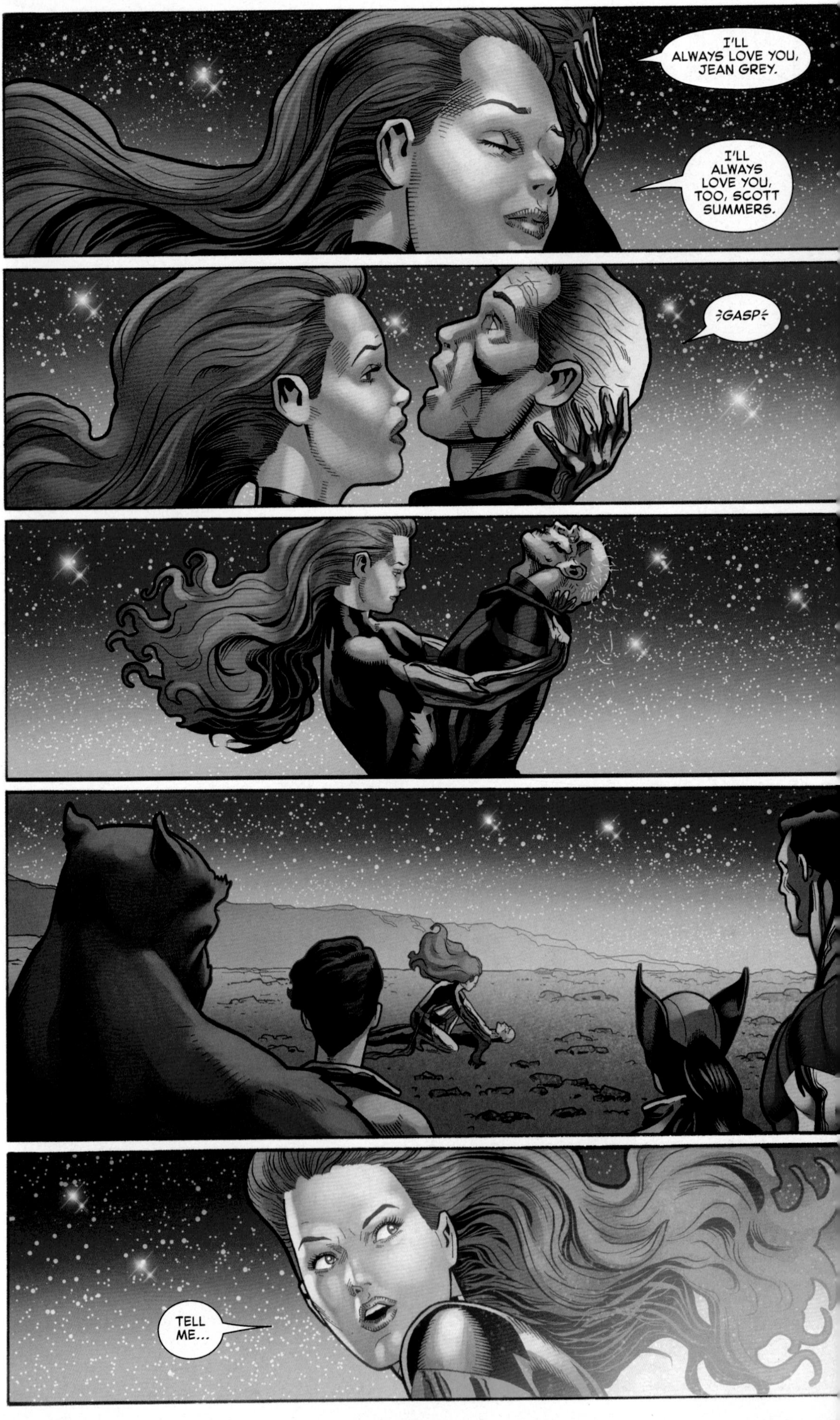
I'LL ALWAYS LOVE YOU, JEAN GREY.
I'LL ALWAYS LOVE YOU, TOO, SCOTT SUMMERS.
GASP
TELL ME...

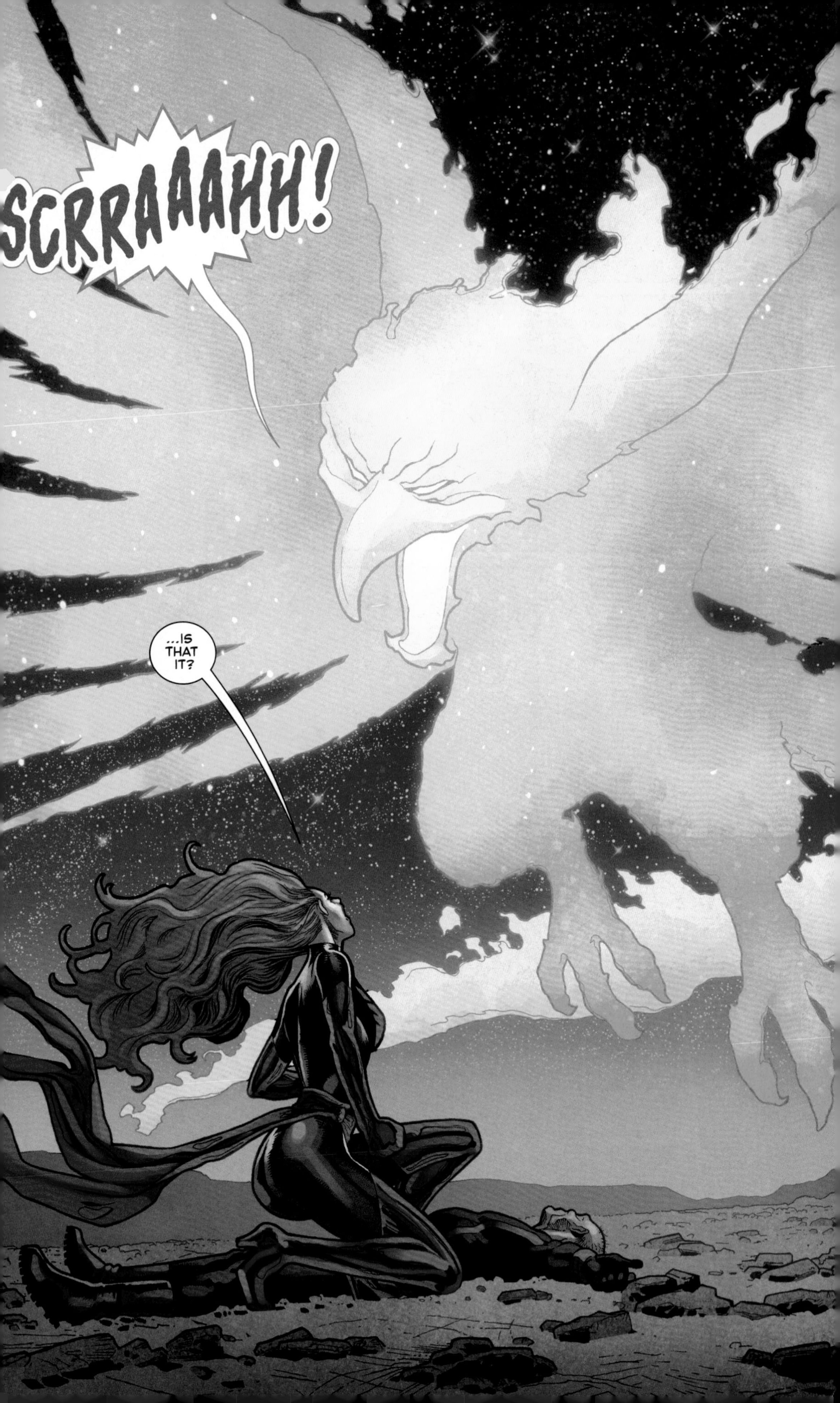
SCRRAAAHH!
...IS THAT IT?

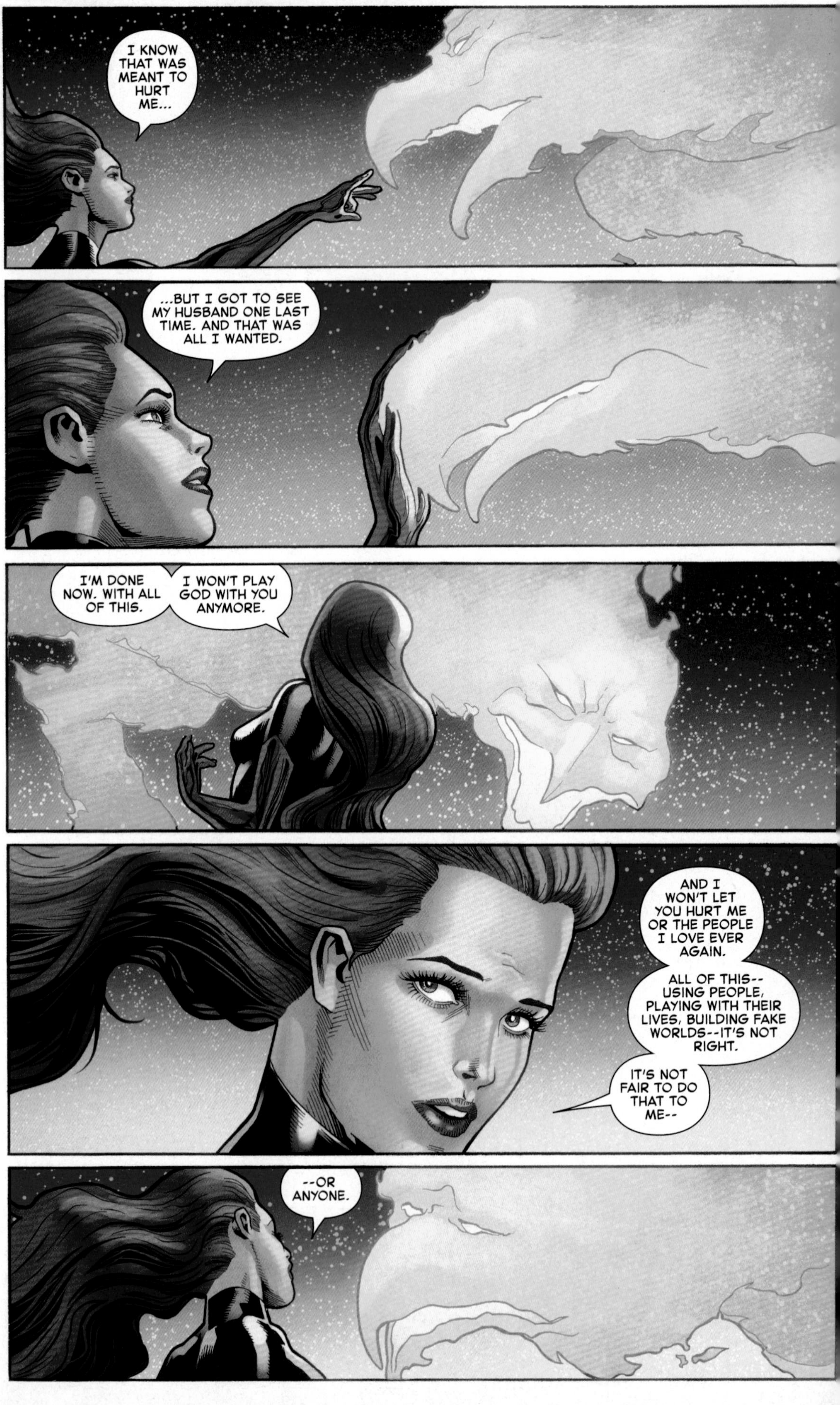
I KNOW THAT WAS MEANT TO HURT ME...
...BUT I GOT TO SEE MY HUSBAND ONE LAST TIME. AND THAT WAS ALL I WANTED.
I'M DONE NOW. WITH ALL OF THIS.
I WON'T PLAY GOD WITH YOU ANYMORE.
AND I WON'T LET YOU HURT ME OR THE PEOPLE I LOVE EVER AGAIN.
ALL OF THIS--USING PEOPLE, PLAYING WITH THEIR LIVES, BUILDING FAKE WORLDS--IT'S NOT RIGHT.
IT'S NOT FAIR TO DO THAT TO ME--
--OR ANYONE.

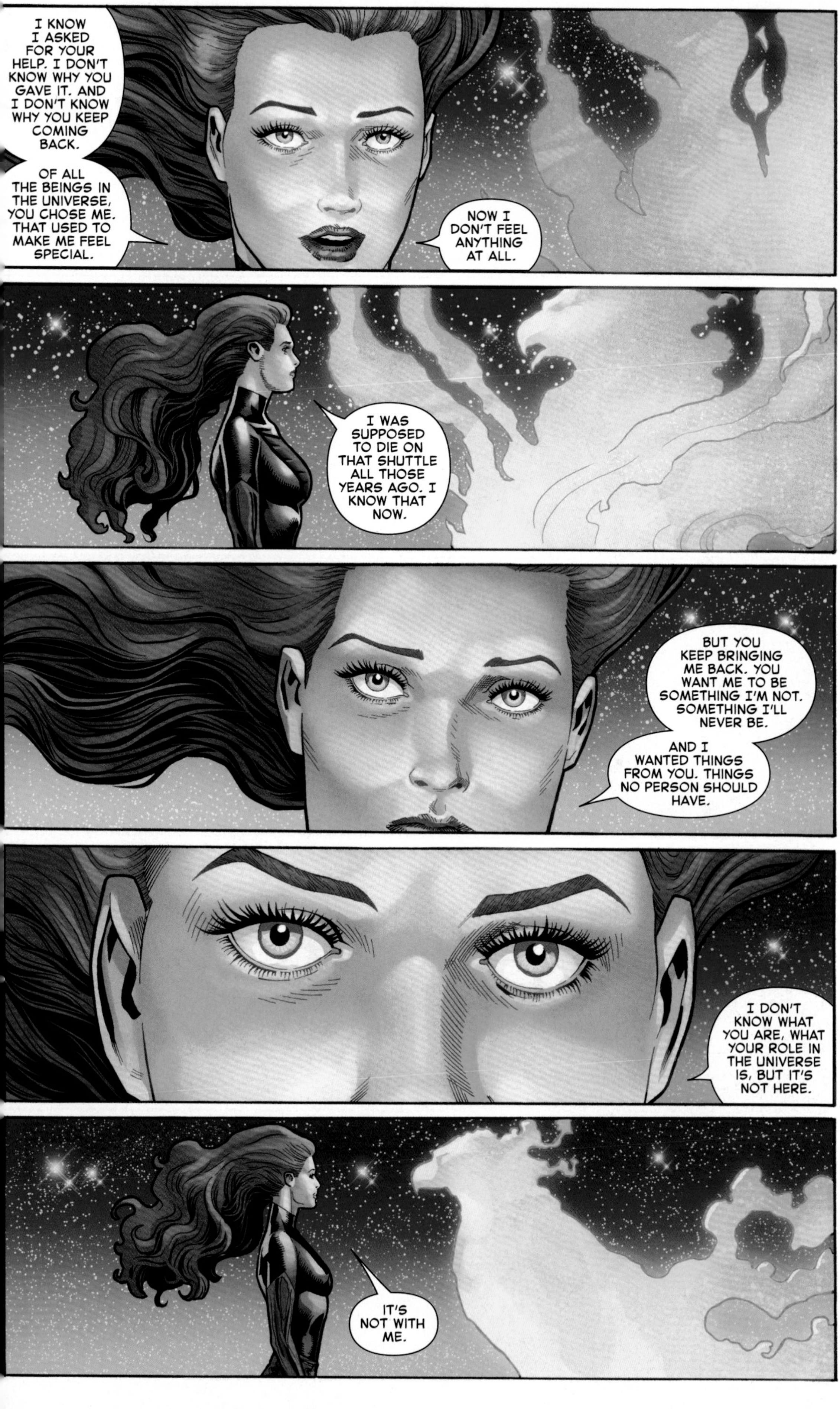

I KNOW I ASKED FOR YOUR HELP. I DON'T KNOW WHY YOU GAVE IT. AND I DON'T KNOW WHY YOU KEEP COMING BACK.
OF ALL THE BEINGS IN THE UNIVERSE, YOU CHOSE ME. THAT USED TO MAKE ME FEEL SPECIAL.
NOW I DON'T FEEL ANYTHING AT ALL.
I WAS SUPPOSED TO DIE ON THAT SHUTTLE ALL THOSE YEARS AGO. I KNOW THAT NOW.
BUT YOU KEEP BRINGING ME BACK. YOU WANT ME TO BE SOMETHING I'M NOT. SOMETHING I'LL NEVER BE.
AND I WANTED THINGS FROM YOU. THINGS NO PERSON SHOULD HAVE.
I DON'T KNOW WHAT YOU ARE, WHAT YOUR ROLE IN THE UNIVERSE IS, BUT IT'S NOT HERE.
IT'S NOT WITH ME.

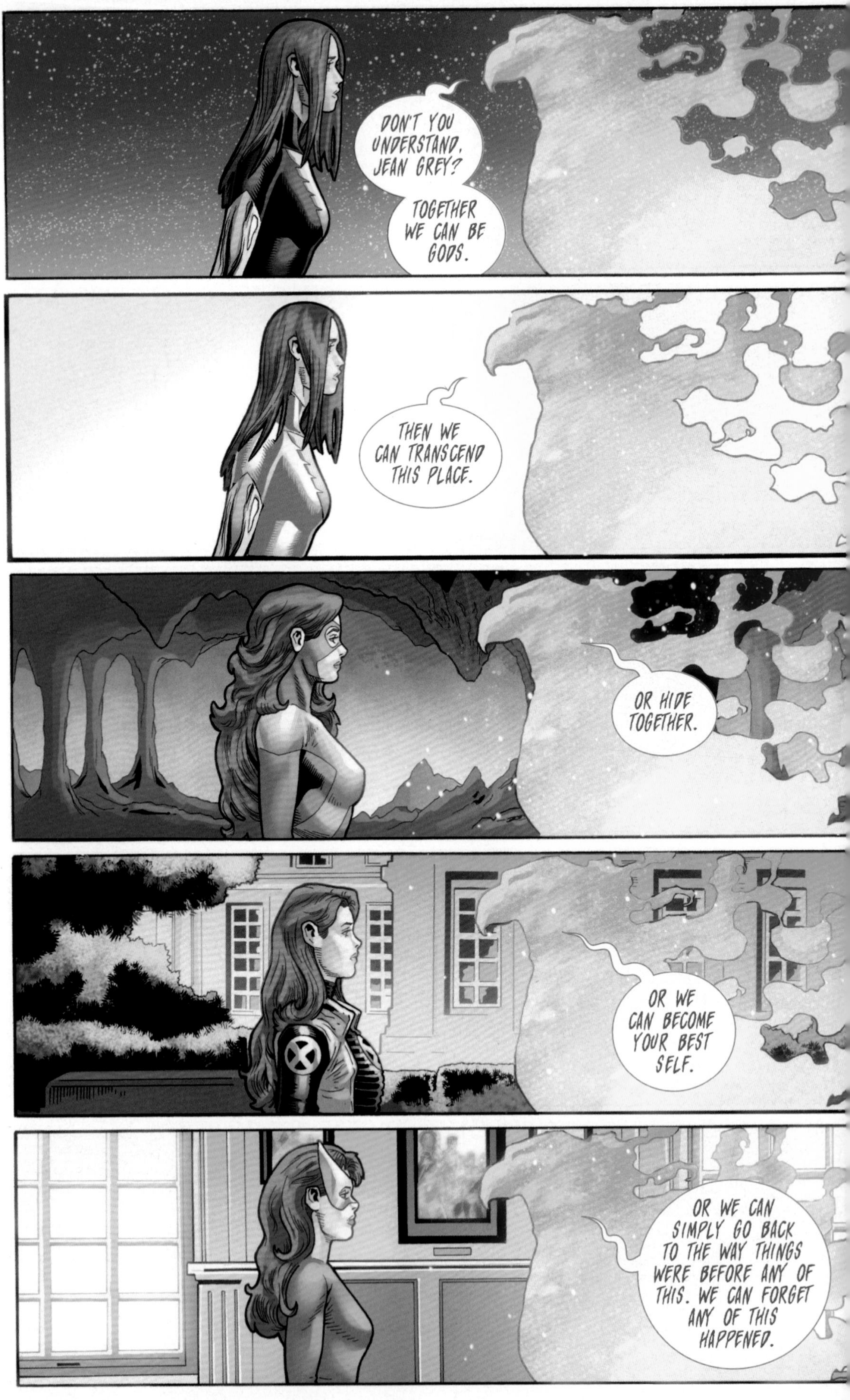
DON'T YOU UNDERSTAND, JEAN GREY?
TOGETHER WE CAN BE GODS.
THEN WE CAN TRANSCEND THIS PLACE.
OR HIDE TOGETHER.
OR WE CAN BECOME YOUR BEST SELF.
OR WE CAN SIMPLY GO BACK TO THE WAY THINGS WERE BEFORE ANY OF THIS. WE CAN FORGET ANY OF THIS HAPPENED.

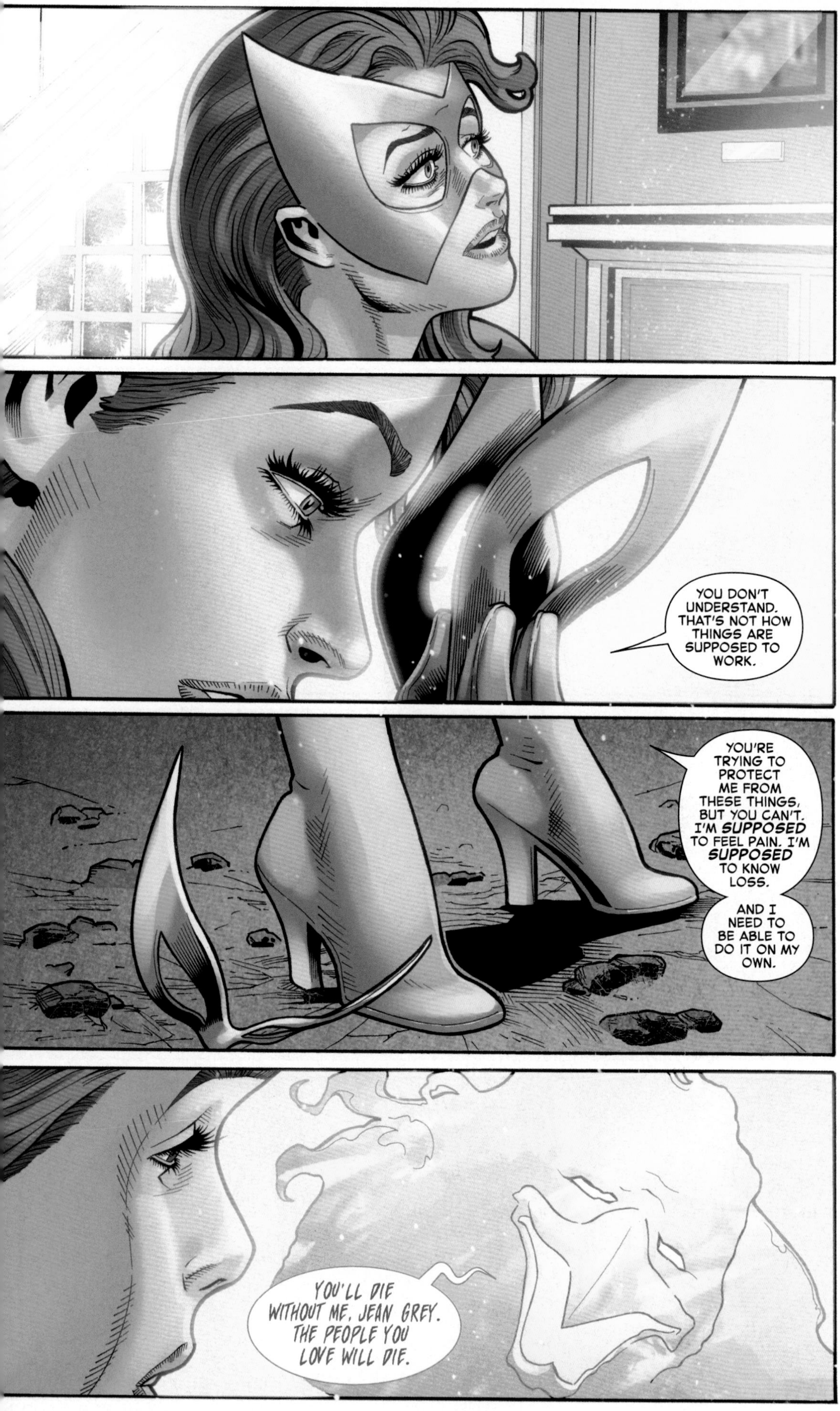
YOU DON'T UNDERSTAND. THAT'S NOT HOW THINGS ARE SUPPOSED TO WORK.
YOU'RE TRYING TO PROTECT ME FROM THESE THINGS, BUT YOU CAN'T. I'M SUPPOSED TO FEEL PAIN. I'M SUPPOSED TO KNOW LOSS.
AND I NEED TO BE ABLE TO DO IT ON MY OWN.
YOU'LL DIE WITHOUT ME, JEAN GREY. THE PEOPLE YOU LOVE WILL DIE.

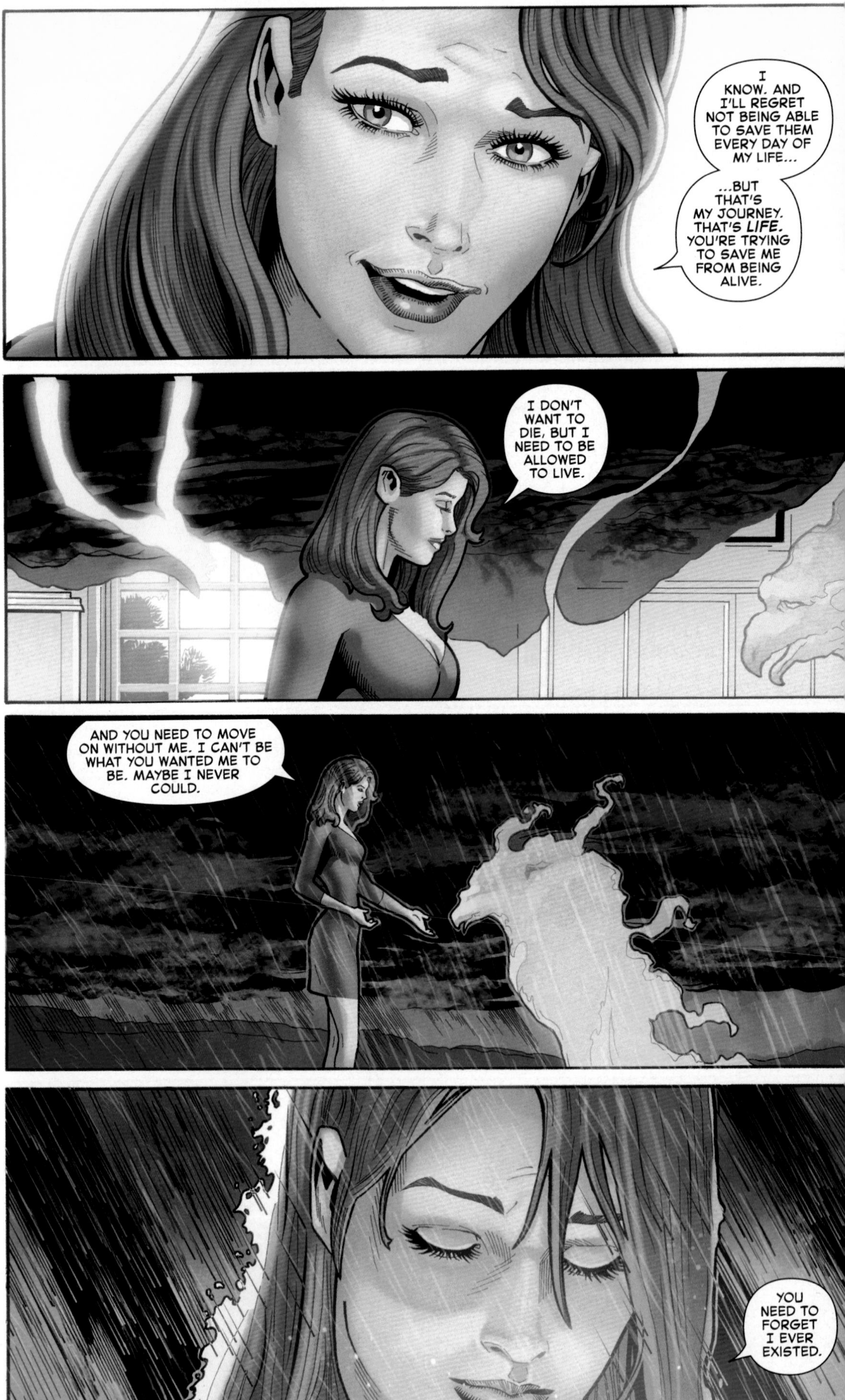
I KNOW. AND I'LL REGRET NOT BEING ABLE TO SAVE THEM EVERY DAY OF MY LIFE...
...BUT THAT'S MY JOURNEY. THAT'S *LIFE.* YOU'RE TRYING TO SAVE ME FROM BEING ALIVE.
I DON'T WANT TO DIE, BUT I NEED TO BE ALLOWED TO LIVE.
AND YOU NEED TO MOVE ON WITHOUT ME. I CAN'T BE WHAT YOU WANTED ME TO BE. MAYBE I NEVER COULD.
YOU NEED TO FORGET I EVER EXISTED.

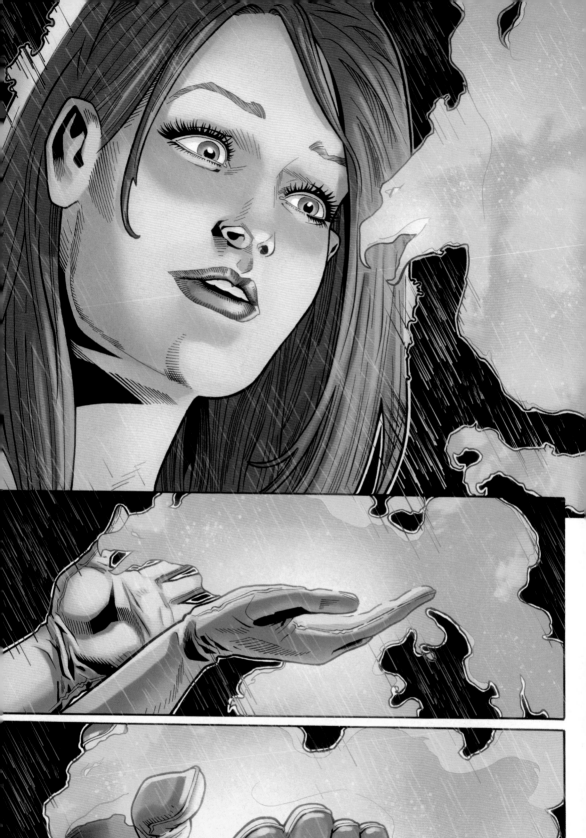

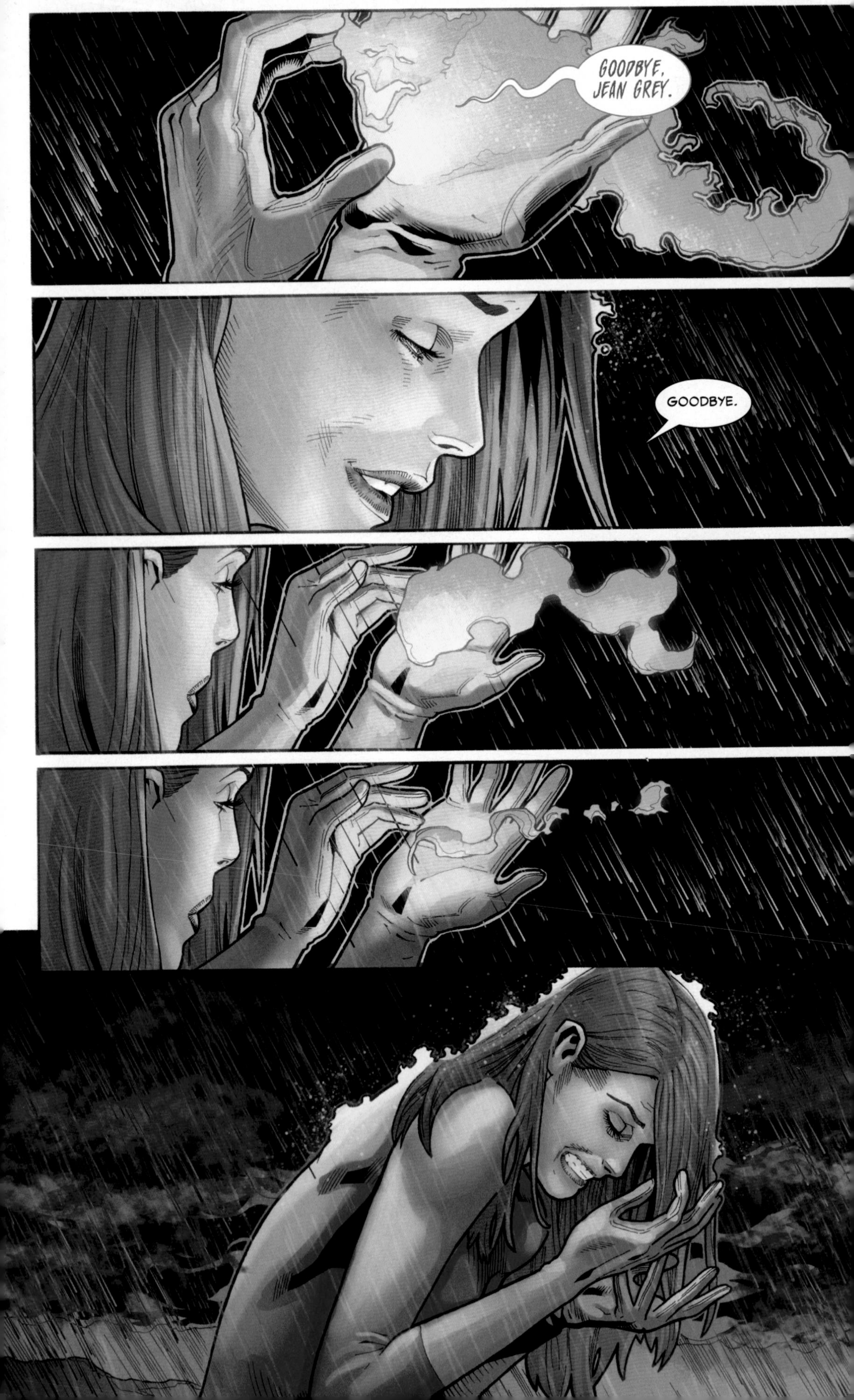
GOODBYE, JEAN GREY.
GOODBYE.

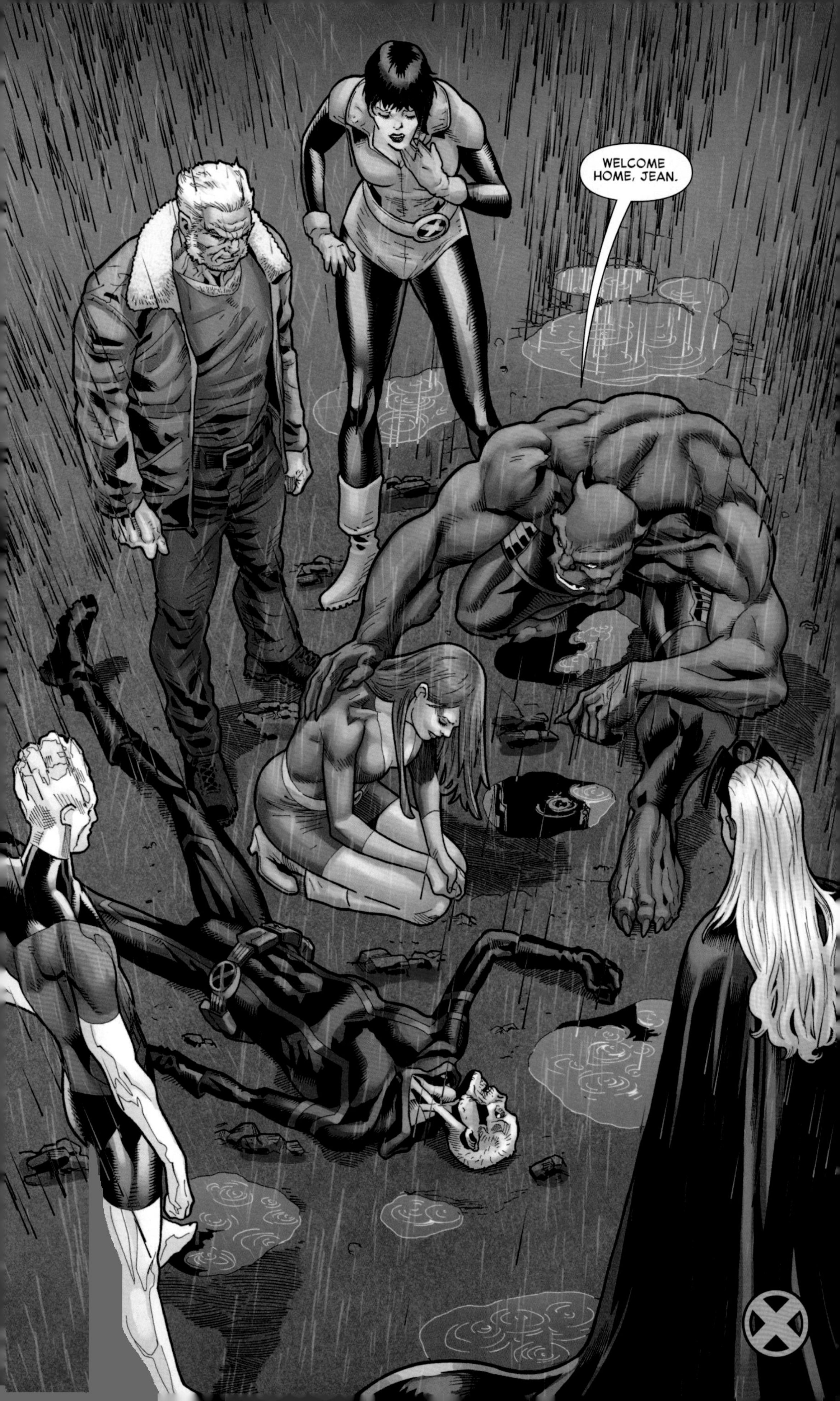
WELCOME HOME, JEAN.

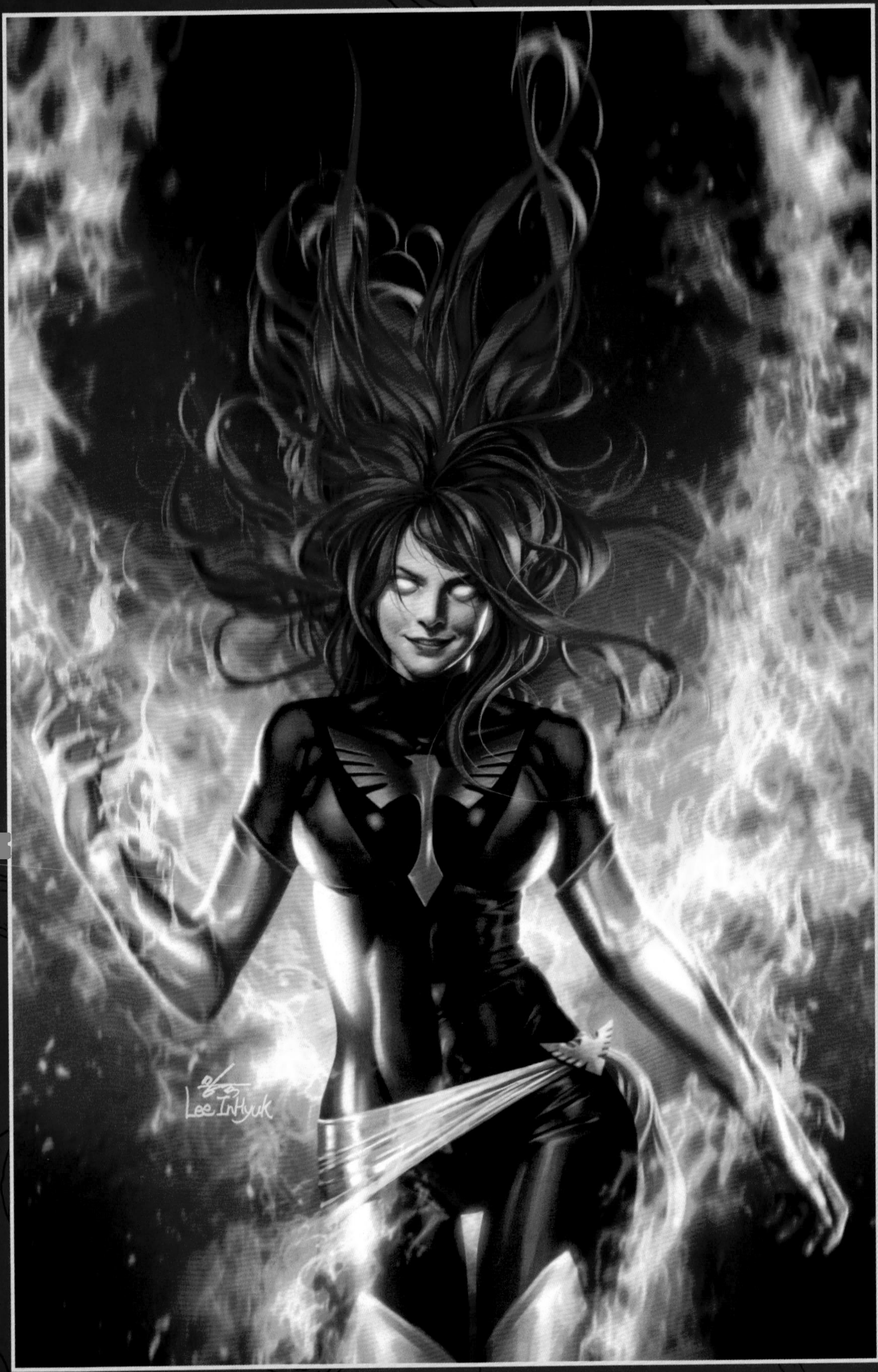
Lee InHyuk

#1 VARIANT BY *IN-HYUK LEE*

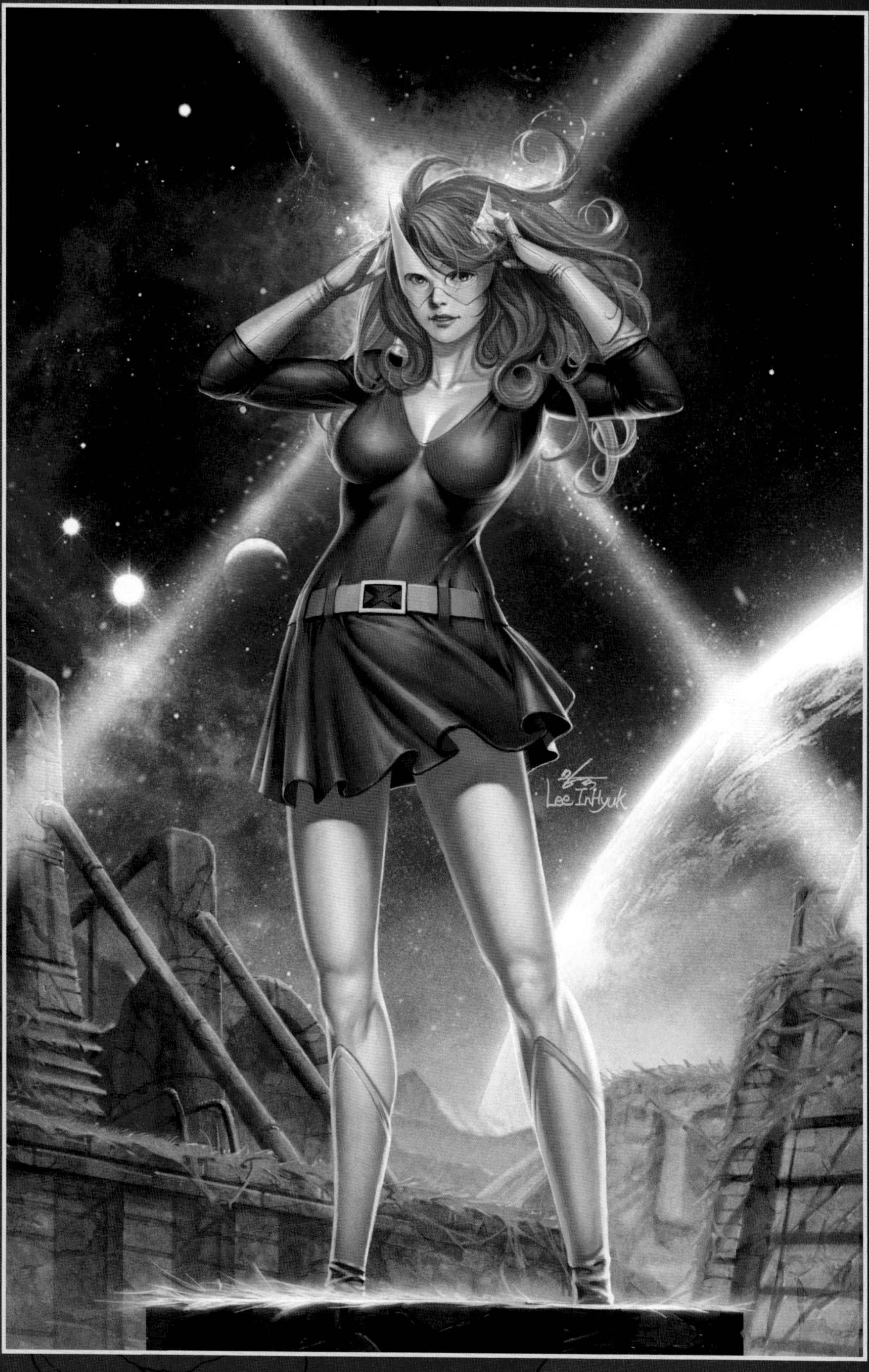
Lee InHyuk

#2 VARIANT BY *IN-HYUK LEE*

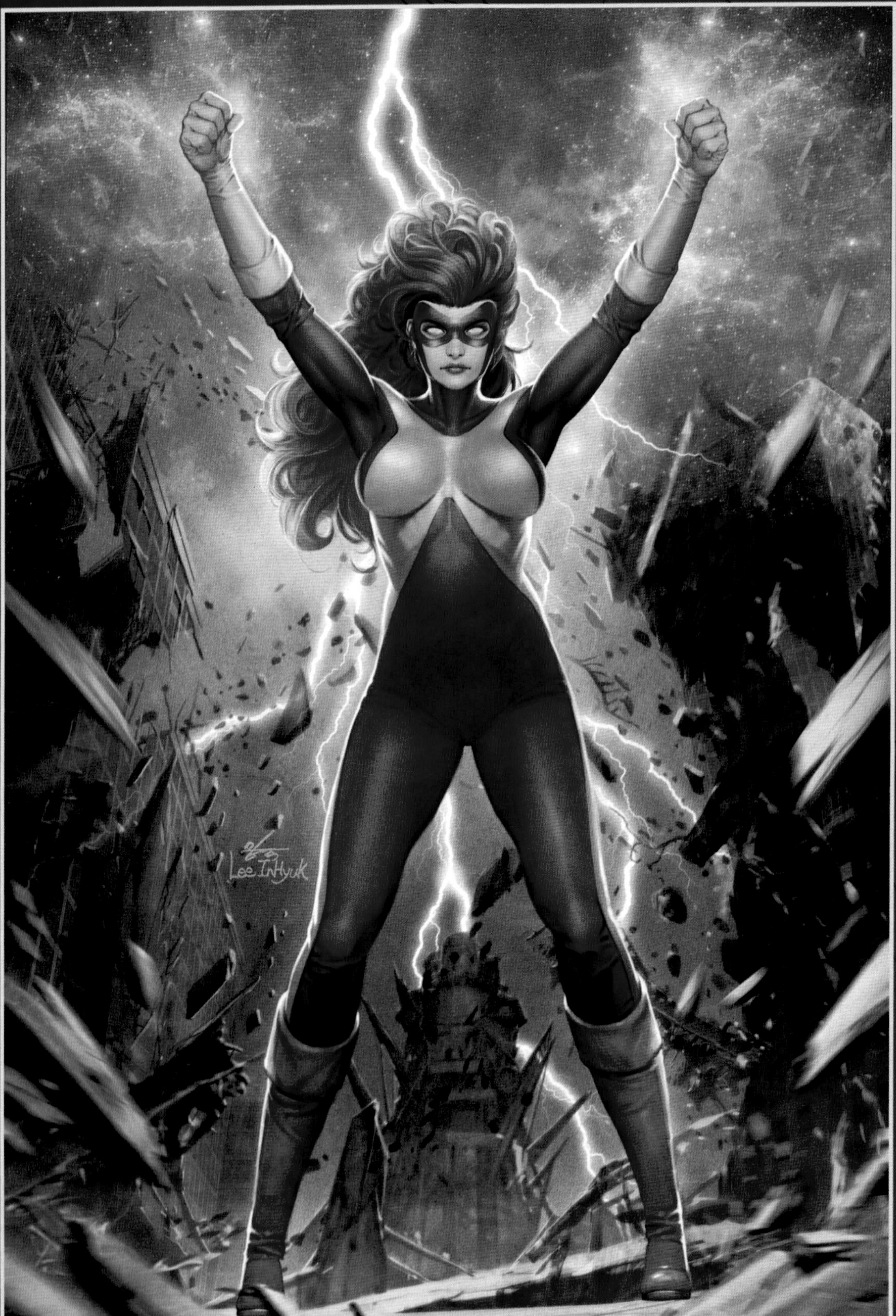
Lee InHyuk

#3 VARIANT BY ***IN-HYUK LEE***

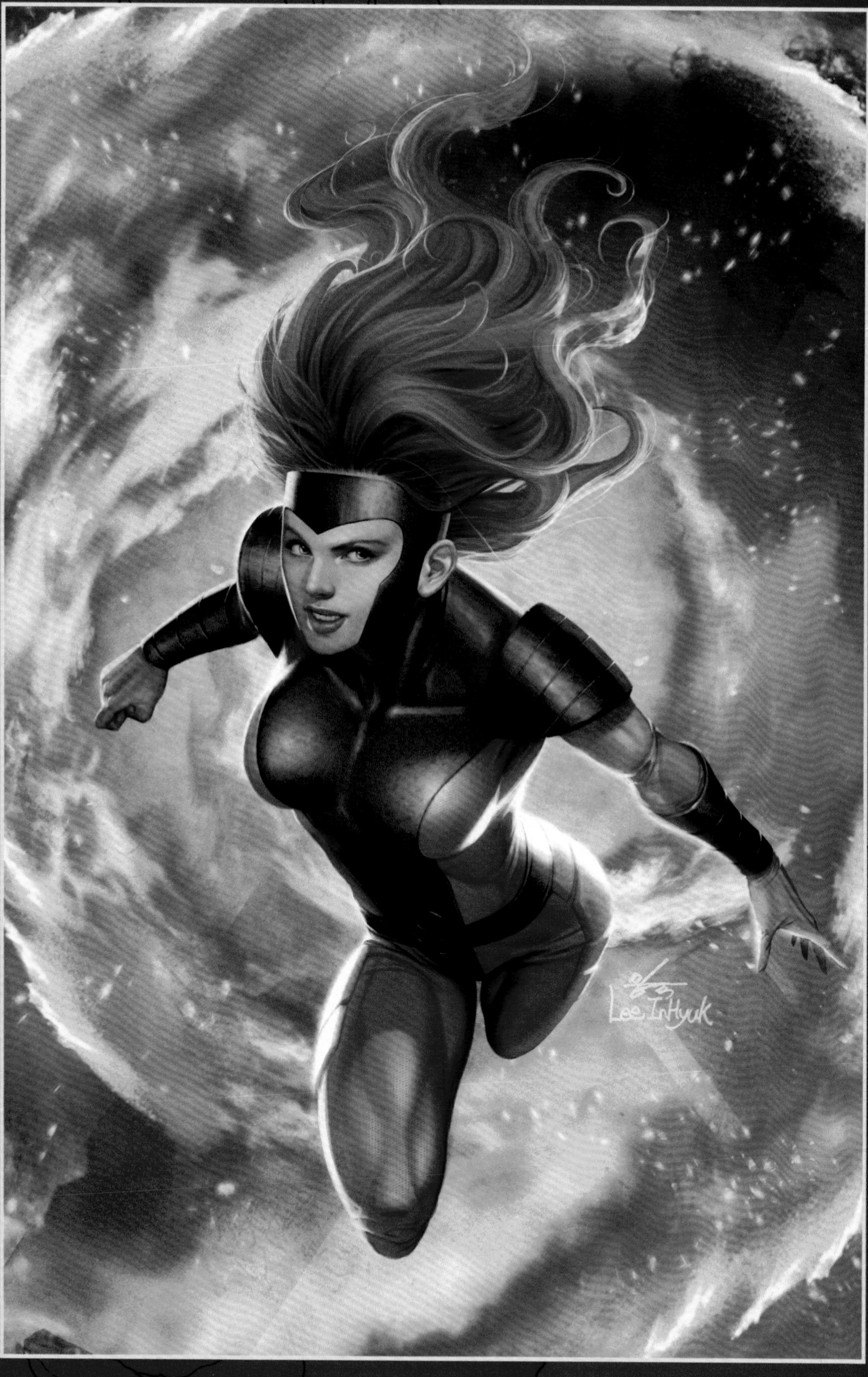
Lee InHyuk

#4 VARIANT BY *IN-HYUK LEE*

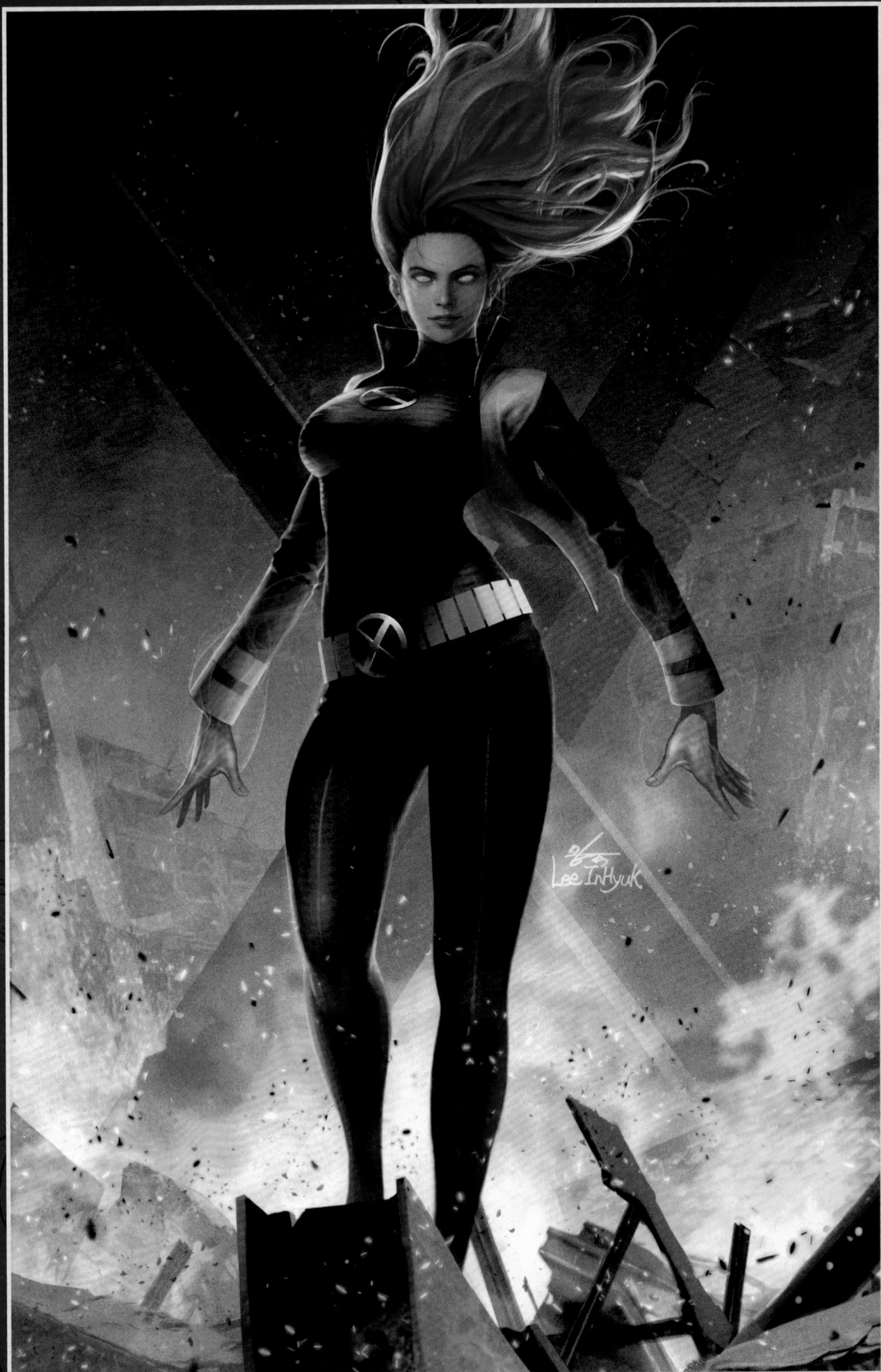
Lee InHyuk

#5 VARIANT BY *IN-HYUK LEE*

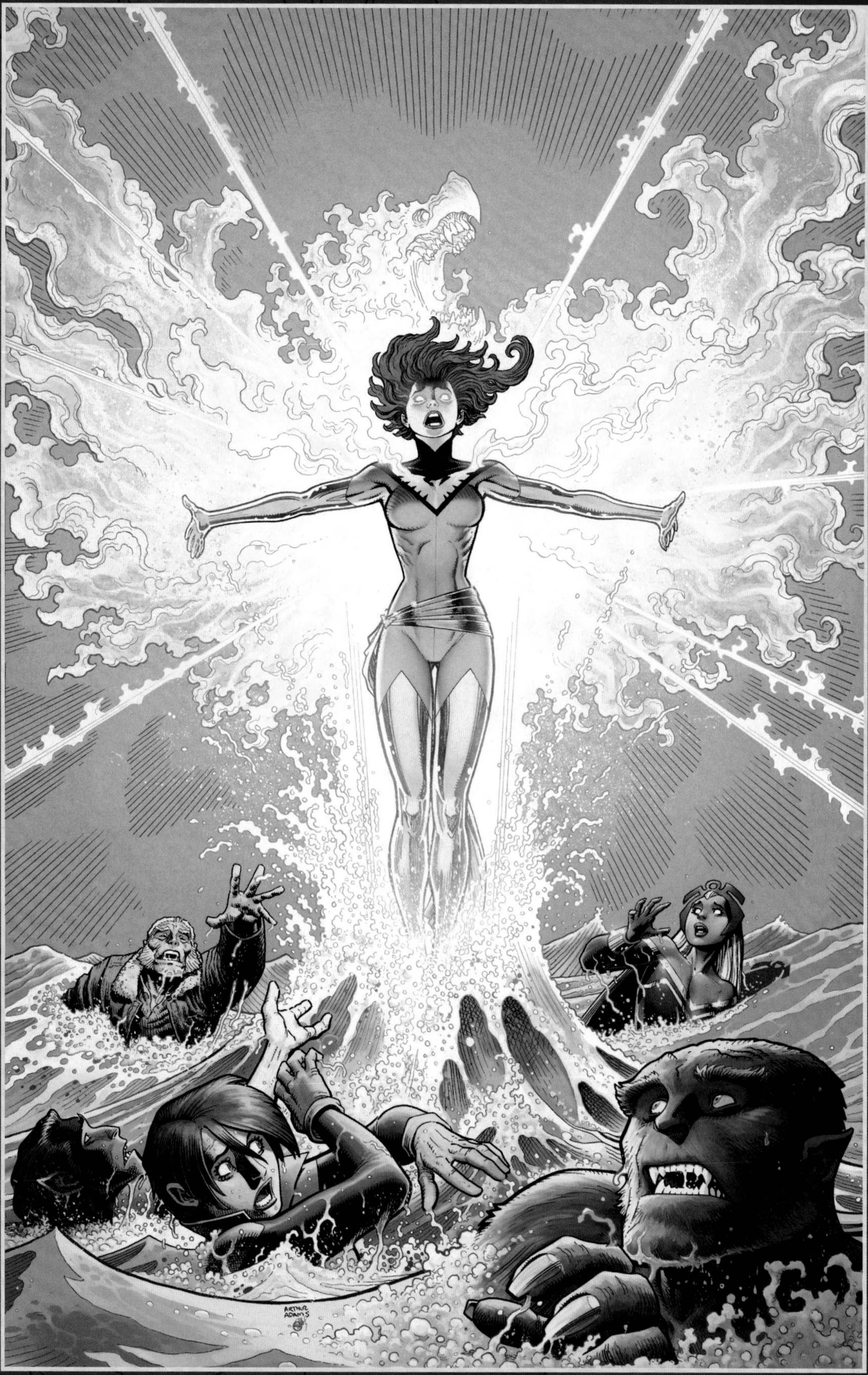
ARTHUR ADAMS

#1 VARIANT BY **ARTHUR ADAMS** & **PETER STEIGERWALD**

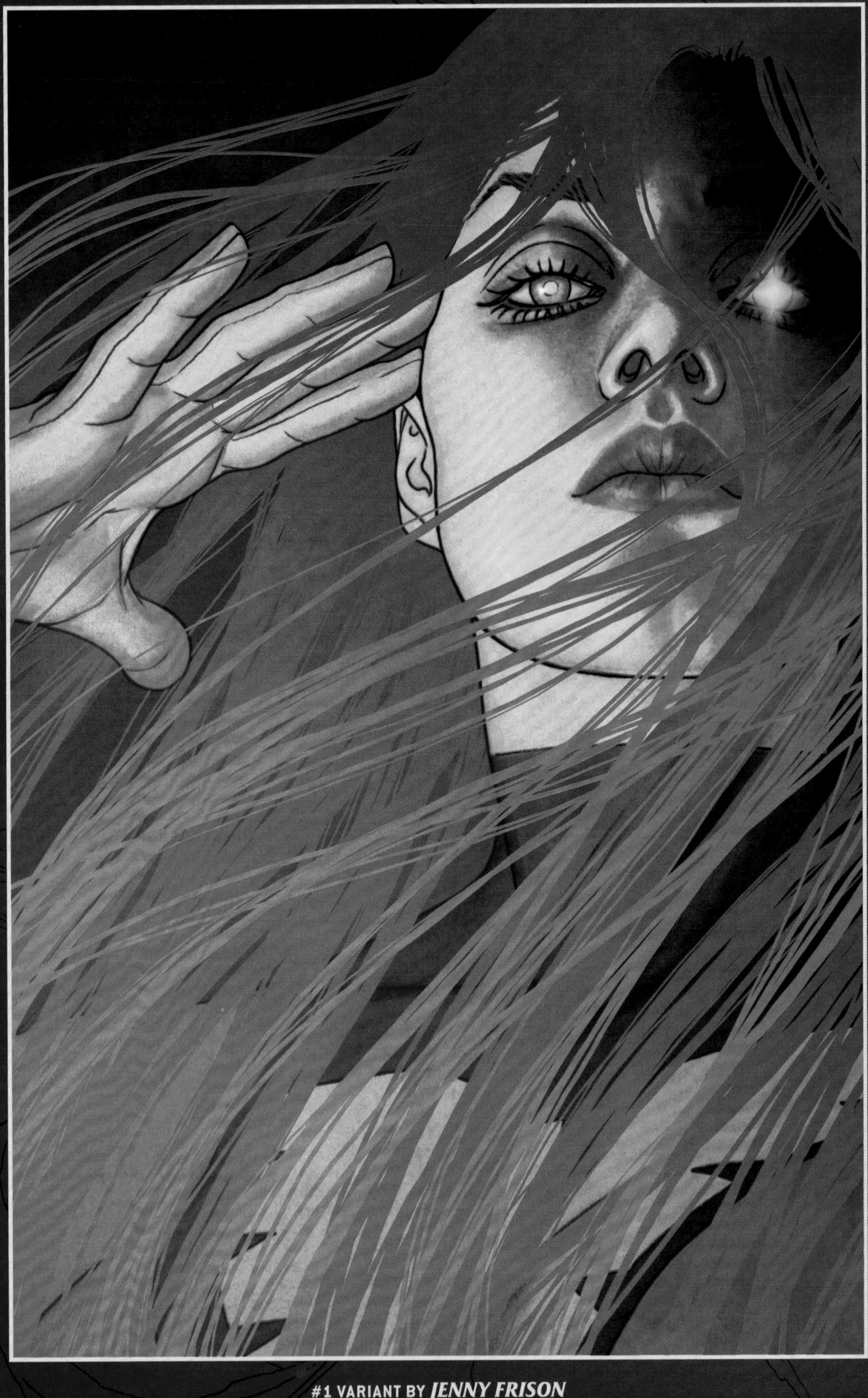

#1 VARIANT BY *JENNY FRISON*

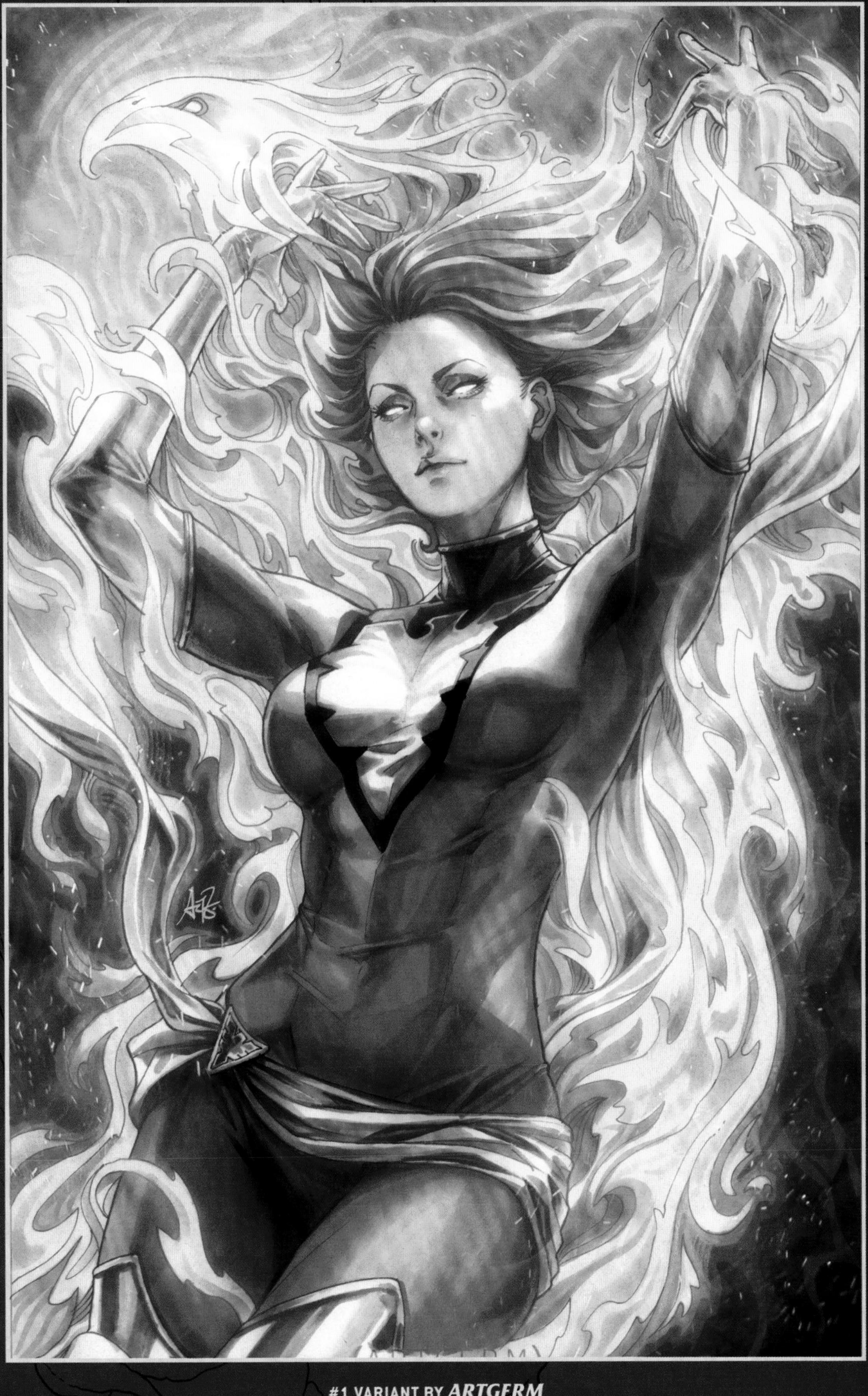

#1 VARIANT BY **ARTGERM**

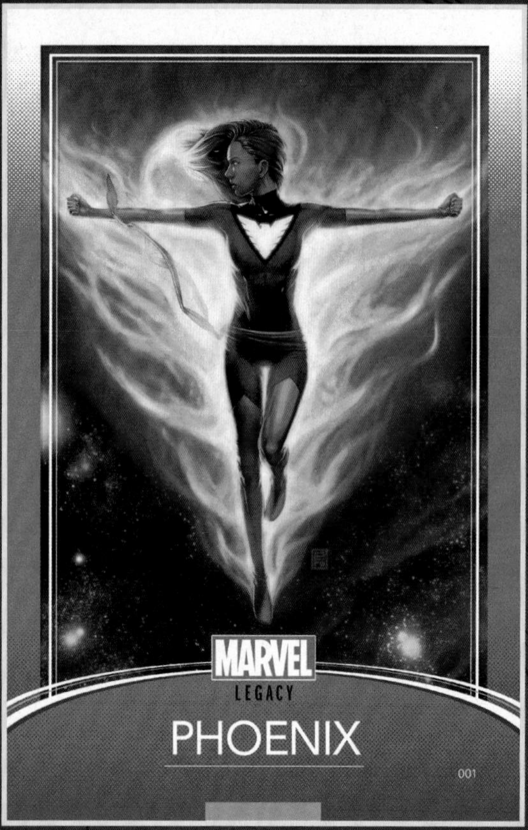
MARVEL
LEGACY
PHOENIX
001

#1 TRADING CARD VARIANT
BY *JOHN TYLER CHRISTOPHER*

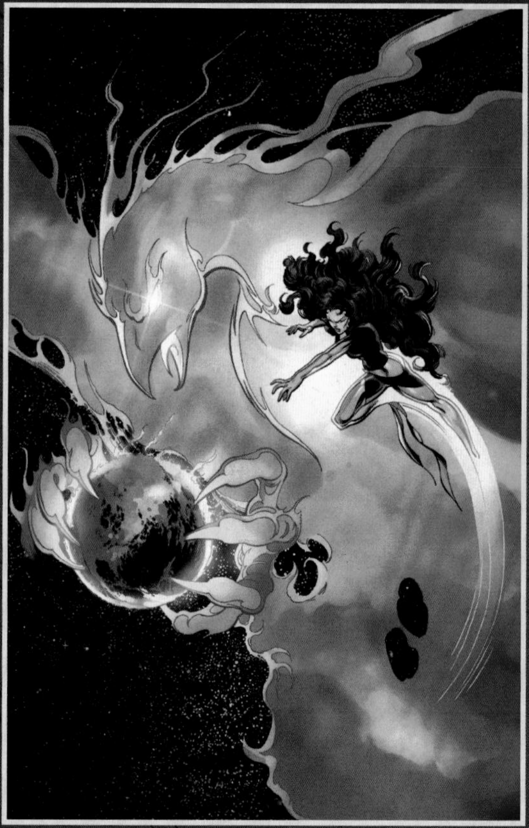

#1 REMASTERED VARIANT
BY *JOHN BYRNE* & *FEDERICO BLEE*
WITH *MICHAEL KELLEHER*

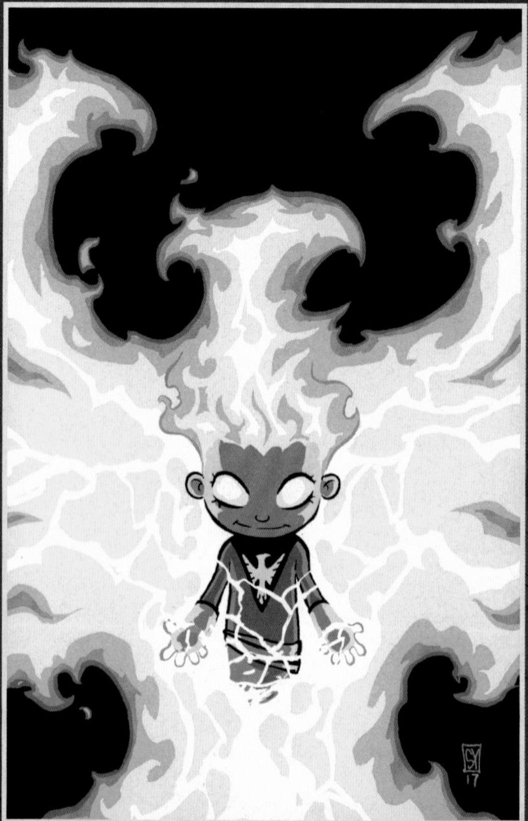

#1 VARIANT
BY *SKOTTIE YOUNG*

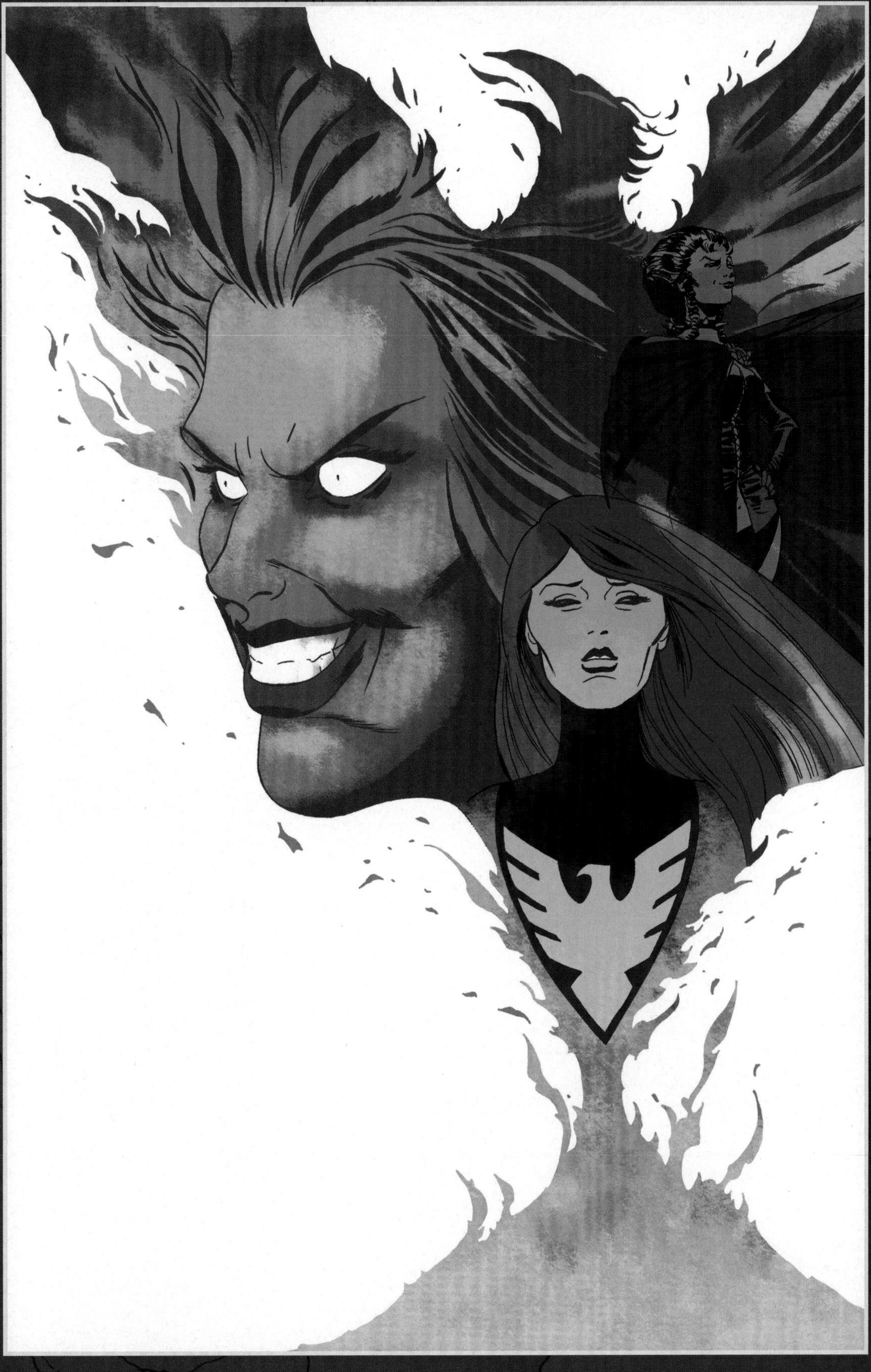

#2 VARIANT BY *MARCOS MARTIN*

PHOENIX RESURRECTION: THE RETURN OF JEAN GREY #2-5 &
JEAN GREY #11 CONNECTING VARIANTS BY *VICTOR HUGO*

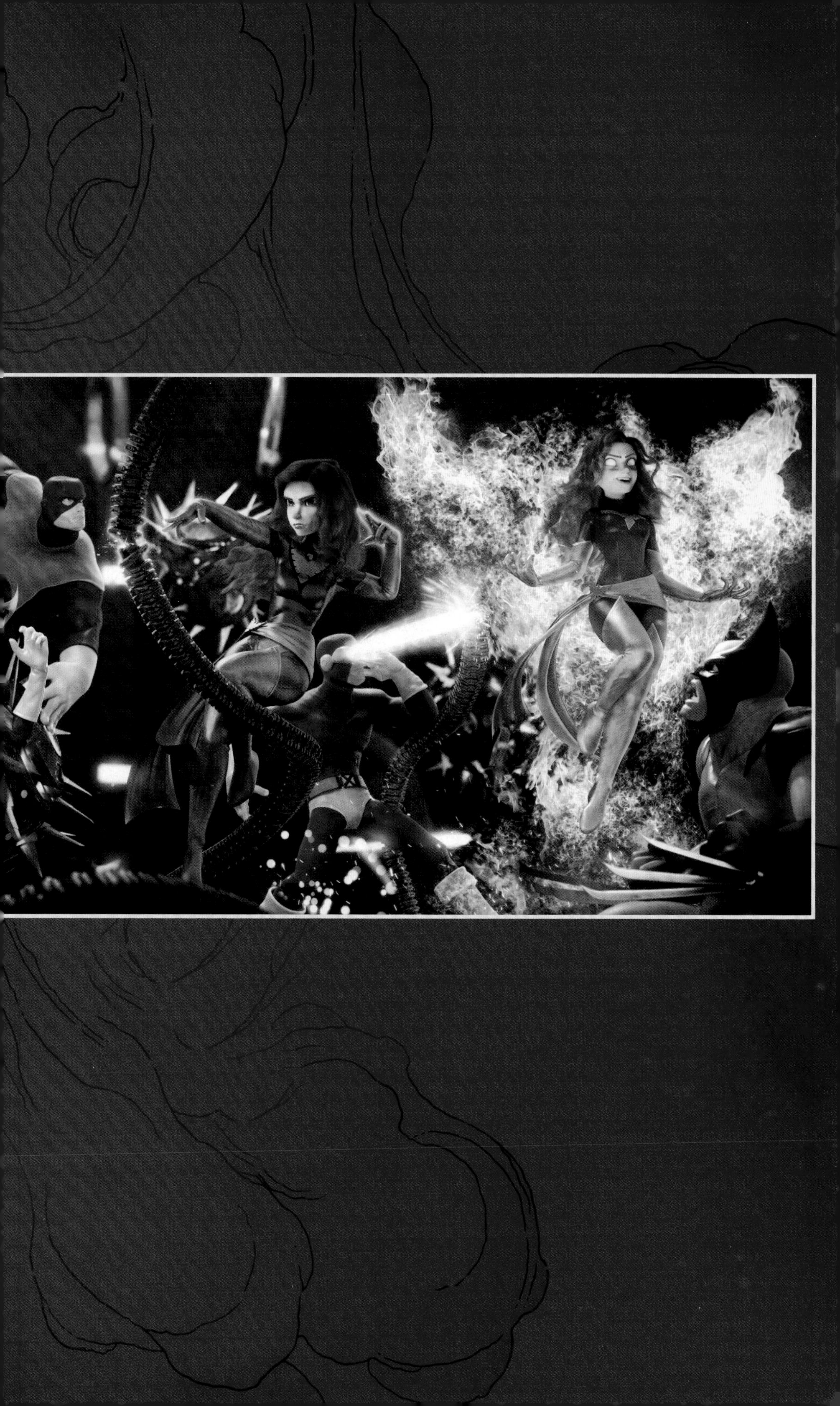

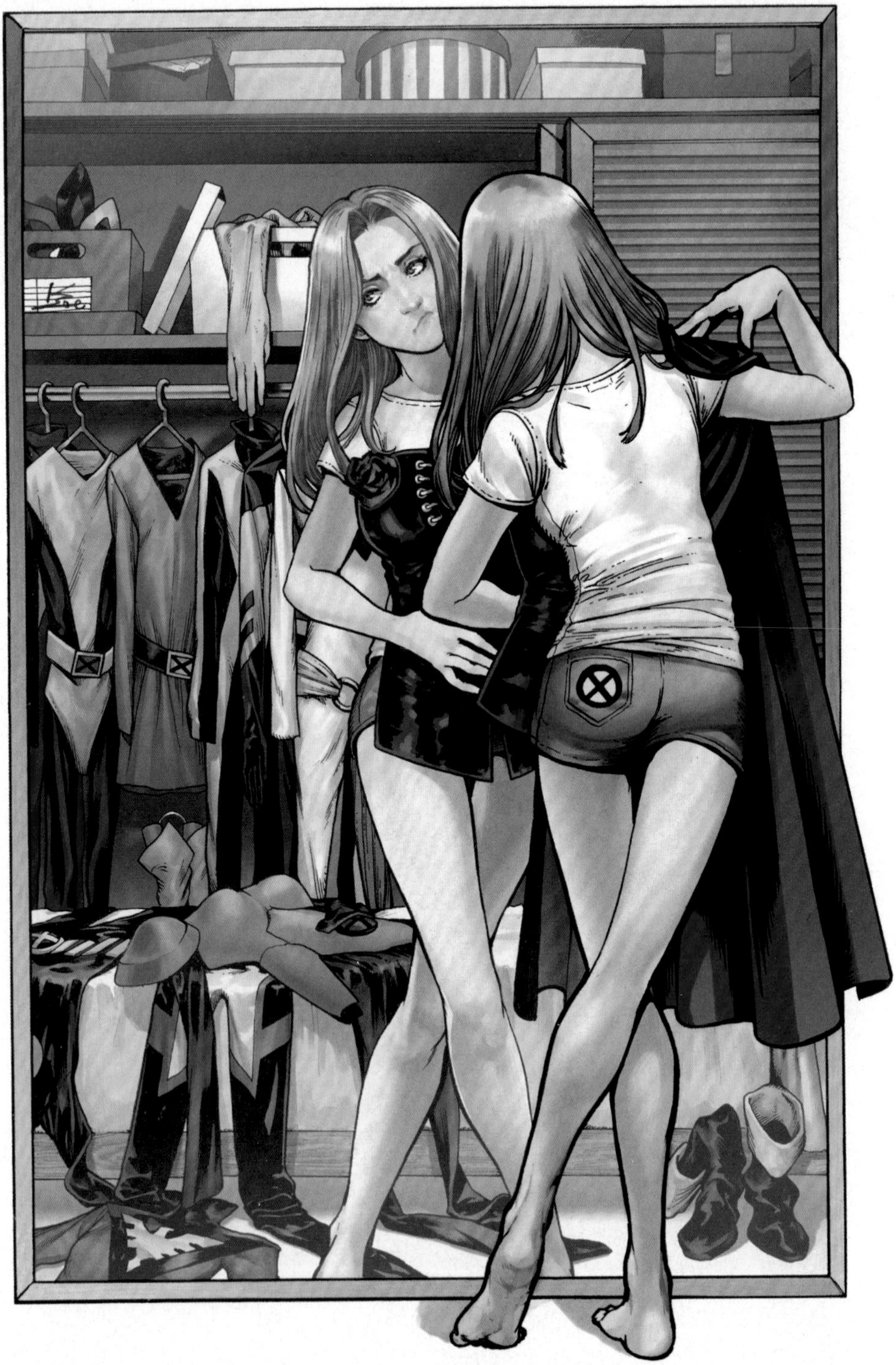

#5 VARIANT BY *KAMOME SHIRAHAMA*